# *Prairie*
## to the
# Pentagon

The Inspiring Story of the Airman
Who Achieved the Highest
Position Ever Held by an Enlisted
Woman in U.S. Military History

## Denise Jelinski-Hall

Foreword by General Craig R. McKinley
Afterword by General Frank J. Grass

Fulton Books, Inc.
Meadville, PA

Published by Fulton Books 2021

ISBN 978-1-63860-320-7 (paperback)
ISBN 978-1-64952-422-5 (hardcover)
ISBN 978-1-64952-421-8 (digital)

Printed in the United States of America

Praise for *From the Prairie to the Pentagon*

Great story! The media and many government officials say the strength of our nation is our military services, and in turn, the strength of our military services is the volunteers who wear the uniform of our nation. Once you read this story, you will know the truth behind that statement. Starting from a life of humble beginnings based on a strong work ethic and a determination to succeed, Denise leads you through the circumstances and ultimate decisions that lead her to serve as the Senior Enlisted Advisor for the chief of the National Guard Bureau. Throughout this journey, Denise magnificently demonstrates how she found balance between her military and civilian careers, being a mother to her children, and a wife to her military husband. This story is an inspiration to those in the military, a role model for leadership in the corporate world, and an example of achievement for those looking for self-improvement.

—Kenneth O. Preston
13th Sergeant Major of the Army
Vice President, NCO and Soldier Program
Association of the United States Army

Working the family farm to leading at the highest level of the Nation's "*Always Ready, Always There*" force. A 'role model-read' that is heartening and inspirational. I finished *From the Prairie to the Pentagon* in two days. Chief Jelinski-Hall's is a life that defines a pure patriot; grit, sacrifice, fearlessness, endurance… I'm proud to call Denise a battle buddy and an exceptional Senior Enlisted Advisor, but more important, blessed to call her my friend. Share in this extraordinary journey.

—Micheal P. Barrett
17th Sergeant Major of the Marine Corps

Outstanding read for all whether you're in the military or navigating the civilian world. First female Senior Enlisted Advisor to lead the National Guard Bureau. The book clearly provides the author's first-hand account of the trials and tribulations along her stellar leadership path to the Pentagon. Meaningful lessons to be learned and real-life experiences as she "walked the talk" to success. Proud to serve alongside her then and now!

—Rick West
12th Master Chief Petty Officer
of the Navy (MCPON)

From the Prairie to the Pentagon is must read for anyone looking for a positive example in service before self and excellence in all they do. Compelling life story from humble beginnings and a complete dedication of service to the Airmen and Soldiers of the National Guard. Her enormous responsibility as the Senior Enlisted Advisor to the National Guard highlights an overwhelming commitment to our National Security and the women and men of America's Armed Forces. Proud to have served with her in uniform and now in the private sector.

—James A. Roy
16th Chief Master Sergeant of the Air Force

Great leaders are lifelong learners. For those interested in gaining insight into how to be a better leader, the plethora of leadership books available may seem daunting. Many of the current crop of books on leadership seem formulaic and provide little real-life help improving personal leadership skills. "From the Prairie to the Pentagon" is NOT such a book. Denise Jelinski-Hall's story goes far beyond catchy formulas and catch phrases. Her narrative provides a unique and real-life perspective on leadership from the ground up. Starting her career as the most junior airman Denise Jelinski-Hall rose to the top enlisted position in the National Guard. Much can be learned from her experiences…this is not just another book on how to succeed as a leader… This book will give the reader insight on how to succeed at life!

—Charles "Skip" Bowen
10th Master Chief Petty Officer of the
U.S. Coast Guard (MCPOG)

This book outlines Command Chief Jelinski-Hall's journey to the top of one of the largest military organizations in the United States. Starting with simple beginnings on the prairie, it's peppered with many personal and professional twists, turns, and hurdles. These challenges never stop her from being the first female to lead the enlisted ranks at the wing, state, and lastly, the national level. This is a must-read book that will inspire and impress both civilian and military readers alike.

—Peter Pawling
Major General (ret.)
United States Air Force

A must-read for all females serving, or those deciding to serve, in the Armed Forces of the United States. My "battle buddy's" story depicts the ability to shatter glass ceilings. It was a true honor to have served alongside Chief Jelinski-Hall, especially visiting our troops in Iraq and Afghanistan.

—Robert G.F. Lee, Major General (ret.)
Hawaii Adjutant General
United States Army

Denise movingly conveys how a strong work ethic on the farm lays the groundwork for a successful future in the Air National Guard. She tells a compelling story where success is laced with strong values of faith and family. This is a great read that will take you from the prairie to the pentagon while looking over the shoulder of Denise Jelinski-Hall.

—Rev. Dr. Kenneth "Ed" Brandt
Parish Associate
Westminster Presbyterian Church,
West Chester, Pennsylvania

This is the most compelling, inspiring example I have ever encountered of how strong core values and an indomitable human spirit can achieve (and surpass) our lifetime goals. Having served thirty years of military service in thirteen enlisted and commissioned paygrades, I can only marvel at the benchmark for success this book provides for our future generations who will so significantly benefit from being made aware of this tough-as-hell, caring and totally dedicated warrior.

—Dwayne N. Junker
Master Chief Petty Officer/
Lieutenant Commander (ret.)
United States Navy

*From the Prairie to the Pentagon* is a thoughtful and inspiring book that provides a deep understanding of the extraordinary rise from humble beginnings to leading our nation's National Guard as the highest ranked enlisted female member in the history of our military. Chief Jelinski-Hall epitomizes the true essence of an *Alaka'i* (leader) who leads with *Ikaika* (courage) and *Ka ha'aha'a loa* (humility). A must-read.

—Robert S.K. Lee III
Command Chief Master Sergeant (ret.)
Sixth Senior Enlisted Leader
Hawaii National Guard

As a woman military leader, Chief Denise Jelinski-Hall redefines standards and shatters glass ceilings. *From the Prairie to the Pentagon* awakens the Spirit of America—that the impossible is possible. Laugh, cry, and beam with pride as she takes you on a unique yet relatable journey!

—Suzanne Vares-Lum, Brigadier General
Army National Guard

Denise is one of the greatest examples of military professionalism and leadership I have seen in over a decade of working closely with the military. The fact that she was the first woman to hold her position speaks to her exceptional qualities. Chief Jelinski-Hall defined and expected the highest level of standards from herself and those she was responsible for, always showcasing the best of the National Guard. Men and women at all levels of leadership, whether civilian or military, will gain a great deal of insight by reading Denise's story.

—Sharlene W. Hawkes
President, Remember My Service Productions
Miss America 1985

A journey like no other—with challenges around every corner. Join Denise, a true warrior, on her history-making adventure to the Pentagon. I am proud to have worked side by side with her while leading the men and women of the National Guard of the United States. Hats off to you, Chief…a job well done!

—Richard J. Burch
Command Sergeant Major (ret.)
Ninth Command Sergeant Major
Army National Guard

Retired Chief Master Sergeant Denise M. Jelinski-Hall has genuinely shared an inspirational memoir that is by far a true example of how perseverance can overcome life challenges by serving pure of heart, having passion, and most of all, maintaining one's faith. She has created a legacy of leadership by "making a difference in the lives of Airmen, Soldiers, and families!"

—Kelly J. Wilkinson
Chief Master Sergeant (ret.)
Airman and Family Readiness Program Manager
133rd Airlift Wing, Minnesota Air National Guard

When you read Denise's book, *From the Prairie to the Pentagon*, you're going to truly feel her courage, determination, and compassion come through in her rich and memorable life lessons. This book will give you a personal account of experiences shared by many but understood by so few. Let her words be an inspiration to all generations and an invaluable lesson to live by.

—Jason Tart-Hisaw
Master Sergeant
Air National Guard

To my loving husband, Gary, and our daughter, Ashley, and to the men and women who have answered the call to serve this great nation.

What I will miss the most is a chance to make a difference.

—Chief Master Sergeant Denise
M. Jelinski-Hall (2013)

# CONTENTS

# FOREWORD

*From the Prairie to the Pentagon* is a true American story of grit and perseverance. Relying on an unstoppable work ethic and a "never give up, never quit" attitude, Denise Jelinski-Hall achieved what no other woman in the history of the United States Armed Forces has ever accomplished.

Chief Master Sergeant Jelinski-Hall's story reflects a life of humility, compassion, and unshakable faith, and her professional career is grounded in selfless service and integrity. Her journey highlights the importance of taking strategic risks and turning adversity into something positive. Growing up on a farm, attending a one-room country school, and giving decades of service at the highest level of enlisted leadership in the Pentagon is truly an extraordinary narrative depicting the American dream.

During our initial interview, I knew I could completely trust Chief Jelinski-Hall. There were many highly qualified applicants for her position, including other women, but her confidence, enthusiasm, and high recommendation from her Adjutant General in Hawaii sealed the deal. She embodies all the qualities we want in our Soldiers and Airmen and is an outstanding role model.

On her first day as my Senior Enlisted Advisor, Chief Jelinski-Hall came into my office, carrying a legal pad with a long list of goals for her tenure. After discussing them, she asked me to call her "Chief" in public, not "Denise," to reinforce her position. That gave me an idea of how she was going to lead—a stickler for protocol, determined, sure of herself, and highly professional.

I came to know our Chief as passionate, indefatigable, and action-oriented, and she left no doubts about her desire to make a difference for the National Guard enlisted corps and their families.

As an ambassador, she represented the National Guard at all levels with thoughtful messaging, firm convictions, and a patriotic fervor.

When you consider all she has accomplished in her career, it's remarkable to realize that women were not allowed to enlist in the National Guard until 1967. Chief Jelinski-Hall inspired an entire generation of women and gave hope to young girls who wanted the opportunity to serve and lead in the military.

Her book is a portrayal of National Guard members across the United States who serve their states in peacetime and unhesitatingly answer the call to serve in foreign lands during times of war. In every circumstance, she led by example and modeled what it means to serve and wear the uniform of the United States Armed Forces with pride and distinction.

I was proud to have Chief Jelinski-Hall serve as my Senior Enlisted Advisor and represent the 450,000-plus National Guard Soldiers, Airmen, and families. She is a pioneer and an inspiration for all of us—enlisted and officers, civilians, men and women, of every age and background.

General Craig R. McKinley
US Air Force (ret.)
Chief, National Guard Bureau (2008–2012)

# ACKNOWLEDGMENTS

A life well lived and a successful career happen with the love, support, and belief of family, friends, and colleagues. Special thanks to Gary, Ashley, Nikki, Nathan, Neili, my parents, and siblings—I owe a debt of gratitude for your love, prayers, support, and unwavering belief in me.

Thank you to the members of the United States Armed Forces and, most especially, to the Airmen, Soldiers, and families of the National Guard. I'm proud to have served and represented you.

I'm tremendously grateful for the leaders who placed their trust and confidence in me.

My deep and sincere appreciation to Donna Mazzitelli for her patience, coaching, and writing efforts and to Elayne Wells Harmer for her professionalism and superb attention to detail in editing my book.

Countless other individuals have touched my life, given me incredible opportunities, and had a positive influence on my journey. Those people are too numerous to list here, but I hope you know how special you are and how much you mean to me.

Above all, I am indebted to God, whose strength I've relied on throughout my life and career. Without my belief and trust in Him, none of this would have been possible.

# INTRODUCTION

On November 19, 2009, *more* than two thousand National Guard Army and Air Force leaders gathered outside Washington, DC, for the first Joint Senior Leadership Conference in National Guard history. General officers, senior officers, and senior enlisted leaders from all fifty states, three territories, and the District of Columbia were assembled to discuss the National Guard's relevance and effectiveness in a post-9/11 world.

Having traveled from Hawaii, I was seated within the first few rows of the audience. General Craig McKinley, Chief of the National Guard Bureau, had recently selected me—the first female and the first Air Guard member—to advise him on the enlisted affairs for the entire Guard.

"I am proud to introduce Chief Master Sergeant Denise Jelinski-Hall as my new Senior Enlisted Leader," General McKinley announced from the stage. With my husband, Gary, and daughter, Ashley, on either side of me, I heard thunderous applause and was humbled by their enthusiastic welcome.

My new position at the Pentagon would require me to serve the second-largest military organization within the Department of Defense; only the Army had more personnel. With General McKinley's introduction, my life would be forever changed. In this role, I would represent approximately 415,000 National Guard enlisted Soldiers and Airmen and have influence and input on programs that affected our Army and Air National Guard members and their families and communities. As the National Guard Bureau Senior Enlisted Leader, I would circumvent the globe, traveling across the country and multiple continents.

Unbeknownst to me at the time, in this position, I would meet people and visit places I had only read about or seen on television. There would be moments of exhilaration, triumph, and tragedy. It would become my life's greatest honor to serve the incredibly brave and patriotic men and women of our National Guard and their families; to work side by side with my sisters and brothers from the Army, Marines, Navy, Air Force, and Coast Guard; and to be mentored and led by some of the most brilliant senior leaders I would ever know.

After General McKinley's public announcement, I stood. As I turned around and acknowledged the audience, the reality that I would soon be working at the Pentagon and representing the entire enlisted corps of the National Guard hit me. *This is really happening!* I thought.

ॐ

I didn't grow up believing that anything was possible—that conviction came much later in life. My childhood upbringing in Minnesota was more practical and down to earth, and my five siblings and I were raised to focus on work and responsibility, not dreams and future aspirations.

My parents were models of an old-fashioned American work ethic. My dad worked a full-time job, performed his National Guard duty once a month, played in a band, and worked on the family farm. My mom managed the finances of our one-income household, tended the farm, and raised six children. By watching our parents, we learned what our family valued: commitment to a job done well, perseverance, keeping our word, being honest, exercising faith in God, protecting and honoring the family name, and acting responsibly in everything we did.

These expectations applied to every aspect of our lives. From our earliest years in the one-room country school, my siblings and I knew we had a responsibility to our family, to school, and to God. I was determined to work hard, be successful, and show my teachers I was willing to give it my all. I graduated from high school, got married, and excelled as a seamstress on an assembly line. In my next job at a local bank, I was promoted from bookkeeper to head teller in just a few years and was recognized as the first Employee of the Month for Little Falls, Minnesota.

But in my early twenties, life hit a series of difficulties. My marriage began to crumble, and my work life stalled. At twenty-four, with a failed marriage and mediocre professional success, I found myself thinking, *Is this it for my life?* I couldn't imagine being a teller for the rest of my career. I was barely scraping by on my meager salary, so starting over at the bottom of the ladder in some other industry seemed impossible. Going anywhere else meant less money, even for a comparable job.

All the officers on the other side of the bank were college graduates. I knew I would never get ahead without a degree, but I didn't have the money for school. I was stuck—and I couldn't imagine what I could do to change my life.

As fate would have it, around this time, I befriended a Minnesota Army National Guard Soldier. One day, she walked into the bank.

"Denise, I see so much more potential in you than what you're doing," she said candidly. "Why don't you join the Air Force and get out of this town?"

I had never seriously considered joining the military. During high school, when a cousin and I talked about it once, my uncle said it wasn't a proper career for women. My dad served in the National Guard, but he never talked to any of us about enlisting, and I didn't know much about what he did.

Within a couple of weeks of her suggestion, my soldier friend drove me to a neighboring town to meet with an Air Force recruiter. He told me about air traffic control, a field I'd never even known existed. I hadn't even flown on an airplane! My eyes grew big as I listened to him describe the duties of air traffic controllers and how the Air Force could pay for college. The prestige of working in a field with great responsibility sounded exciting, and I was sold.

This one female National Guard soldier had recognized that I could do more with my life. She saw in me a strong work ethic, self-discipline, and the commitment to do the best job possible and knew I would be a great fit in the military. Almost thirty years later, as I stood on the stage of the Women in Military Service for America Memorial at Arlington National Cemetery for my retirement ceremony, I was overwhelmed with emotion and mixed feelings. I recognized the significance of this moment. Having achieved the highest position ever held by an enlisted woman in the history of the US Armed Forces, as the Senior Enlisted Advisor of the National Guard, I also wondered where life would take me next.

Throughout my journey, I had relied on four bedrock principles: a strong work ethic, a determination to make a significant impact, a patriotic heart filled with love of country coupled with a desire to serve, and a belief that God's will would never take me where His grace would not protect me. Each day, when I stood in uniform in front of the mirror, I had but one thought in mind, "Dear God, let me serve You and my country well today." Whatever accomplishments I attained on this extraordinary journey, I achieved as an answer to that prayer.

As I looked at all that had unfolded throughout my life, I was filled with awe and gratitude. Here I stood, a little girl who came from humble beginnings, grew up on a farm on the prairie of Central Minnesota, worked hard, refused to quit, and had a historic career in the US Air Force and National Guard.

I was proof that no matter your age, sex, family origins, or social background, if you believe in yourself and have a desire to do your best, in America, anything is possible!

# Part One

## The Prairie Years

# CHAPTER 1

# A Traditional Family

I grew up on an eighty-acre farm in Central Minnesota, a region full of wooded hills and sparkling-blue lakes. My dad called it a "hobby" farm because he had a full-time job, but trust me, there was nothing "hobby" about it.

My five siblings and I worked on the farm six days a week—after work and school and on Saturdays. Dad usually got home around four o'clock each weekday afternoon and took charge of what we needed to accomplish that day. During the school year, we all worked at our assigned chores until suppertime. After supper, the three girls took care of cleaning up the kitchen, dishes, and sweeping the floor. The three boys typically had their chores done before supper and were free for the rest of the evening. Homework had to be done after all home and farm responsibilities were finished.

My siblings and I were typical farm kids. We worked, played, and had fun together, but we also had our squabbles and even fought with each other. Of course, we had to be careful—the last thing we wanted was to hear Mom say, "Just wait until your dad gets home." Dad was a strict disciplinarian and kept us in line with a stern look. We knew we couldn't question him, let alone talk back. As I watched my two older siblings try to argue or win over Dad in some type of discussion, I came to understand where the line was with him. I learned to not cross it; life was easier staying well within the boundaries.

Dad was a truck shop foreman at a boat manufacturing company, where he oversaw a handful of mechanics and the maintenance of eighteen-wheel rigs. He had picked up technical skills in the Korean War, when he served as a mechanic in the Twenty-Third Regiment, Second Infantry Division of the US Army. Like most men, he came home from the war, found a job, and started a family, and it was only much later in life that he shared a few brief comments about his time in the war.

His footsteps had been all over the hills of the Kumhwa Valley in North Korea and around Old Baldy, adjacent to Pork Chop Hill, just above the 38th Parallel. Dad talked about the bitter cold in Korea—he didn't have warm clothes, his worn-out fatigues had holes in them, and they had no cold-weather gear like parkas or snow boots. When he returned home, he vowed he would never let himself be cold again. To this day, the thermostat never dips below eighty degrees in my parents' home.

One afternoon, Dad and I had been talking for some time about his experiences in the war when he got choked up and abruptly said, "That's enough. Don't ask me anymore." I knew by the changed look on his face that the war had left deep emotional scars.

But despite the difficult memories, Dad continued to answer the call to serve our nation. He joined the Minnesota Army National Guard and worked his way through the enlisted ranks until he became a First Sergeant. He was tough—some would even say he "spit tacks for breakfast"—but he was fair. I've often commented that my siblings and I were raised in true First Sergeant fashion.

Later in his career, my father was commissioned and retired as a Chief Warrant Officer 2 with twenty-two years of service. I don't recall much about Dad's service with the Minnesota Army National Guard since he never talked about what he did. My siblings and I only knew that Dad was gone one weekend a month and two weeks in the summer for annual training.

Truth be told, we were happy when Dad had Guard duty. When he wasn't home, things were significantly more relaxed. From time to time, we had spaghetti or frozen pizza, which we never ate when Dad was home. In the evening when chores were done, Mom let us watch something other than news—usually sitcoms like *The Beverly Hillbillies*, *Gomer Pyle*, and *Bewitched*. When Dad was gone for his two-week training, the younger kids argued about who got to sleep with Mom. Frankly, I'm surprised any of us got to sleep with her, as I suspect she would have enjoyed the peace and quiet to herself.

There was a real sense of freedom when Dad was at training. As I got older, I took great advantage of his absence by talking on the phone longer and staying up later.

ॐ

My parents' roles were traditional and clearly defined. My mother was a farm housewife, and for most of my childhood she did not work away from the house. Mom was in charge of the inside of our home, and Dad had responsibility for the outside—although Mom also managed the huge garden and flower beds. I recognized that these were the traditional roles of my parents' generation, but I resolved that *my* marriage was not going to look like that. I was determined that I would not be the one solely responsible for all the household duties, laundry, yard, and garden.

Doing the laundry was a huge, time-consuming task since we had an old-fashioned wringer washing machine and no dryer. During the summer months, we hung the laundry outside on clotheslines. Living on a dirt road, we despised it when big trucks drove by and blew dust from the road onto the laundry. In the winter, we hung everything on clotheslines in the basement, and the heat from the furnace dried them.

Most everything had to be ironed and starched—including my dad's handkerchiefs. Around the age of ten, I desperately wanted to learn how to iron clothes. That turned out to be a big mistake. The clothes for eight people had to be ironed weekly—and that took an entire afternoon. I did that for the remaining years I lived at home, and I grew to hate it.

We ate and canned everything from our garden. I wasn't fond of canning because it never seemed to end. We canned tomatoes, cucumbers, corn, carrots, beans, and more, all picked from our garden. On summer weekends, when my family went to our cabin, I occasionally stayed home to babysit for a nearby family. Since I was the only one home, I had to pick and clean the cucumbers, tomatoes, and other vegetables to prepare them for canning on Monday. Having to do it by myself made me mad, but I knew there was no point in complaining…on a farm, you just do what has to be done.

Thanks to our backbreaking continuous efforts, weeds never had a chance to survive in our garden. My mom and siblings and I spent hours pulling them until our garden was completely weed-free. Later in life, this standard of perfection would come back to haunt me—when we lived in Hawaii, I spent fifteen to twenty minutes each day during the week, and longer on weekends, walking the entire yard to eliminate the nut grass. It had to be dug out by the root, or else it would take over the entire yard. My Hawaiian neighbors called me the "nut grass weed hunter"—I have my Minnesota farm upbringing to thank for that.

For a short time, while I was growing up, Mom worked in a senior care home. She usually worked the 3:00 p.m. to 11:00 p.m. shift and seemed to enjoy it. I think it was a reprieve for her to get out of the house, socialize with coworkers, and be able to help others, as she had a warm and caring spirit. It was a treat when we were allowed to wait up for her, but that only happened on Fridays, Saturdays, or during the summer. Sometimes we would bake a frozen cherry pie and have it waiting for her when she got home. Because we didn't get a lot of "special treats," we all wanted to enjoy both the warm cherry pie and special time with Mom. Whoever got to be with her on those nights felt extremely lucky.

As my siblings and I began to play musical instruments, Mom would arrange for us to occasionally play for the senior residents on Sunday afternoons. I can't say we enjoyed it at the time, but today we all look back fondly on those memories. None of us understood it then, but these informal recitals taught us to serve and give back to those less fortunate. We learned to give or play music for others with no expectation of anything in return.

When we entertained the residents, my brothers played piano accordion, I played guitar, and our baby sister shook the tambourine.

All of us still remember the senior citizen who would stand in front of us as "Bud, the band director," and conduct our little group each time we performed. These experiences later helped shape my thinking about being kind and helpful to senior citizens.

꙳

My mother's parents, Roy and Rose Moe, lived in the farmland area of Glenwood, Minnesota, about an hour's drive from where I grew up. We didn't see them very often, but it was always fun to go to Grandma and Grandpa Moe's big farm. They had a small lake behind the house, where we often played, and a lot of big farm equipment. I especially remember their red tractors and watching Grandpa Moe milk their cows. Grandpa always wore bib overalls and a smile, smoked a pipe, and gave us "shag"—when he hugged us, he rubbed his whiskers on our cheeks. We hated getting shagged from Grandpa, as it really did hurt.

When I think about Grandma Moe, I remember how she wore her wristwatch way up on her arm, which seemed a little odd. I think she wore it that way so it never got wet or soiled. Grandma always drank tea, and she reused her tea bags several times so that eventually the liquid in her cup looked like pure water. We all remember Grandma saying "oh hell" a lot.

Grandma and Grandpa Moe were both hard workers. Grandpa was an avid hunter who trapped fox and hunted birds, and Grandma cleaned and processed all the ducks and geese that he brought home. She also baked plenty of goodies. Any time someone came to visit, she would immediately invite them to sit down for coffee, tea, and something sweet she had prepared.

Grandpa Moe died when I was fairly young, and Grandma eventually moved into the city of Glenwood. After she moved to town, she babysat to earn money. She was also well-known in the community as a big bingo player who usually won.

My paternal grandparents were John and Helen Jelinski. Although they were born in the United States, both were 100 percent Polish. They lived on a homestead—President Benjamin Harrison signed the land deed on October 21, 1859. Today the land is called a "Century Farm"—it has been continuously owned by a single family for more than one hundred years—and my parents live on that same plot where my father grew up. He purchased it from his parents when they got older because it was important to Grandpa John and my dad to keep the original homestead in the family.

We were all very close to Grandpa and Grandma Jelinski since they only lived about a quarter mile up the road. Somehow, we seemed to know when Grandma was baking homemade bread or cookies, and we'd manage to show up at just the right time. We always got to enjoy something sweet, whether it was cookies, leftover fried dough rolled in sugar, a Polish pastry called *pączki*, or a piece of cake. Grandma usually gave us candy when we visited too: pink peppermint candy or circus peanuts, a soft orange candy shaped like a peanut. Sometimes she would tie a couple of nickels in a strip of rag or dish towel and give us the treasure to safely carry home, along with a homemade loaf of warm bread. As we left, Grandma would always remind us to pay attention.

"Be careful that you don't fall in the creek!" she would warn us every time.

As my grandparents got older, our family helped them out more and more. We mowed their lawn, took them to mass, and helped to do whatever needed to be done around their house. Grandpa was the strong, silent type: he sat in his chair, spit Copenhagen snuff into a brass spittoon, and repeated the phrase "ho-hum" over and over. Grandma was the energetic talker. She ran their household until she and my grandfather moved off the farm when they could no longer manage it on their own.

Grandpa and Grandma Jelinski were tremendously influential and important in my life. Because of their close proximity and accessibility, they were role models and an integral part of our family life. They helped instill strong family values in all their grandchildren, including a strong work ethic and the importance of worshipping and practicing our faith. They were kind and honest, and we grew up wanting to never be a disappointment to them.

Both sets of grandparents also had traditional and well-defined roles—as husband and wife, as parents to their children, and as grandparents. They had been raised with a strong faith and belief in God. They were honorable, humble people who worked hard, helped their neighbor, and believed it was important to know, serve, and love the Lord. We witnessed them honoring the Lord's day and the practices of their Catholic faith in their daily lives. They believed strongly in "until death do us part"—Grandma and Grandpa Jelinski were married for sixty-three years. Although it's been decades since they passed, I get very emotional when I think of them—I miss their presence and guidance in my life and wish I could have more conversations with them.

∾

My siblings and I grew up with that same strong belief in God, and we did not work on Sundays because that was the Lord's day. Even if hay was down in the field and it promised to rain on Monday, we understood that Dad would rather let the hay rot than allow any of us to dishonor the Lord by working on Sunday.

We strictly observed Sundays, holy days, feast days, and religious holidays. On Easter and Christmas, we all wore our Sunday best to mass. Sometimes we got a new outfit for Easter—along with sweet treats from the Easter Bunny. Like most kids in the sixties, we thumbed through the thick Sears or J. C. Penney catalogs that came in the mail twice a year. At Christmastime, we went through the special Christmas edition and dreamed about what Santa might bring us. As I got older and understood there was no Santa Claus, it became pointless to even look at the catalogs and dream. With more awareness about our family's circumstances, I understood there was no extra money for the beautiful things on the colorful pages.

The Christmas gifts we received were usually things we needed, like clothes or pajamas, although we also got something small that we could play with. One Christmas, I remember getting a black plastic wig, and my older sister got a brunette one just like it so we could play dress-up.

Dad and Mom believed in equality—we were all treated the same and received gifts of equal or comparable value. When we reached a certain age, our parents gave us a special keepsake: the girls each received our last doll, and the boys received a special toolbox from Dad. (My brothers still have theirs today.) Many years later, the boys all received a .30-30 Winchester lever-action rifle from Dad, and the girls received identical jewelry boxes with an inscription from him. This was a special gift that will always have a prominent place on my dresser.

In 1967, we received the most special Christmas gift of all: a baby sister! Shannon was born on December 21, and on Christmas Eve, Dad brought Mom and our new sister home from the hospital. When they arrived, Dad placed our baby sister under the tree in a laundry basket. Just like baby Jesus, she was our true Christmas blessing.

The values my family and community instilled in me form the foundation of who I became and the life I've lived. I continually reach back to that bedrock base. There is no doubt that throughout my life, my faith in God and my Christian beliefs have been a lifeline for me during many trying times.

# CHAPTER 2

# Farm Life

Although we grew up on eighty acres, our home was modest and small. When it rained or snowed, we took off our wet boots and coats on the porch and stored them before entering the main part of the house. No shoes were allowed in the living room, and we couldn't even go in there unless we had bathed and were dressed in clean clothes. Understandably, we spent most of our time in the kitchen.

The basement was made of concrete and frequently leaked, so we stored things in two attics on the second floor. They were mostly filled with boxes of old memorabilia. My siblings and I made up stories about what was in those attics—including a resident boogeyman lurking within. Since attics are typically scary places for kids, we sometimes locked each other in there and said, "The boogeyman is going to get you!" No one wanted to be in the attic for long.

The eight of us used three bedrooms, two on the main floor and one upstairs. We played musical rooms over the years. Initially, I shared a bedroom with my older sister on the second floor of our farmhouse, and the three boys shared the bedroom downstairs next to our parents. Once our baby sister came along, Mom and Dad put her in a crib in the boys' room but moved my oldest brother upstairs by creating a semiprivate space with a curtain next to the railing. When my brother left home, the curtain came down. After my older sister married and left home, my little sister moved upstairs with me, and the two younger boys had the downstairs bedroom to themselves.

Eventually, when everyone but my younger sister had graduated high school and moved out, she took the downstairs bedroom. Personally, I think my parents wanted to keep a closer eye on her.

৵

A typical day while growing up began with Mom making Dad's lunch and a hot breakfast. Dad was up early and out of the house by 6:30 a.m. We had one bathroom with a tub on the main floor and a shower in the basement for all eight of us. I learned from a young age to get up early. When Dad was finished in the bathroom, I made sure I got it next. I knew that if I wanted extra bathroom time, I needed to get up before my siblings.

Our farm was not on the city sewer or water system. We had a well, so water was precious, and showers were limited to three to five minutes. A "Navy" shower meant you got wet, shut off the water, soaped up, and then rinsed off. I got five minutes to shower because of my long thick hair. Dad liked long hair on girls, so he wouldn't allow my sisters and me to cut our hair, except for an occasional trim. As a teenager, I resented Dad's prohibition. After all, it was my hair! I often told him that if he allowed me to cut it, I wouldn't need as much time to shower. Rational thinking never worked, however, and I had long hair until well after high school graduation.

My siblings and I would sometimes pull a prank when one of us was in the shower. We would turn on the water in the kitchen, which made the shower water run cold, and within a couple of seconds, we'd hear a loud "Shut the water off!" from the basement. Whoever was in the bathroom often heard pounding on the door. Since screaming and yelling were never allowed in our small home, the sibling who pounded on the door would firmly state, "Get out! I need to go the bathroom!" as they banged on the door. Sometimes that "someone" was fibbing just to get a turn in the bathroom sooner.

The boys had the responsibility of tending to early-morning farm chores, such as feeding the cows or ensuring they had water. While we got ready for school, Mom prepared lunch for us and packed it in a round plastic ice-cream bucket with a handle. We took turns carrying the "lunch pail" since no one wanted to be seen with it. Most of the other children carried metal lunch boxes with cartoon characters on them, so our ice-cream pail stood out like a sore thumb. I suspect all of us wished we could have our own cool lunch boxes, but none of us ever expressed such a desire—we all understood that we didn't have extra money for such frivolous things.

Usually, Mom packed a sandwich, cookies, and, on occasion, a piece of candy for each of us. Most of the time, sandwiches were white bread with either peanut butter and jelly or butter and sugar. After breakfast—which typically consisted of Kellogg's Corn Flakes or Wheaties with dry powdered milk, or thick, creamy unpasteurized milk from the neighbor—we walked to school. When school was over, we didn't waste any time getting home since we all knew our afternoon chores were waiting.

Overall, my mom was an okay cook, but we still tease her about her cooking methods. Back then, everything was fried in lard rendered from a pig and cooked until it was more than well done. Even the fresh vegetables were cooked until they became mush. Based on what we now know about the nutritional value of raw or al dente fresh vegetables, I am sure most of the nutrients had been cooked out—although we did all grow up to be healthy individuals. I must admit that it took years for me to enjoy a good steak, as I thought they had to be cooked until they tasted like shoe leather. When I finally tasted a superb steak that was pink inside and not cooked in lard, what a difference! No matter how the food was prepared, though, we never went hungry, and we ate what Mom put in front of us. And, of course, we always cleaned our plates.

When it came to farmwork, we all pitched in, no matter what time of year it was. I especially remember the springtime, when it was rock-picking season. Dad first plowed the fields and then went back over the ground to smooth out and level the furrows. When the field had been readied for seeding, we spent days going up and down the fields, picking up the rocks that had been overturned in the process.

The only good thing about picking rocks was that we could get a great suntan from being outside all day. In fact, many times we got sunburned since we didn't use sunscreen back then.

Bailing hay and putting it up in the barns was another family teamwork event. As a teenager, I enjoyed the workout, but it's amazing that none of us ever fainted from heat exhaustion. Ninety-degree heat and humidity take a real toll when you're loading heavy, dusty hay and stacking it in a three-sided metal-roofed pole barn.

We also had a large yard that required mowing once or twice a week, which often turned into an all-day process. We used push mowers, and from time to time, we'd comment about how nice it would be to have a riding lawn mower. Although my allergies bothered me, I much preferred working outside than being in the house and doing the cooking, cleaning, dishes, canning, or laundry. I recall one time in the winter when I told my dad it wasn't fair that the boys got to do the outside chores and feed the animals while the girls had to cook the meals and do the dishes. In response to my protest, he switched the job responsibilities between the boys and girls. Unfortunately, that only lasted one night. The boys revolted, and everything went back to the status quo. Although I still didn't feel it was fair, we all understood that when Dad set the rules, we didn't argue. I had to accept his decision, and that was the end of it.

☙

While we were young, my siblings and I found plenty of time for fun. We played hide-and-seek, cops and robbers, tag, built forts with branches, and found other ways to entertain ourselves. Unlike kids today, we didn't have toys. We ate our fair share of mud pies with grass, played in our homemade sandbox, and made our own fun using sticks, can, pails, jugs, bottles, and twine. Using five-gallon pails as drums and firm branches as drumsticks, we even created our own little "junk-band" orchestra. A thicker, longer branch became our guitar, and we tied twine from one end to the other to create the strings. My siblings and I were proud of our little orchestra and the sounds we created.

My dad nicknamed me "Bug" when I was a toddler because I used to crawl inside cabinets or other small spaces. I was apparently quite a rascal in my younger years. The nickname embarrassed me when I was a teenager, but by the time I was out of high school, I decided to embrace it. To this day, everyone in my family, including nieces, nephews, and cousins, calls me Bug. My grandchildren affectionately refer to me as "Grandma Bug."

❧

We raised beef cattle on our farm, and in the spring, Dad typically bought a couple of pigs and some chickens to fatten up. In the fall, my dad, brothers, and grandfather would butcher a steer, a pig, and the chickens. The steer and pig were cut up and packaged by a local butcher, but the entire family participated in the cleaning and plucking of the chickens. I absolutely hated that task.

We ate everything from the animals we killed, including the heart, liver, gizzards, and tongue. My grandmother used the head of the pig to make head cheese, which isn't cheese at all but more like meat jelly. I *never* became a fan of liver or head cheese. When supper was served, everyone ate what was on the table. On liver nights, however, most of my siblings and I would wear clothes with pockets in them. We then carefully tried to hide the liver in our pockets without being caught and later fed it to the dog. To this day, I swear there is nothing worse than well-done fried liver!

❧

Growing up in a rural farming community, we had "party lines" for our telephone, which meant that the neighbors and our family shared a phone line. I think there were five to six families on our party line. If someone wanted to be sneaky, you could listen to the neighbors' conversations and vice versa. If someone was on the phone and you needed to use it, you tapped the cradle of the phone down—which meant "get off the phone."

In our family, we had a limit of three minutes per phone call. Three minutes meant three minutes. If we didn't hang up in three minutes, Dad would hang up for us. This rule was partly out of respect for the others on the party line, but mostly, it was because Dad really didn't like us being on the phone. He figured that if what we had to say couldn't be said in three minutes, we were just wasting time. From his perspective, the phone was meant for short conversations and business matters—mostly the latter.

Unfortunately, this was a tough rule for teenagers to follow. As I got older and had a boyfriend, I waited until Dad fell asleep in his chair, which was usually around 9:00 p.m. or 9:30 p.m. I would then ever so quietly dial the number and move as far away from Dad as possible so he couldn't hear me talking. We had a long cord on our phone, about ten to twelve feet fully stretched out, so I pulled the phone into the bathroom, closed the door as far as I could, and talked as low as possible. However, I still got caught and scolded many times. Dad's three-minute phone rule used to make me mad. As embarrassing as it was to explain to friends, however, I certainly couldn't argue with him.

# CHAPTER 3

# Early Challenges and Commitments

Growing up, my father attended a one-room country schoolhouse almost two miles from home. Each country school throughout the surrounding farmland around Little Falls had one teacher who taught all grades and all subjects; families were assigned to schools based on their location. My father, aunts, and uncles all went to the same one. As a child, I also attended that very same country school for grades one through five. Just as when my father and his siblings attended, the school did not have indoor plumbing—we had to use outhouses.

We've all heard stories of parents who tell their children, when the kids complain about the inconveniences in their lives, how they walked to school through all kinds of extreme weather conditions and over all types of terrain. Well, my siblings and I actually did: we walked a mile and a half to and from school every day. It didn't matter if it was twenty below zero, snowing, or raining. We dressed appropriately, in layers of clothing when the weather was extremely cold, and we didn't waste any time going from home to school and back again.

At the beginning of each school year, my siblings and I got new clothes. Along with a few items of clothing, socks, and underwear, we usually got one pair of shoes for the year, and we knew that was going to be it—no frills or extras. One year, my mom bought me a pair of very sensible, sturdy, ugly shoes. They looked like the kind nuns wore, and I hated them so much that I purposely walked on the backs to ruin them. Eventually, the back of the shoes split, and I thought, *Aha! This is my chance to get new shoes.* However, I learned a priceless lesson that day. My dad fixed my shoes with black electrical tape, and I had to wear them for the rest of the year.

ॐ

Mrs. Boros, our teacher, was nothing short of a saint—she was responsible for teaching all subjects to about thirty-two children in eight different grades. Every day she would call each grade separately to a table for instruction in the core subjects: math, science, history, and English. We only had time for a few minutes on each subject.

The school had no phone, so when a child got sick and had to go home, Mrs. Boros had to drive that student home herself. She always placed an older student in charge, but it didn't matter—there was total chaos while she was gone. The kids raided her desk for thumbtacks, rubber bands, and paper clips. Once Mrs. Boros was gone, we all knew to carefully check our desk seats for thumbtacks. I was not one of the hellions since I was too afraid of the ramifications of being caught. It was one thing to be in trouble with the teacher and quite another to be in trouble at home.

I did well in school with the exception of mathematics. By about fifth grade, my ability to comprehend math changed, and I could not understand anything above basic math. It was humiliating going to the blackboard. I often stood there as if I were frozen.

Like many kids, recess was my favorite time at school and consisted of playing softball, dodgeball, tag, or jump rope. But all too often, while everyone was outside playing, I was held in from recess, and Mrs. Boros tried to help me with math.

Everyone had their own wooden desk with a top that lifted. The storage well under the desktop held our books, pencils, and other school supplies. Many times when I had to stay in from recess to do my math, I'd put my desktop up and just sit there quietly. Mrs. Boros said I was "spunking"—which meant I was being stubborn or obstinate. The truth was I just couldn't seem to grasp the concepts, no matter how hard I tried. I wasn't being disrespectful—I just didn't understand the equations, and staying in at recess to work on them seemed pointless. I felt like no matter what she did or said, I would never understand how to do the problems.

I always did my best to be courteous and polite even when I didn't like having to stay in and work since we were raised to listen to our elders. However, it was humiliating having to stay in at recess—the other students teased me for being dumb. I didn't like that one bit! Thankfully, even though I had a tough time with math, I was never held back a grade for poor performance. No one was.

✌

Although Mrs. Boros did her best to accommodate the needs of every student, my country-school education was poor. Receiving just a few minutes of daily instruction in each core subject did not provide a strong foundation for moving into upper grades. At the end of fifth grade, our "Laura Ingalls Wilder Little House on the Prairie" school closed. All the country-school kids were bused to the city school, where I began sixth grade. Although many of the country-school kids were smart, I suspect the Little Falls school system assumed that we had not been taught to the same standard as the city kids. At our new school, each class had three different levels in each core subject, and students were assigned to a level based on their ability or past grades.

At the beginning of sixth grade, I was placed in most of the lower-level classes—not an auspicious start in a new school. Everyone called the lowest level "the dummy classes." Kids were ruthless with name-calling and made fun of those who struggled. I didn't want to be that kid who was labeled "dumb," so I worked hard to get good grades and fit in. Rising from the lowest level of academics to the middle or highest was hard work. Fortunately, I knew about hard work from growing up on the farm.

Because my parents had taught me to continually strive to do your best and to never quit, I had a strong desire to succeed. I wanted to do better and *be* better. Failing at anything, especially a class, would have brought great shame to my family. I would do everything I could to avoid that. In time, I was able to move out of the dummy classes in science, history, and English. Ultimately, despite tremendous effort and frustration, I was never able to get out of the math dummy class. Nevertheless, I managed to do well enough to pass and move on to middle school.

⁂

While in sixth grade, wanting desperately to be one of the cool kids and fit in, I decided to join the school band. The previous year, following in my father's footsteps and doing exactly what he'd done when he was my age, I saved up the small weekly allowance my parents gave me plus money from babysitting to buy my own acoustic guitar. Just like my dad, I began to play and take lessons.

It turned out, however, that to be in the school band I'd need to take up a new instrument since the band didn't take guitarists. As I considered the various instruments, I really wanted to play the drums, another instrument my father played. My dad, Willie, was part of a Big Band ensemble called "The Dave-Willie Orchestra." Dad was the drummer and occasionally sang and played his guitar. When I asked my parents about playing the drums, Dad said, "No, one drummer in the family is enough." When I considered other options, I decided the saxophone case would be entirely too big to carry to and from school, so I settled on the clarinet. My parents agreed. This was a big deal since it was expensive.

Dad laid down the rules for practice. My parents believed in commitment—you said what you were going to do and then were held accountable. If I wanted to play an instrument, I had to make the commitment to practice thirty minutes every day, no exceptions. Mom and Dad would make the sacrifice to pay for the instrument, and in return, I would practice daily. This also meant there would be thirty minutes of practice on the guitar as well as the clarinet—I would be playing both. There would be no compromise on this obligation.

My siblings and I were also required to play our chosen instrument until we graduated. That was commitment! One of my younger brothers and my younger sister also joined the band in elementary school, and they, too, made the same commitment. There was no going back or quitting. I remember when my younger brother wanted to quit band in high school because he had other interests he wanted to pursue. Needless to say, Mom and Dad gave him no option: he remained in band through the rest of high school and practiced every day.

# CHAPTER 4

# More New Schools

Middle school meant transferring to another new school, starting in seventh grade. Having only attended a one-room country school and a one-floor elementary school, the middle school was intimidating. Would I get lost? How would I find my classes? What if my teachers didn't like me?

The middle school was a two-story building, which at the time seemed very big to a country girl. Two elementary schools fed into the middle school, so we had a much larger student body. I had attended Lincoln Elementary on the west side of town. I didn't understand the social class system back then and didn't know that many of the kids from Lindbergh Elementary on the east side of town were from upper-income families. To me, we were all just a bunch of kids coming together to attend a new school. It soon became apparent that there were big differences between us.

Lincoln students were labeled "the farm kids" while many of the Lindbergh students were the children of doctors, dentists, lawyers, and businessmen. However, because I played in the band and sang in the choir, I mixed well with all types of students and got to know kids from both the east and west sides. My seatmate in band was the school superintendent's daughter, and we became good friends.

In middle school, I continued to play in the band and sing in the choir, but I was not allowed to attend any of my friends' parties. The only time I got out of the house was to babysit and attend an occasional football game. In seventh grade, I caught the interest of an eighth grader who lived in town. He asked me out to the movies and other social gatherings with his friends, but Dad's "You can't date until you're sixteen" rule meant "Don't bother asking." Every time Rick asked me to do something, my response was the same: "No, I can't." Needless to say, at some point, he found a different girlfriend.

Being stuck on the farm and not able to attend fun things with friends became a real source of frustration. I said "I can't" so many times that my friends just eventually stopped asking. While it hurt to not be included, it almost made it easier to not be asked and have to tell them I couldn't go. My close friends kept me up-to-date on the happenings and gossip, but I still remained somewhat on the outside. Since Dad's rules were nonnegotiable, it would have done no good for me to tell my parents how I felt. Instead, I internalized my frustration and accepted that "this is just the way it is." At times, I was so angry that I would sit in my room and think about running away. But where would I go? There was no place to go, so I internalized my anger as well—I certainly could not display how mad I was. I had to push down my feelings and keep going. Decades later, I would describe this process as putting hurtful things in a box with a bow on top and storing them on a shelf in my mind.

During those years while I was in middle school, my brothers played league baseball each summer five miles down the road in Bowlus, Minnesota. To get to practice and games, they rode their bicycles. My younger brother, Bryan, and I wanted to attend their games, so we decided to buy a banana-seat bike from the Montgomery Ward catalog. We both saved our money. I babysat for fifty cents an hour, so it took a long time to save up the money we needed. Once we got our bike, though, it was worth the wait, and we put a lot of miles on it riding back and forth from our brothers' games. Having wheels in the form of a bicycle gave me freedom to get off the farm and meet new people.

After my final middle school year, another summer of hard work on the farm passed. Soon it was time to enter high school. As with middle school, there were now many more new students in my class since the private Catholic school kids also entered our high school. As a freshman, I continued to play in the band, sing in the choir, and became interested in student government.

In the fall, the high school band played at the football games, which I really enjoyed. Playing in the band enabled me to attend the games and socialize, and it also gave me the chance to take center stage with the other band members. As I learned the marching band movements for our halftime performances, I realized how much I enjoyed performing for a crowd.

Getting involved with various activities gave me the opportunity to get to know different groups of kids and created a sense of belonging. Once I became more active in school and attended practices, events, and group activities, I didn't feel like that farm kid who could never do anything or go anywhere. I was able to hang out with friends at the sports events and felt accepted and a part of social groups. Whenever our band performed, I also had a deep sense of accomplishment—band gave me the knowledge that I could perform well and helped me realize that I was actually good at some things.

⚮

Our band director, Mr. Nelson, had incredible vision. He took an ordinary band and challenged us to excel. After football and basketball seasons came to an end, our band performances were mostly over for the year. As a fairly new band director, Mr. Nelson wanted to create something special for the community and something to challenge the band, so during my junior year, he planned our first spring concert. This gave us all something more to look forward to and work toward.

My brother Bryan and I were part of the inaugural Little Falls Community High School Spring Concert. When the night of the performance arrived, the air was filled with electricity. The lights were dimmed, and the disco ball flashed and illuminated the packed auditorium. My flag squad started the evening with the music from *2001: A Space Odyssey*. The night was magical as the band played music from *Star Wars* and other pieces that created an otherworldly feeling. One of our band members even played a synthesizer to create space-like sound effects. In my opinion, it was the best band performance ever.

Mr. Nelson challenged every one of us to become a better musician. As a result of his inspiration and our hard work, our band went to the state music competition. In preparation, we had to learn a difficult piece, and I struggled with its complexity. Mr. Nelson gave us time to learn the music but got frustrated with our slow progress. After one bad rehearsal, he told us all to go home and practice. At the next rehearsal, he planned to call on individuals to play in front of the entire band. This put the fear of God into every single one of us.

I practiced that music nonstop and by the next rehearsal was able to play it fairly well although I hadn't perfected it. Fortunately, he didn't call on me. By the time of the performance, though, our band had mastered that piece, and Mr. Nelson was pleased with our performance. We won the state competition.

During my sophomore year, I tried out for the new choir ensemble and made it. We practiced after school, performed at a few small local events, and during my junior year, we won the state competition.

The seniors had a musical group called "The Jubileers." I really wanted to be a part of this group as well, but they performed at a lot of evening and weekend events, and I knew transportation and additional outfits would be a problem. Several of my ensemble friends asked me why I didn't try out, and it was difficult to admit my parents couldn't take me to all the practices and events—let alone buy additional ensemble attire. My parents did, however, manage to get me to and from play practice at school, so I was able to perform in *My Fair Lady and the Mikado*.

❧

Wanting to challenge myself to learn a new sport, I asked my parents if I could try out for the girls basketball team during the summer between my sophomore and junior years. The team practiced on weekday afternoons in the summer, yet that was the busiest time on the farm, with crops, gardening, and canning all requiring hundreds of hours. There was no way my mom could take me to and from practice, but my parents said I could ride my bike as long as I helped out once I returned home.

Our high school was about ten miles from our farm, and the first four were all dirt road. I did farmwork in the morning, rode my bike ten miles, practiced basketball for two hours, then rode my bike back another ten miles. Once I got home from practice, I jumped back into whatever chores still needed to be done. I did my best to manage both my responsibilities at home and to become a good player on the team. Sadly, I only made it onto the C squad, which was a bitter pill to swallow for a high achiever like me. It was like being back in the dummy class. I have to say, though, that I was definitely in great shape as a result of my rigorous schedule!

As I attempted to branch out, I continued to look for activities held during school hours. In my sophomore year, I ran for class representative and soon found myself involved in student government. Initially, I wasn't an active participant in the meetings since I was just learning what student government was all about. By my junior year, I began to find my voice and started to take on a more active role. As an upperclassman with some experience under my belt, I had ideas to share and was willing to speak up. Each time my peers accepted my ideas, I felt validated and could see that I liked being in charge.

Our senior year, my good friend Debbie Czech decided to run for class president and encouraged me to run for vice president. The current vice president was very popular and active in many different school activities, but I chose to run against her anyway. The elections were nerve-racking, but Deb and I both won. I was excited to be her teammate.

During our tenure, I chaired a "stomp out smoking" campaign. Having never smoked a cigarette, I was pretty passionate about it. My parents smoked, and I didn't like the smell. To prepare for the campaign, I spent countless hours thumbing through magazines and newspapers to find anti-smoking pictures and articles. I cut out letters and words that pertained to our campaign and placed them with the pictures on a large wall by the student commons area.

I remember feeling anxious about the success of the campaign, so I took complete responsibility on my shoulders and did most of the work for the group. I learned a valuable lesson about what it means to be a leader when Mr. Bates said to me, "You have to trust your committee to help." I was embarrassed that he'd recognized I was primarily working on my own. As the chairperson, I wasn't asking for my fellow committee members' participation. That experience stuck with me. After that, I learned to delegate and trust my classmates when we worked on projects together.

There was one defining moment in high school when I had to make a tough decision regarding friendships and the people with whom I associated. My childhood best friend and I had grown up on neighboring farms, went to school and church together, hunted squirrels together, and spent nights at each other's house. There was nothing I couldn't tell Cheryl. In high school, however, we were on slightly different paths, and she was part of what I considered a rowdy crowd. They were good kids, but they smoked and were boisterous. I got along with that crowd but recognized that I could not hang out with them during school. I couldn't afford to get in trouble at school—my teachers liked me, and I wanted to keep it that way. I was especially unwilling to risk the consequences I might face at home if anything happened.

So one day, during study hall, I talked with Cheryl about our situation. I needed her to understand that I wasn't snubbing her or that I thought I was better than the rest of the group. Because she knew my parents were strict in comparison to hers, she understood.

After that, I spent most of my time in the library, studying and doing my homework alone. Cheryl and I still rode the bus together, had some of the same high school classes, went to the same catechism classes, and had sleepovers. Our one-on-one friendship continued, and Cheryl and I remain best friends today. Having that difficult conversation with my best friend put me on an entirely different path throughout high school. I most likely would have been labeled "rowdy" and might have even taken up smoking or other questionable behaviors had I continued to hang out with that group.

Decades later, I heard some great advice: "You will be the same person in five years that you are today except for the people you meet and the books you read."[1] Since then, I have encouraged others to choose their friends wisely. Spending time with negative people or people who don't have goals and dreams can potentially bring you down, lower your standards, diminish your dreams and goals, and influence what you choose to do. Somehow, although I was a young high school student at the time, I already had a sense of this significant wisdom.

# CHAPTER 5

# The Worst Days of My Life

A few months after my brother Jeff graduated from high school, he was in a near-fatal car accident. The memories of that traumatic time are seared into my mind, and even today are difficult for me to revisit.

Jeff was two years ahead of me in school and had just turned eighteen years old on August 23, the week before. Around one o'clock in the morning, he fell asleep while driving and hit a bridge about three miles from our house. Jeff had been on the graveyard shift, working from 11:00 p.m. to 7:00 a.m. that week, and he'd had little sleep. His best friend, Kenny, found him pinned in his car. Kenny stayed with him, making Jeff recite his ABCs until the emergency vehicles arrived.

Dad happened to be on National Guard duty in another city about an hour away. My Uncle Ron was on the Little Falls volunteer fire department squad and was one of the first responders on the scene. When he recognized my brother's car, he left the accident site and came to our house in the early hours of the morning to tell us. This was before people in Little Falls locked their doors, so my uncle walked into our house and right into my parents' bedroom. He woke my mom and told her to get to the hospital as quickly as possible.

I was the oldest at home, so Mom woke me with the news. In tears and full of fear, we got dressed and left within minutes. Right before we took off, the phone rang. Mom answered, and a few seconds later, she simply said, "Catholic." My heart sank because I thought this meant that Jeff either had died or was near death and that he would need last rites. Fortunately, the staff merely wanted to be prepared with his full name and religious preference. Mom tried to contact Dad at the National Guard Armory, but she didn't have the phone number of his drill location. The Princeton Police Department started looking for him.

While Mom got the car, I quickly called Jeff's girlfriend, Ann, and told her to get to the hospital. I ran to the car, and Mom was so distraught that she started to drive off before I was all the way in. Neither of us spoke.

As we came upon the scene of the accident, we both fell apart. It was horrific.

"I can't drive any farther," my mom said through her tears.

Even though I had no idea how I'd manage it, I asked her if I could take over. I could see how upset she was, and I wanted to help her. She wouldn't let me. At that moment, one of the highway patrol officers came up to our car and asked who she was.

"I'm the boy's mother, and I can't drive anymore," she answered.

The highway patrol officer said he would get someone to drive us the rest of the way to the hospital. As we waited, we stared in disbelief. Jeff's car was in two pieces—mangled and intertwined with the metal of the side of the bridge. I got out of the car to try to take in the scene, but another highway patrol officer ushered me back to the car, telling me I really didn't need to see the wreck any closer.

We arrived at the emergency room just as they were about to transport my brother to St. Cloud Hospital thirty miles away, where they would be able to care for his severe injuries. The attending doctor met us and said there was nothing they could do for him at the Little Falls hospital. He sounded bleak as he described Jeff's condition—he had sustained multiple critical injuries.

When we saw Jeff, his face was cut and bloody. There was dirt and blood in his teeth, and his head rolled back and forth as he tried to tell us something. He was restless and agitated, and no doubt in severe pain. They covered him with a warming blanket and put him in an ambulance. Mom got in with him and told me to go home and be with my younger siblings.

Dad called the emergency room just before the ambulance left, and I sat down with Kenny. It was heart-wrenching to listen to him talk about finding my brother. Jeff had been pinned in, and Kenny had been helpless to get him out. As Jeff screamed, all Kenny could think to do to keep Jeff's mind off the pain was to have him recite the ABCs.

We both cried as we waited for Jeff's girlfriend, Ann. I felt completely alone, facing a situation I wasn't sure how to handle. My siblings and I hadn't been to the doctor much as kids. We had very little experience with hospitals, especially emergency situations, so being in this environment was frightening.

My earliest childhood memory of seeing a doctor was when I was about four or five years old and diagnosed with asthma. My only other memory with a doctor was after an accident while climbing a tree one summer. My mom did her best to remove a piece of tree branch sticking out of my leg, but the wound got infected. The doctor couldn't find anything on the X-ray, but a few days later, my dad pulled out a two-inch piece of wood from my leg with a tweezer. I still have a large dent where that piece of wood came out.

Waiting in the Little Falls ER and worrying about what was happening to my brother was the most frightening experience I can recall from my young life, yet I knew I had to stay strong and help take care of my family. I didn't go home, but I called my younger brother with the news. I also called my older sister, and she and her husband left immediately for the hospital. Because I didn't know if my big brother was going to live or die, I wanted to be there too.

I drove with Kenny, Ann, and her parents to St. Cloud's emergency room and found my parents. There was no news, so we all sat quietly and waited. At 3:50 a.m., a doctor came out to the waiting room. He said it would be a long surgery and that Jeff was in really bad shape. He told us as kindly as he could that it did not look good and that we shouldn't get our hopes up too high. Hearing that was like a sucker punch to the stomach. It hit hard and hurt worse than anything I can ever remember. We sat and cried, prayed, and held on to hope. Waiting to hear about the surgery seemed like an eternity. The hospital held mass at 6:00 a.m., and several of us attended the service to pray for Jeff. When we returned, there was still no word.

At 8:30 a.m., Jeff's doctor finally came to talk with our family. Dr. Gilchrist explained that Jeff had two compound fractured legs, one where the artery was torn so badly he might lose that leg. His right hand had been crushed, and his thumb had been hanging on by a couple of tendons. The doctor was able to reattach his thumb, which had a fifty-fifty chance of recovery. All his right fingers and wrist had been smashed into tiny pieces, and the doctors had pieced his hand back together like a jigsaw puzzle. He had 120 stitches in his face, and his fingers and arms were badly cut. He was still unconscious, and the doctor said it could be days, weeks, or even longer before he came to. Jeff had also suffered head injuries, but he had not sustained any internal injuries. They told us the next few hours would be critical.

Before the doctor left, Dad asked, "Will he live?" The doctor put his head down and said, "It does not look good…but he's lucky to be alive. He has been through a lot. It's all a shock to the body, and the body can only handle so much. He is in critical condition and needs a lot of prayers."

After a short time, another doctor came to speak with the family about Jeff's left leg. The tear in the artery was bad, and he anticipated the leg would have to be amputated. Dr. Brown also discussed Jeff's thumb and what to expect. I've only seen my dad cry a couple of times in my entire life, and this was one of those times. The news was devastating, but we all tried to hang on to the fact that Jeff was still alive.

The hours in recovery passed slowly. Once Jeff had been wheeled into the ICU and settled into his room, we were told we could visit him in pairs of two. No one could have prepared us adequately for what we were about to see and for the overwhelming emotions we would experience when we were taken to his room. We'd been told Jeff would be lucky if he survived the night.

Tubes and machines surrounded his unconscious body. Both legs were in traction, the right leg had a cast and a screw through it, which was anchored by weights. The left one looked the same, except that it was wrapped, and his foot looked dead. His hand and arm were wrapped with so much gauze that it looked like a club. He had lots of minor cuts and stitches covering his face and severe cuts on his fingers and arms.

After seeing him, our family sat quietly in the ER and prayed. I went home around one o'clock that afternoon, gave my brothers and sister the update, and returned the long list of phone calls. After giving instructions to my three younger siblings about lunches and school, I returned to the hospital with Kenny around 5:00 p.m. Nothing had changed during the time I was away. I sat with Jeff for a long time and watched for any sign of life or movement. My parents insisted I go home that night because I had school in the morning.

Leaving the hospital at 10:30 p.m. and arriving home to yet another long list of phone calls, I began dialing. It was difficult to talk about and relive what had happened, but I knew that others needed to be informed about Jeff's current condition. And since my parents remained at the hospital, I understood that I had to be the one to communicate with them. After I was finished returning calls, my younger brother Bryan and I talked until two thirty in the morning. I had been up for over twenty-four hours, but I wasn't tired. I apparently dozed off at some point, however, because the alarm rang at 6:00 a.m. and woke me. It was a new day, but I knew Jeff's fight for his life was far from over.

I prepared breakfast for my younger siblings and got them on the school bus on time. I drove to school, got a two-day pass to be excused from classes, and went to my teachers to get homework. It was hard talking to them, but they were understanding and helpful. It was my parents' anniversary, so I stopped to get them some roses and also got one for Jeff. I took care of other errands as well before I returned to the house.

As I was getting into the car after leaving the bank, my aunt stopped me and said she had just gotten a call from my mother. Jeff had taken a turn for the worse. I stood there—once again frozen—not knowing what to do or where to turn. I ended up in a furniture store and asked to use their phone. I called Mom, and she explained that they'd found a lot of brain damage. They didn't know if it was permanent. I asked if Jeff was going to make it. In a very shaky voice, my mom answered, "It doesn't look good, but there is hope." I told Mom I was on my way, and she reminded me to keep the speed limit.

After seeing the speedometer hit eighty-five on my way home, I remembered my mom's words and slowed down. Ann joined me ten minutes later. When we arrived at the ICU, we found out there had been no change. We spent a lot of time in the chapel that day and many hours pacing the hospital corridors.

The next day, the doctor reported that the skull looked good—there was a fracture at the base but no clots. This was good news, but his neurosurgeon warned us that anything could still happen. They did find a large clot in Jeff's left knee and decided the leg had to be amputated that evening.

A few days later, the doctors told us that Jeff would need a second surgery to remove his leg above the knee. That night, Mom was holding Jeff's hand when she asked him, "If you can hear my voice, squeeze my hand." He did. The next day, when a nurse asked him a question, he answered, "Yes, ma'am." Jeff also began squeezing my mom's hand in answer to questions she asked him. These were all good signs.

The morning of his second surgery, Jeff said, "Good morning, Mom." She tried to explain what was going to happen in surgery, but Jeff didn't understand. Surgery went well, and the doctor was thankful they hadn't waited any longer. They found that the knee was much worse than expected.

Over the next few days, Jeff spoke but was confused about where he was or what was happening. He was stable but still in a lot of pain. We were told that we should begin to see significant progress. The part of the brain that had been damaged was his memory, and the neurosurgeon explained that it would improve overtime. On September 20, after three weeks and two days, Dad took Mom home for the first time since the accident.

More time passed, as everyone adjusted our schedules to be with Jeff at the hospital as much as possible. During the following six weeks, Jeff went through a lot and endured many painful physical therapy sessions. Finally, his doctors had a conference and decided that on November 6 or 7, he could go home, as long as he returned every day for physical therapy Jeff didn't care what had to be done. All he wanted was to come home. That's all any of us wanted at that point.

⤳

Looking back at what occurred during this time, there's no question that this was the most painful time of my entire life. Of course, the situation was devastating for everyone. Jeff's recovery process was long, and he and our family experienced many ups and downs. As I watched my parents make the difficult decision to amputate his leg, I was overwhelmed with the pain of this situation and agonized along with them. I believe this was the hardest decision my parents ever had to make.

While my brother was unconscious for two and a half weeks, my mother stayed at the hospital constantly. Since I was the oldest at home, the situation put me in charge of cooking, cleaning, laundry, grocery shopping, and making lunches. No one had to ask me to step up. Admittedly, being a teenager, it was a lot of extra responsibility to manage our home along with schoolwork, but I knew I'd do whatever it took to lighten the load for my parents and maintain some sense of stability for my younger siblings.

Jeff came home about two and a half months after his accident, and we count our blessings every day that we still have our big brother with us. His road to recovery, however, was long and often taxing on the entire family. Mom took Jeff to his physical therapy treatments several times a week and to all his medical appointments during that first year after the accident. Because of the prior brain seizures, Jeff was not permitted to drive. He had memory loss and needed a lot of extra help. He also became easily agitated. As kids, we didn't understand everything that was happening, and many times, we did or said the wrong things. As a junior in high school, I wrote about this experience as part of a creative writing class. I still have that paper, handwritten in pencil.

Today, Jeff is able to speak about his accident and shares his perspective at schools and safety-related events. I am proud of him for doing this—it may very well save someone's life. We know today that drowsy driving can have the same effect as drunk driving.

Up until Jeff's accident, I never had to stand up for anyone outside our home. During the early days of my brother's hospitalization, my mom and dad were there with him round the clock while my siblings and I went off to school each day. Bryan, my younger brother, was a sophomore at the time. One day, the vice principal marked Bryan unexcused for a day he'd missed while visiting Jeff in the ICU. The entire town, including our high school principal and the school staff, knew what had happened to Jeff, so I couldn't understand the vice principal's insensitivity. I marched into the vice principal's office with Bryan.

"Do you really want me to call my dad, ask him to leave his oldest son's bedside, not knowing if he is going to live or die, and come here to write my brother an excuse note?" I demanded.

Needless to say, Bryan was excused.

# CHAPTER 6

# Becoming an Adult

Throughout high school, I worked hard, got involved in many activities, and wanted more than just an average life. I was proud of what my parents and grandparents did, but farming was not something I wanted to do for the rest of my life.

We never discussed attending a four-year college in our home because we simply didn't have the money. My parents taught us that you don't borrow money, and you work for everything you want, so higher education was not in my sights.

During the last two years of high school, I had been dating a young man named Mike. Before my senior prom in 1978, we became engaged to be married a year later. That meant I would need a full-time job, so the morning after graduation, I began working at Munsingwear, a clothing manufacturing plant. Employees received a base hourly wage plus extra for what was called "piecework"—which meant that the faster you worked and the more pieces you produced, the higher your earnings. One of my sisters was already working at the plant, so I thought it would be a good idea to join her.

Truth be told, I was not very excited about this job. I didn't know how to sew, and quite frankly, I had no desire to learn. Having watched my older sister make most of her clothes, I had never wanted anything to do with sewing. I thought that if I learned to sew, I, too, would have to make all my own clothes. In high school, I wanted store-bought clothes—not items that might look homemade.

Deep down, I believed I should be doing something better than this job. My friends were going off to college, and I resented having to work at Munsingwear. One of my friends from high school advised me not to take the job. I think she was embarrassed for me—she knew how much I wanted to go to college.

As a member of a blue-collar family, I was supposed to be happy and grateful I had a job, so I tried to accept that this was my lot in life. And because my father and family were well-known in town, along with the fact that my sister already worked at the plant, I knew I needed to do my best. I did not like the work at all, but I was grateful to be earning my own money while I still lived at home. I bought my first car from my aunt for two hundred dollars, a 1967 four-door Ford. It sounded and looked like a tank in need of repair, but it got me safely back and forth to work for the next two years and allowed me to save money for my upcoming marriage.

※

In June 1979, Mike and I got married. I also decided it was time to find other work, and I was hired at First Bank (NA)—Little Falls as a bookkeeper. In time, I moved to the teller line, became the head/vault teller and eventually became the backup loan teller. I earned a net income of about six hundred dollars a month.

During my time at the bank, my young marriage of two and a half years fell apart.

I could no longer trust my husband after all the lies, deceit, and the secretive financial hole he dug for us. My parents and family knew things were not right, yet they didn't try to interfere. There were weekends, though, when they would pick me up to go to our lake cabin, and Mike would stay behind and hang out with his friends. He liked to party, drink, smoke cigarettes, and marijuana—and I did not. When I caught him in a big ongoing lie, I knew I'd had enough. I wanted out, but in our family, divorce was not an option. I had to suck it up and deal with it.

Mike thought we should have a child, believing it would help our failing marriage—as if that was the answer. I was dead set against having a child until we could figure out our marriage. We were worlds apart on many issues: for example, I believed in paying bills ahead, or at least on time, and saving for a rainy day, but Mike believed in partying first. On payday, he would stop at a bar and stay out late drinking.

One night, I found him sleeping behind the house, at nearly three in the morning. I managed to get him in the house, and the doorbell rang a few minutes later. I opened the door to find my cousin Bruce with my brother Jeff, both in their sheriff uniforms. Mike had hit a mailbox of the neighbor I used to babysit for.

I couldn't take any more and began to hyperventilate. Once I was able to speak, Jeff took me to our parents' home in the middle of the night. Crying, ashamed, and feeling like a complete failure, I sat with Mom and Dad at the kitchen table at 3:30 a.m. and told them everything that had been going on. My dad's words gave me strength and unspoken permission to file for divorce.

"Bug, I learned a long time ago that in farming, your first loss is your best loss," he said. "Get rid of him."

And so, at the young age of twenty-one, I moved back home for six months and soon was divorced and single.

Living under Dad's roof meant I had to once again follow his rules. I wasn't allowed to date—not that I had any interest in doing so. In the eyes of the Catholic Church, a couple is still married until officially annulled. When I wanted to go out dancing with friends or to a movie, I had to ask permission. It was like high school all over again. Once again, I was stuck—I had no money and no place to go. Even though I was thankful for their help, I was now dependent on my parents, and I hated it. The little money I had gone to my divorce attorney.

As we considered the division of our property, Mike said he wanted the house, and I responded, "Fine. I'll take everything in it." After all, he had spent all our money and drove us into debt. I figured it was a fair trade and knew he would never be able to keep the house.

We went to court. He said he wanted our nineteen-inch colored TV but did not contest my getting the rest of the furniture. I said no to the TV. It was a matter of principle, which cost me more in attorney's fees than the price of a TV, but I had to stand for what was right. The judge assigned Mike his debt, and we were to split the smaller household items between us—which we did by taking turns tossing a coin.

I clearly remember the day I received my divorce papers that awarded me the furniture, TV, and my freedom.

"I won," I said to my coworker at the bank.

She looked at me sadly and said, "No one won."

I was taken aback and realized she was right. This was not a happy occasion. We were both losers with a failed marriage.

As a Catholic, I felt that receiving an annulment from the church was necessary to truly find peace and move on with my life. The eighteen-month process was extremely emotional and painful.

During the annulment hearing, family, friends, and I had to testify and relive events of our courtship, engagement, and marriage. It was difficult to examine what had transpired in our marriage that led to the need to end it, but it was well worth the emotional journey to me so that I could remain in good standing with the Catholic Church. Being in good standing with our church was not only important to me but to my parents and grandparents as well.

⁊

After the divorce, but prior to starting the annulment process, I moved into my own apartment. Six hundred dollars per month did not go very far with rent, food, and insurance for a single person. I walked to work for about six months before I was able to afford another car. Eventually, I bought a Ford Maverick, but neither the heater nor the defroster worked. This proved to be quite a challenge, living in Minnesota.

I can remember one year when I went to visit a friend for Thanksgiving in the middle of a blizzard. I was dressed in boots, a heavy coat, gloves, and layers of warm clothes. My father had previously looked at my car to try to fix the defroster and heating problems, but he couldn't solve it. At the time, I didn't have the money to take the car to a shop. So I did what I had to do: as I drove down the freeway, I scraped my windows from the inside each time they froze over. There was very little traffic on the freeway since most people had the good sense to stay off the roads. I drove so slowly, I could have crawled faster. At that superslow speed, it wasn't difficult to keep one hand on the wheel and scrape the window whenever it became necessary.

☙

I worked at the bank for five years and was selected as the first Employee of the Month for the city of Little Falls in recognition of my friendly and professional customer service. Although it was difficult to live on the pay I earned, I loved working at the bank, enjoyed the interaction with our customers, and felt good about how well I did my job.

In fact, one year, I went the entire 365 days with my cash drawer balanced to the penny. It was not unusual for tellers to be off a few cents from time to time. I didn't realize it at the time, but my parents' emphasis on attention to detail had already influenced my work habits. This attention to detail would one day have a significant role in my military career and growth as a leader.

Another time, I realized how much I'd learned from my parents when a loan company contacted me about a bill. My ex-husband had stopped paying the debt, so the company came after me. Not wanting to hurt my credit or bring shame to my family name by not paying the loan, I made arrangements to begin paying the debt. The loan amount was thirty-two dollars a month. I did not have an additional thirty-two dollars in my budget to pay the loan, but feeling cornered and responsible, I applied for a second job as a waitress at a nearby restaurant. It had not been in my plan to work evenings and Saturdays to pay a bill that my ex should have paid, but I was a responsible adult. I needed to do what was necessary to meet my obligations, even ones I unexpectedly inherited.

I paid the thirty-two-dollar-a-month bill until the debt was paid in full. Once it was paid off, however, I didn't stop there. Just as I'd done in high school for my younger brother, I stood up for myself. I tracked down my ex, had him served, went to court, and had his unemployment wages garnished to repay me. I had to stand on principle and do what was right for me. This had never been my debt, but because I cared about my reputation and my family's name, I had taken it on as my responsibility. It probably cost me more to find him, have him served, and collect what I'd paid than what the amount of the original loan balance was, but it was a matter of principle!

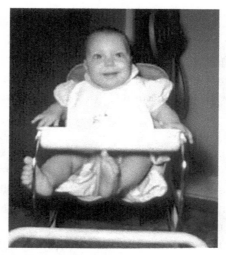

Baby Denise, 1960

Denise, first grade

With Mom and Dad, first Holy Communion, 1968

Family farmhouse

Interior of country school, 1959

Mrs. Boros and students

High school band

High school graduation, 1978

# Part Two

## The Wild Blue Yonder

# CHAPTER 7

# Welcome to the USAF!

About five years after I began working at First Bank, Minnesota Army National Guard Staff Sergeant Joyce Madsen, who'd become a regular customer at my window, posed that fateful question, "Why don't you join the Air Force and get out of this town?"

Joyce offered to take me to the Air Force recruiter's office in St. Cloud. On impulse, yet with a sense of curiosity, intrigue, and the thought of something bigger and greater out there, I said yes. When the recruiter described the air traffic control career field, I got excited. I could see myself doing something prestigious and exciting that didn't require a college degree. He also painted a picture of being able to later pursue higher education. How could I say no? Other than leaving my family, I had no responsibilities or obligations to hold me back.

At twenty-four, I finally saw a different vision of where my life could go. Without seeking anyone else's advice or approval, I decided to join on the spot. The decision to enter the military was the first time I distinctly remember listening to my intuition. My gut told me this was the right direction for my life. One could say it was a calling.

The recruiter explained that I could either wait for a guaranteed air traffic control opening or go in "open general." Open general meant that the United States Air Force (USAF) could assign me to any career field since the needs of the USAF always come first. Because I was all in and ready to commit, I made the decision to go in open general. Six weeks later, I had sold my car, furniture, stored my personal possessions at my parents' home, and resigned from the bank.

Although I was excited for where this decision would take me, I'll admit I had some trepidation about the future. I was about to take my life in a completely different direction from what any of my family or friends had done. My friends had either gone off to college or stayed in our local area. Although I was about to enter the uncharted unknown, the intrigue of unfamiliar territory beckoned. I was off to the wild blue yonder, where I expected to discover adventure, new possibilities, and the chance to create a new life for myself.

❧

After saying farewell to my family, my good friend Dorian Allen drove me to Minneapolis, where I took my first airplane flight to San Antonio, Texas. It was November 14, 1984. I remember being very nervous about the flight—actually, I was scared to death. I had never flown before and was unsure about where to go or what to do when I arrived at the airport. I had packed an oversized duffel and knew nothing about checking baggage, so I hand-carried that duffel from the beginning to the end of the trip.

At the San Antonio airport, things were a bit chaotic with scared and hopeful future Airmen flying in from all over the country. We eventually ended up on a bus to Lackland Air Force Base (AFB). As we got close to the base, we were instructed to not talk and to follow instructions. I was accustomed to listening, being quiet, and doing as I was told, so this leg of my journey was easy for me; however, it was obvious that others were having a hard time with the change of atmosphere.

When we arrived on base, training instructors (TIs) yelled at us to quickly get off the bus and be quiet. They barked orders: no talking, eyes front, feet at a forty-five-degree angle. It was very late by the time we got to our barracks. TIs told us to dump all our belongings onto the beds and to hold out any money or items of monetary value. Not realizing the stamps on my bed were equivalent to money,

I got a good chewing out from a TI for not holding them out. Once the TIs had collected everything "illegal," such as knives, scissors, or other articles that could do harm, we were able to go to sleep.

But how could anyone sleep? I'm not sure anyone did that night—I know I didn't. Fear of the unknown, nervous anticipation of what the morning would bring, plus the residual anxiety after our informal "initiation" into the Air Force left me restless and wide awake. Reveille sounded early, and we jumped to our feet, not knowing what to expect next. As processing continued throughout the day, I wondered what I had gotten myself into.

From day one, we learned what "hurry up and wait" meant. We seemed to spend an inordinate amount of time standing in lines and waiting. For example, when it was time to get our ID cards, we were marched to a building where we had to stand in line quietly—no talking, no whispering, and obviously, no complaining—as each person was processed. Many of the women were extremely young—some of them right out of high school. Being surrounded by immature, inexperienced females who didn't know how to be quiet, listen, or follow orders frustrated me. I was almost twenty-five, and I had been taking care of myself since I was eighteen.

I also understood that this was serious business—this was the military. I didn't mind being told what and when to do things, and I wanted everyone else to do their part as well. I felt impatient—after all, no one "made" them join the USAF. I expected these women to know they needed to follow orders exactly.

I realized almost immediately that my success was somewhat reliant on others' performance. Up to this point in my life, it had been completely up to me to make something of myself—now there was an entire flight (group) of forty women whose performance would affect me. Their mistakes, lack of attention to detail, attitude, or refusal to follow orders would be a reflection on me and on my successful completion of basic training. Quite frankly, I didn't like that. I wanted to be responsible for only me. I quickly learned that a person comes to basic training as an individual but soon discovers that successful completion of basic training is based on the success of the entire team.

On day three, we went to the base exchange (BX) to purchase items we needed for basic training, like irons, towels, and extra T-shirts. As my fellow trainees and I came out of the BX, my TI said, "Jelinski! You're going to be my dorm chief."

*Oh nuts!* I thought.

Although I was one of the oldest and most mature women in my flight, I knew nothing about what being a dorm chief meant. To me, it sounded like an assignment no one wanted—not that we had a choice.

Up to this point, I had kept my head down, done as I was told, didn't volunteer information or volunteer for anything, and tried very hard to just blend in. For instance, when they asked if anyone had marching band experience, I didn't let anyone know I'd been in band for four years. Although I'd tried to stay inconspicuous, here I was being singled out and assigned as our flight's dorm chief. As we'd already been taught to respond, I answered, "Yes, ma'am," firmly and without hesitation, but inside, I felt the immediate weight of this impending responsibility.

Like the others in my flight, I was still just beginning to learn about our Air Force. With this new assignment, I would be responsible for overseeing the flight whenever our TI was not present. Without any additional training, I was now being asked to step up to the plate. All I could do was rely on the values my parents and grandparents had instilled in me. Sometimes when I didn't immediately have the answer to a situation, I had to trust my gut intuition to guide me.

As dorm chief, I worked directly with the four assigned squad leaders under me, who were each responsible for a squad of about nine women. I quickly came to understand our chain of command. I was ultimately responsible and had to answer to the TI for everything that happened within the four squads. Even though there were challenges within our flight, I followed the Golden Rule and treated everyone with dignity and respect, doing my best to instill a culture of teamwork.

For a variety of reasons, our flight was what I called "somewhat dysfunctional." Besides having three different TIs in a short period—

each with a different leadership style and expectations—some women did not want to be in the Air Force. By the middle of basic training, a handful of them realized what they'd gotten themselves into and wanted out. Since we had all signed a contract, that wasn't an easy option; I spent several nights on suicide watch, overseeing those who were struggling to adjust. Although I did my best to be a good dorm chief, it was difficult for me to understand how some of them seemed afraid and acted as if someone had made them join the USAF.

Our flight's dysfunction showed up in a variety of ways. For instance, we had one trainee who refused to shower. Things got so bad that her body stench began to reek even from her locker. One of the other trainees brought it to my attention, so I took the matter to our TI. Later that day, the TI came in, made the trainee open the locker, and ordered her to wash all her uniforms. Someone was assigned the duty to ensure she actually washed them. The TI then assigned me the duty to oversee and ensure that she took a shower. The trainee and I both remained silent as she washed herself, and I kept my eyes averted.

Although no one spoke about it, I'm sure everyone felt a sense of humiliation on her behalf. Who knew what event in her past had caused her to avoid bathing? Whatever her reasons, thankfully, we never had to repeat the episode again.

As time went on, I continued to struggle to understand why some of the trainees had joined the Air Force. I expected I would have to work hard, do as I was told, apply myself, and do my best— all of which were second nature to me because of my upbringing. It was mystifying to me how anyone could have believed it would be different or easy. Perhaps some of the women were trying to escape some type of "hell" that I couldn't comprehend. Admittedly, I'd lived a sheltered life prior to entering the Air Force. Having been raised on a farm in Central Minnesota, my frame of reference and knowledge of inner cities was almost nonexistent. I didn't know about abusive families, drug addiction, or other social problems.

As I assumed the role of dorm chief, I noticed the change in my personality during basic training. I had to become more forceful and direct and take on a tougher persona. I began to find a different voice, which at times meant I had to yell at the flight. I had grown up with my father barking orders at us, using a strong, firm voice to give directions, but my parents had never yelled at us. During basic training, the consistent yelling I had to do to get the flight to act and perform their duties was extremely uncomfortable. All I wanted the flight to do was listen, do their assigned tasks on time, be responsible, and work together. Additionally, I didn't want my TI singling me out for not being able to control the flight or accomplish the required tasks. Most of all, I wanted to successfully graduate basic training.

Some of the trainees showed their ability to become true leaders, but there were others who couldn't even pass their physical fitness test or training. A couple of trainees were medically boarded out, which meant they had some type of medical condition that didn't allow them to successfully complete basic training or disqualified them for continued service. In general, basic training had a way of showing us whether we had the ability to continue forward.

At some point in basic training, those who came in "open general" received their assignments. One day, the TI approached me.

"Jelinski, do you like pilots?" she asked.

"Yes, ma'am!" I responded automatically.

"Good, because you got air traffic control," she said.

*Yeeessss! Thank you, intuition, and thank you, God!* was all I could think at that moment.

Our first TI, a female Senior Airman, was reassigned after a few weeks. We were then assigned a male TI, Staff Sergeant R. Earnest. On his very first day, I approached him and explained that our flight hadn't been able to shower in three days. It was my responsibility to bring the matter to his attention to ensure the well-being of the flight. He allowed time for us to shower.

A short while later, we had a uniform and locker inspection. To prepare, we were required to cut off all loose threads, remove quality-inspection stickers from our uniforms, and ensure they were ironed, starched, and evenly spaced within our locker. Our boots had to be shined to a high gloss with not a speck of dirt or dust on them. Our laundry bag that hung on a bedpost could only have a certain amount of items in it. We also had to fold our towels, T-shirts, underwear, pantyhose, and socks in certain dimensions. All the items in our wall-locker drawers had to be evenly aligned and flush to the locker. We had a small area for a comb, hairbrush, toothbrush, toothpaste, soap, and soap container. All items had to be clean, dry, and serviceable—this meant that our brushes and combs could not have any hair or dust in them, and the plastic soap containers could not have water or soap scum in them. After a short time, we caught on, and most of us threw away our hairbrushes prior to inspections and switched from bar soap to liquid. Our irons could not have any water in them when the TI tipped them upside down. Many of us got caught with a few drips of spray starch in the cap or water in the caps of the shampoo and conditioner bottles. The standard of "clean, dry, and serviceable" was strictly enforced and became engrained in every one of us.

As the dorm chief, I helped others get their lockers and drawers squared away in preparation of the first inspection by our new TI. After I'd assisted some of my fellow trainees, I quickly spaced my hangers and aligned the clothing in my drawers. Then I waited, like everyone else, for the results.

With the entire flight in the dayroom, Staff Sergeant Earnest called me to my locker. I suspected this was not going to be good. He quietly explained that he could have redlined, or failed, me because of the quality-inspection stickers that had not been removed and the excess threads that had not been cut off my uniforms. As I stood before him, I was scared of being "recycled" or put back a class. I was afraid of failure and of being humiliated.

But Staff Sergeant Earnest went on to say that he would not fail me because he recognized that I was the only thing holding the flight together. He understood that with all the turmoil as a result of the change in TIs, I provided the stability for the flight. With an overwhelming sense of relief, I thanked and assured him it would not happen again. Through these experiences, I realized that Staff Sergeant Earnest was fair. I also came to believe that he trusted me.

What I learned from this experience—besides getting my locker squared away for the next inspection—was that while it was important as dorm chief to help others, I needed to take care of my individual requirements as well. I had spent a great deal of time to ensure that others were ready, yet I had failed to properly prepare myself. After the inspection, I quickly got my uniforms and locker in order.

I was embarrassed, but fortunately for me, Staff Sergeant Earnest practiced and modeled what he'd been taught—a good supervisor is supposed to criticize in private and give praise in public. Rather than feeling sorry for myself after this episode, I committed to work harder, do better, and be the best example possible, no matter what. I understood that our flight of trainees was looking to me to lead the way. Instead of letting the fear of failure paralyze me, it drove me harder to succeed.

⁂

After a short time, we were assigned our third training instructor—Sergeant D. R. Fox. Sergeant Fox had just returned from maternity leave. She stood all four feet something and was a real firecracker. Her orders were short and crisp. Like my previous TIs, she quickly trusted me and my judgment. She asked for a nightly report on what had transpired each day. This was before computers, so every night, I handwrote a lengthy report and finished around midnight. Mornings seemed to come earlier and earlier as I managed these additional responsibilities.

All trainees are issued a basic training manual they must study and are tested on toward the end of basic training. This book contained everything enlisted personnel needed to know about the USAF and all that was necessary to become an Airman. Late one evening, during the final days before testing, Sergeant Fox called up to the flight through the speaker, which we called the "squawk box," to check in with me. I had been in her office writing the usual report and bawling over the fact that the test was quickly approaching, and I had not even cracked open my basic training manual. While the other trainees were required to study as they waited in line for various appointments, our TI gave me the task to watch over them and ensure they were in fact studying, which did not allow me the opportunity to study. Writing the lengthy reports in the evening also took away precious night study time. On routine evenings, it was my responsibility to oversee the flight and ensure that all assigned nightly duties were completed before "lights-out." Once lights were out, I went into the TI's office to write my report.

When the TI heard in my voice that I was upset, she came up to the flight deck to talk with me. I explained that I had not had the opportunity to study, and I was certain I would fail the exam. This was so uncharacteristic of me—I always overprepared for exams—but my responsibility to stand guard over a dysfunctional flight, combined with the task of writing nightly reports, had left no time for me to study. Sergeant Fox, not realizing that this had been happening, understood and took immediate action to help.

The next day, she chose one of the smartest trainees in our flight and told her to go to the library with me and cover the most important points in the basic training manual. Airman Basic Elizabeth T. Henderson did just that. I was pleased that I passed the exam, but I knew in my heart that given the appropriate amount of study time, I could have been an honor graduate.

There wasn't time to dwell on the end result, though, because I needed to start focusing on what lay ahead. I had to get to my tech school base and get through Air Traffic Control (ATC) school. This was a big lesson in learning to let things go and focus on what was important, which happened to be the next leg in my journey.

Looking back, I realize this experience helped me learn the first principles of what it means to be a leader. I needed to take care of my Airmen first and do my best to support them. I needed to assure them that I had their back. Little did I know then, but this first experience with balancing my personal requirements against the needs of others set the stage for my future career. Sergeant Fox also showed me how a good leader behaves: she took care of me, listened to my concerns, and then took swift decisive action on my behalf. Her leadership example stuck with me throughout my career.

Although I didn't recognize it at the time, being dorm chief was my very first leadership opportunity in the United States Air Force.

Sergeant Fox wrote in my graduation book, and over the years, I have reflected on her words many times:

> To my best dorm chief,
>
> What can I say but thank you for your support and excellent leadership towards this flight. It's been hard and you still did it. I'm really proud of you. You have earned something very few AMN get from me—my respect and admiration for a job well done. If you ever need some support you know where we are. I wish all my AMN were as super as you are and tried as hard as you have. I'm proud to say that I helped train you and guide you in your AF career. When things get rough believe in yourself and always strive for that little bit extra from everything you try. Smile when you think of us here in the 43rd and don't forget what you have been taught. You're good, and no one can take that from you. Your leadership is sound and one of the best I've seen in an AMN. Be the outstanding AMN that you are and continue to shine. Don't hide behind the bushes when you leave but glow like a bright light that guides others. I expect you to excel in your AF career and look forward to news from you and life in Tech School. Be good and take care of yourself. You're the best.
>
> Sgt. Fox

I didn't tell Sergeant Fox, but hiding behind the bushes was pretty much what I planned to do after graduation.

# CHAPTER 8

# Air Traffic Control School

On December 30, 1984, I boarded a bus at Lackland and headed for Keesler AFB in Mississippi. Fortunately, one of my squad leaders and I had become good friends in basic military training, and we arrived at Keesler together. Airman Christine Garcia was like my younger sister. She and my sister Shannon were about the same age and even shared the same birthday. Airman Garcia was assigned to attend Wideband Radio technical training, and I would be attending Air Traffic Control (ATC) training.

I desperately wanted to succeed in ATC school, but it did not come easily for me. Several classmates, including James A. Cody, seemed to effortlessly grasp the concepts. Little did I know that about twenty-five years later, Jim and I would reconnect at a conference and ultimately compete for the most senior enlisted position in the Air Force.

I studied nonstop—literally using every waking moment I had. That included studying at two thirty in the morning under my blanket with a flashlight, as well as during evenings and on weekends. After my experience as the dorm chief, I chose to not volunteer for any additional duties. Many former dorm chiefs became what were called "ropes." Ropes had different responsibilities, such as assigning squad bay duties, leading physical fitness training, or marching their flight to and from school. When I was asked to become a rope, I declined, sticking with my intent to "hide behind the bushes."

I also chose to not get involved with any extracurricular activities. So while friends were out having fun at the beach, going to the movies, or spending time in the Airman's Club, I spent my time at the library or "fish bowl." We called it the fish bowl because it was mainly made of glass. Christine would come by the fish bowl, peer at me through the glass, and tease me to come out and do things with her, but I'd always tell her I needed to study.

In ATC school, our instructors threw a lot of information and reading at us daily. On our very first day, we received a manual on basic air traffic control concepts and terminology—and were tested on it the following day. We had to quickly grasp concepts and pass frequent tests. Each test was important since most of what we were taught was foundational to what we learned next. With no knowledge about the ATC career field and no prior aviation experience, this was all new to me. It was like learning a foreign language.

On top of that, I had been out of high school for more than five years and had to relearn study habits. After school, there were days when our flight had extra duties, as well as physical fitness training and inspections, which all took away from our nightly study time. Having no frame of reference for the specific ATC language in those early weeks, I couldn't discern what was most important for me to memorize. I spent many hours trying to memorize large amounts of information that went way beyond the scope of what ultimately showed up on the test. In addition to the foreign subject matter, it was difficult to absorb new information during class after staying up late at night to study. I soon realized I needed extra help, and I was committed to do whatever it took to be successful.

The curriculum consisted of six learning blocks, some of which were more difficult than others. Those of us who were struggling were teamed up with prior active-duty service members or with students who were doing exceptionally well and used their help during certain blocks. They were my lifelines, and I'm not sure I would have passed ATC school without their assistance. After performing well on the first couple of block tests, I saw the possibility of being an honor graduate. Because I graduated high school with honors but did not achieve honors in basic training, the goal of achieving that recognition in ATC school became extremely important to me.

Going through ATC school reinforced my guiding principles of "never ever quit, stay focused, and work hard." Once more, I knew that perseverance and commitment to everything I did would pay dividends. I understood that instant gratification was overrated and usually meaningless. Anything worth having took extra effort. I was not afraid of hard work, and I accepted that I had to work harder than others in my class—I'd done that before. I was all in: ready, willing, and able to do whatever it took to excel. I recognized that the USAF was paying for me to go to school, learn a new set of skills, and be a good Airman. I felt a deep sense of duty to do what the Air Force asked of me and to even go beyond those expectations.

About midway through ATC school, students received notification of the base, where they would be assigned upon graduation. I was elated when I found out I was assigned to Laughlin AFB, Texas. I later came to realize I was the only person in the entire USAF who was excited about being assigned to Laughlin AFB! Laughlin was known as "the pits" of an assignment because it was out in the middle of nowhere in a hot and dusty area, where there wasn't much of anything to do. As a Minnesotan, though, I was excited about being in a warm climate with lots of sunshine and no snow.

My excitement was short-lived, however. Within a few days of my assignment, I received a second set of orders, diverting me to Offutt AFB, Nebraska: back to the tundra. I could not believe the United States Air Force was doing this to me. I immediately thought, *What happened to the pitch "Join the Air Force, travel, and see the world"?* Here I was being stationed five hundred miles away from my hometown, where the weather was just as bleak in the winter.

My attitude plummeted. I didn't show my dissatisfaction to anyone, but inwardly, I felt deflated. I had hoped to see another part of the United States, where I wouldn't be shoveling snow for the next few winters. Somehow, though, I knew I had to change my attitude and make the best of this new assignment. I needed to find the silver lining. Besides, there were more pressing things for me to worry about—like getting through ATC school.

During the latter part of our ATC training, we had a short five-day block of instruction. For four of those days, I was hospitalized due to a severe infection that required intravenous antibiotics. My classmate Sergeant Bud Stewart, a prior service member who was retraining into ATC and with whom I'd been partnered, came to the hospital every night and went over the material they had covered each day in class. He taught me what I needed to know to pass the block test. My instructor gave me an option to take an academic "wash-back," which meant I'd be placed in the class behind me without receiving a permanent stain on my record. An academic washback is for something other than poor performance—like a hospitalization.

My other option was to take the block exam and hopefully pass and stay with my class. If I failed, I would be recycled, or put back with the class behind us, and it would reflect on my record. This was block five of six, so I chose to stay with my class. I took the risk and tested as scheduled. Up to that point, I'd carried about a 93–95 percent average. On the block five exam, I got a 78. It was a passing grade, which allowed me to stay and graduate with my class, but once again, my score completely knocked me out of the running to be an honor graduate. I was naturally driven and wanted to excel, so this was difficult to accept gracefully.

After the test, I sometimes questioned my decision. I was disappointed in my performance since I had worked so hard to do well and score high on all the other block tests. Eventually, though, I understood that it was more important for me to stay with my class than to be an honor graduate. I saw that our class had bonded and come to rely on each other as we went through the academic challenges of ATC school. Being part of a team and graduating with that team was important to me, as we had helped and encouraged one another through difficult experiences. We had been there for one another—no matter what! I could not imagine falling back to a class of strangers after being with my classmates for five blocks. I know I would make the same decision today.

Much like my experience with Staff Sergeant Earnest, I once again saw a noncommissioned officer (NCO) leading and going above and beyond to help a fellow Airman be successful. Sergeant Stewart did not have to come to the hospital four nights in a row to help me. This was another example of what leaders do for their people. I may not have aced the exam, but because of his help, I passed and was able to stay with my class.

After graduation, controllers had an option to apply and stay at Keesler as an associate instructor. I applied and was accepted. As a new Airman, this was a second leadership opportunity. I was able to help other students in the ATC simulator. My primary reason to stay at Keesler as an associate instructor was that it gave me an opportunity to study and learn my "part one" or Local Area Knowledge (LAK) for Offutt AFB, Nebraska, which would give me a head start in my future training. The LAK contained runway lengths/widths, taxiway and navigational aid information, pattern altitudes, frequencies, reporting points, coordination procedures, and so on. Being an associate instructor also showed my supervisor and new crew at Offutt that I was working hard to learn the material.

One of the side benefits was the time it gave me to rest after my illness and hospitalization. During my time as an associate instructor, I had the freedom to go out after my duty day and do things I'd not had time for during ATC school. During the day, I worked with students in the ATC simulator, and at night, I studied the LAK at my own pace. After six weeks as an associate instructor, armed with knowledge of Offutt AFB, I was on my way to a new adventure.

# CHAPTER 9

# Offutt AFB, Nebraska

In the days leading up to my departure to Nebraska, I visualized what would be next. Although my assignment to Offutt AFB was not the one I'd dreamed about, that was where the Air Force was sending me. I realized I did have one choice I could make, though: I could bring my disappointed attitude with me or make a conscious decision to change my attitude. I chose the latter.

I decided I was going to arrive at Offutt, in process to my new unit, settle in my dorm, and begin to be the best Airman possible. I was going to do everything the United States Air Force asked me to do: train and work hard, learn the material, become the best air traffic controller I could be, volunteer wherever possible, and do all the things required and expected of a new Airman.

Changing my attitude was a very conscious and deliberate decision. At the time, although I didn't understand how my attitude could affect my career, I intuitively knew that bringing a negative attitude would lead to trouble. I didn't want to be labeled a bad Airman or viewed as a problem.

The great thing about attitude is that no one can give it to you, and no one can take it away. You get to decide what type of attitude you're going to have. Motivational speaker Zig Ziglar famously said, "Your attitude, not your aptitude, will determine your altitude."[2] I wholeheartedly agree! Consciously changing my attitude was a pivotal and significant decision as a young Airman—a decision that set me on an entirely different path for the rest of my career and life.

At Offutt AFB, I was one of a handful of women in ATC, and I placed a tremendous amount of pressure on myself to learn more and excel faster than my male counterparts. I studied hard, went to work, went to the gym, and enjoyed free time—all the while doing what the Air Force asked me to do. I volunteered for the Airman's Advisory Council and held the treasurer's position, served as a big sister through the Big Brothers Big Sisters program, and volunteered at holiday events. One year, I even played an elf and Santa's helper at the Airman's Christmas party.

Every month, our squadron held award boards. Whoever won the monthly board went on to the quarterly board competition. The winner at the quarterly level competed at the base level for Airman, Noncommissioned Officer, and Senior Noncommissioned Officer of the Year for Offutt AFB. In each competition, a panel of three to four senior military members questioned participants. They graded the Airmen on customs and courtesies, military bearing, uniform standards, and on their responses to specific questions. Most of those questions were on Air Force history, but a few required opinions in response. I was successful in the Airman of the Month and Airman of the Quarter board competitions and won many of the awards. Through those experiences, I learned a great deal about our Air Force and how to prepare for and face boards. All that preparation paid significant dividends later in my career.

One year, after winning quarterly boards, I faced the Airman of the Year board for the base. My good friend Senior Airman Thomas Scott and I faced the same board. We had studied, prepared, and practiced. When the final results came in, Senior Airman Scott was chosen as the Airman of the Year for Offutt AFB—and I was just half a point behind. While extremely disappointed to lose, I was happy for him. I believed he deserved the honor and knew he, too, had worked hard for this recognition. Understanding the effort it took to come that far, I remained dedicated to my studies and determined to prepare for future opportunities.

# CHAPTER 10

# It's Official

In order of increasing complexity, the three positions in the tower are flight data, ground control, and local control. Even though the level of complexity increases, each position is critical and essential to the other and to the safe and effective flow of air traffic. In flight data, the controller learns the layout of the airport, how to request and receive clearances and operate the majority of the tower equipment, how to acquire and relay weather, and how to coordinate various procedures between local and ground control. After mastering the flight data position, a controller moves on to the ground control position. This position has the responsibility (with the exception of the active runways) for all movement on the ground, taxiways, ramps, and run-up areas. The ground controller approves the movement of all vehicles and taxis all aircraft to and from the active runway, often in coordination with local control. After mastering the ground control position, a controller moves to the local control position, the most complex and challenging position to master. Tower local controllers have responsibility for the active runway and airspace within a five-mile radius of the airport from ground level up to approximately three thousand feet.

In preparation for each position, I worked an eight-hour shift and studied for another two to three hours, either before or after my shifts, including weekends and days off. There could be no shortcuts or half steps. I knew lives would depend on my mastering every detail of each position.

ᕦ

For an air traffic controller, certification day is a big deal. Once certified in flight data, ground control, and local control, an Airman receives a facility certification and is upgraded to a five-skill level. Receiving a "five-skill level" certification means that an Airman can work as a controller without the need for another controller to be plugged in and working alongside them. And, at that level, controllers are then able to officially wear the coveted ATC badge.[3]

Like most trainees, the anticipation of undergoing my local control and facility certification process was nerve-racking. What if I blew it? What if I sequenced aircraft wrong? What if I didn't use the precise phraseology? My nemesis, the fear of failure, was ever-present. What if I had a separation or wake turbulence error? To diminish my anxiety, I spent as much extra time as possible studying the ATC rules, procedures, and standard phraseology. After the written exam, I knew that within a few days the training, standardization, and evaluation controller (TSN) would be plugged in with me, watching and listening to every word I spoke and every action I took.

The day of my local control and facility certification finally arrived—the day a TSN would assess my skills. It was a clear blue-sky day for flying and for being certified. There was adequate air traffic that day, allowing the TSN to gauge whether or not I was ready to be certified as a fully rated controller. It just so happened, though, that Offutt AFB's primary tower was under renovation and we had to work out of an alternate fixed facility. Right through the center of the alternate tower cab, a large square pillar obstructed our vision. It stretched from the top of the tower cab to the floor. Facing the runway, controllers had a partial visual of the entire tower pattern. To see the portion of the pattern behind us, we had to continually get up and physically move around the pillar. When there wasn't much air traffic to control, working around the pillar was manageable. But during a period of high-volume traffic, it became extremely annoying to get up and peer around the pillar to see where each plane was located.

Because I had dealt with this situation during my training, though, moving around the pillar was just one more obstruction to deal with. For about an hour, the TSN watched and listened to me. When he finally shook my hand and said "Congratulations," I was elated. With an adrenaline rush and a huge sigh of relief, the rating exam was over.

Within a few days, the chief controller, TSN, and fellow controllers gathered in our training room, and I was awarded my five-level ATC badge. I wished in that moment that my parents had been there to witness this event. As I received my badge, I pictured them there, standing proud. My mom had been my number one supporter, and when I was asked to make brief comments afterward, I spoke about her as I choked back tears. While in ATC school, she had listened for weeks as I talked about how scared I was that I might fail the upcoming block tests. In response to my concerns, she always told me, "You can do it." Now that I had, I wished more than anything that she and Dad were standing in the training room to witness this achievement.

Thinking back to the day I enlisted, I knew this moment was what the AF recruiter had talked about when he described what I could accomplish in the Air Force. Although what he'd described sounded incredibly exciting, to be completely honest, I had never in my wildest dreams envisioned this actually coming to fruition. This farm girl from Central Minnesota, who'd continually struggled with math and never got out of the dummy class, who received little encouragement in school to achieve, and who struggled with a deep fear of failure since basic military training, was now a full-fledged air traffic controller.

ꜱ

Everything transmitted on a frequency and landline in the tower and radar facilities is recorded and maintained for thirty days. As part of the ceremony, I received a cassette tape of my recorded time in position during my certification with every transmission and response to and from every aircraft that I worked in the tower pattern. To this day, I still have that recording. It represented the pinnacle of all my hard work and was the prize for the endless hours of studying and training at ATC school. The recording also represented the end of my training and the beginning of a new chapter in my career.

One of the rewards of receiving a facility rating was the opportunity to fly in a T-38 jet trainer, which we called a "fam flight," or familiarization flight. I was superexcited about the actuality of this flight but also nervous that I would get sick. Many controllers told stories and made fun of others who got sick and threw up in their masks. I did not want to turn out to be one of *those* controllers!

On the day of my T-38 flight, I ate very little—only saltine crackers. During the preflight check, the pilot asked what type of ride I wanted.

"Certainly not like a corkscrew roller coaster!" I responded firmly.

Yes, I was tough, but I also knew my limits. Let's just say I'd had a bad experience on a corkscrew-like roller coaster as a teenager—and I had no desire to repeat anything like it again.

Taking this opportunity seriously, rather than for pure pleasure, I told the pilot I wanted to spend some time in the tower pattern to get a visual from the air of the local Offutt AFB flying area. Even though I knew I could go up and focus on the pure joy of the ride, which was the reward for all my hard work, I wanted to learn something. Although this was a chance to experience barrel rolls, sightsee, and take in the countryside, I wanted to see from the pilots' perspective what they saw at the various reporting points and to experience the traffic pattern they flew. This would help me visualize what the pilots experience and would make me a better controller.

After the preflight and safety briefing, we headed to the jet. The pilot went through the aircraft prechecks, and we listened to the automatic terminal information service (ATIS) recording. The ATIS is an hourly recording that airports broadcast to reduce frequency congestion with reports on weather, notices to Airmen (NOTAMs), the active runway, tower frequencies, and other pieces of useful information. The ATIS is updated hourly and when weather and airport conditions change.

Once we were ready to taxi to the active runway, the pilot allowed me to contact the ground controller for taxi instructions. Sitting on the runway, with engines running and me in the backseat of a T-38, was surreal. Over the frequency, the tower controller said, "Ace 1, [call-sign], wind, cleared for takeoff." The roar of the engines was charged with adrenaline as our flight took off.

Flying in the T-38 was completely different from my two previous flights in a commercial aircraft. Once we climbed to an appropriate altitude, we got a block of airspace from ATC that was all ours to play in. The pilot let me take control of "the stick" and fly the aircraft. It was unimaginable that I could actually take control—yet there I was, flying the T-38. As I sat in the back seat with the stick in one hand, I felt the exhilaration of controlling such a powerful and magnificent machine. Of course, I knew the pilot was in full command of the aircraft and ready to take control at a moment's notice, but it didn't matter. I was flying a USAF jet and having fun!

We did a few barrel rolls, and as we were flying back to the airfield, he pointed out various reporting points. Once we landed and taxied in, I thought to myself, *Who gets to do this?* The flight was thrilling, and I felt a bit giddy. I realized I would never have had the chance to fly a T-38 if I'd stayed in my hometown. And one of the best parts was...I did not exit the plane with a barf bag!

# CHAPTER 11

# The Marine

In the summer of 1986, a friend of mine stationed with me at Offutt AFB drove me home to Minnesota. We both had leave, and he was going to continue on to Michigan to visit his family and then pick me up on the way back. We had a seven-hour drive and lots of time to talk about our lives.

"You're going to meet someone, fall in love, and get married," Mark teased me.

"Be still, my heart!" I responded with a laugh. "In Little Falls, Minnesota? I don't think so."

I knew pretty much everyone and was not interested.

As fate would have it, though, one night while out with friends, I met a young Marine. We danced to a few songs, and I tried to lead. The Marine wouldn't have it.

"I'll follow you anywhere, but not on the dance floor," he said with a smile.

His name was Gary, and he was an amazing dancer. It was easy to fall in step with him. However, as much as I enjoyed dancing with him, I made it clear I was not interested in anything more. He was persistent, though, and wouldn't give up. Over the course of the evening, after declining several invitations for dinner, I finally gave him a reason.

"I don't date troops," I explained.

Gary stood up very tall and squared his shoulders.

"I am not a troop," he replied, a little indignant. "I am a Captain in the United States Marine Corps."

It was quite obvious that I had offended him, which had not been my intent. Feeling bad and somewhat embarrassed, I agreed to meet him for a drink the following evening. When he asked me to the movies after that, I also said yes. Because I didn't really know him, I asked my older sister to accompany us—Gary was not expecting that when he picked me up!

I did agree to a solo dinner later that week. Over the course of a few short dates, this young captain had swept me off my feet—on and off the dance floor. It made me a believer in the concept of "love at first sight." We had known each other for three weeks and had about five dates when we got engaged. We were married six months later.

It was apparent to both of us that our first meeting was fate. I had requested leave two weeks prior to the actual time I went home. My leave had been denied because I was required to work in the tower during an airshow. Had I gone home as originally requested, Gary and I would have never met. We believed we were meant to meet each other, but we wondered how we could ever overcome the obstacles to be together.

Although we were obviously drawn to each other, the deck seemed to be stacked against us. Gary was a United States Marine Corps officer; I was enlisted. He was a Republican, and I, at the time, was a Democrat. He was Protestant, and I was Catholic. He had been raised in a white-collar family, and I had been raised in a blue-collar family. He had three children from a prior marriage, and I had none. I had an annulment, and he did not. We were stationed five hundred miles apart and in different branches of the military. Who would believe this marriage was ever going to work?

With both of us on active duty, one an officer in the Marine Corps and the other enlisted in the Air Force, we didn't see how we could ever be stationed at the same location, or even in the same state, at the same time. More importantly, we had to deal with the issue of breaking the fraternization rules—the military prohibits dating between ranks. Although the Air Force was not going to kick me out, the Marine Corps told Gary that one of us had to get off active duty, or else we'd face disciplinary action.

Once we knew the Corps' position, the answer was clear. At the time, Gary had ten years in the Marines while I'd been with the Air Force for just under two years. Gary also paid child support, which we would not be able to manage on my pay. For Gary to stay active duty, I had to transfer to either the National Guard[4] or the Reserves. I decided to apply for "Palace Chase," a program in the Air Force that allows Airmen to leave active-duty service and transfer to the Guard or Reserve. If approved, an Airman has to serve double the time remaining on their active-duty contract. Not everyone gets approved for the program, as the needs of the Air Force always come first.

Gary had decided that if I were denied approval to Palace Chase, he would get out of the Marine Corps. Fortunately, we never had to consider that. I was approved for Palace Chase and transferred into the Air National Guard (ANG). It was up to me to find a slot or position within the ANG in whatever state I would be living, so I began to look for positions within the California Air National Guard in Southern California. Gary would be stationed at Camp Pendleton, near Oceanside.

It was an extremely difficult decision to leave active duty and transfer to the Air National Guard. I loved the Air Force and embraced the culture, comradery, and structure. I knew in my heart that if I worked hard, did what was asked of me, and was a good Airman, I could have a successful career in the Air Force and could also pursue higher education. The Air Force was my niche, and I was proud to be enlisted. Deep down, I really did not want to leave.

"The Air Guard needs good people too," my flight commander told me. That reassured me that I could be equally successful in the Air National Guard.

As difficult as the decision was, ultimately, the power of love won out. Also, I felt like I could have my cake and eat it too—I could marry Gary, and he and I could continue to serve. My intuition told me the transfer would be approved and marrying Gary was the right decision. I was fortunate—my request was approved.

Gary Hall and I were married on February 14, 1987, in Sobieski, Minnesota. That's not a good month for a wedding in Central Minnesota, but we were fortunate to have good weather and no snowstorms. Gary came to Offutt AFB to get me, and we drove to Illinois. His children flew in from California so they could see their grandparents, who lived in Illinois. We then jumped in his two-door, five-seat Nissan Pulsar with luggage, wedding dress, and three kids and drove from Illinois to Minnesota for the wedding. We hardly had room to breathe, let alone move, but we all weathered the trip.

Gary and I had worked with Father David Benz, an Air Force Captain and former Marine, at Offutt AFB on our premarital requirements to marry in the Catholic Church. When Father Benz unexpectedly showed up at our wedding, Gary and I weren't the only ones surprised—the entire church gasped in unison when he walked out onto the altar. Father Benz is African American, and I don't believe there had *ever* been a Black man in that church. My dear eighty-plus-year-old grandmother, who wore thick glasses, asked rather loudly, "Is that a Black man?" God bless her! We were honored that Father Benz took the time and drove the five hundred miles to co-officiate our wedding.

We have continued to see him throughout our marriage while living in California, Hawaii, Washington, DC, and Colorado. It was an honor to have now *Monsignor* Benz attend my retirement ceremony in DC and visit us in Colorado, where we asked him to bless our new home.

After the wedding, the kids went with their grandparents to Illinois, and Gary and I flew off to the Bahamas. Following a wonderful honeymoon, my new husband drove me from Minnesota to Offutt, then returned to Chicago to prepare for a deployment to Norway. One day, Gary waited until the wee hours of the morning and climbed a hill in subzero temperatures to call his new bride on a brick telephone all the way from Norway. After the brief hellos, my response was, "Hurry up. I have to get to aerobics."

That was probably not the best thing for a new bride to say to her husband, but Gary knew I was driven in my work and physical fitness. He had witnessed this on many occasions when he would drive to Offutt to see me, and I would make him power walk with me in all types of weather.

There he was, in the freezing conditions of Norway, being his selfless, romantic self…and I was more concerned about aerobics. Hindsight being twenty-twenty, I should have skipped aerobics that day! Admittedly, it was not my finest hour.

# CHAPTER 12

# The Air National Guard

My last day in the Offutt AFB Control Tower turned out to be one of my best days in the tower. Once the supervisors learned that I was transferring to the Air National Guard, I didn't get much time in Local Control. On my final day, however, the watch supervisor gave me several hours to work in that position. Everything clicked, and when I left the tower at the end of my shift, I felt exhilaration and pride in a job well done.

Although I was looking forward to transferring into the Air National Guard and excited to start my life with Gary, I also felt a sense of loss. After spending a short time in the Air Force, I began to understand all that the Air Force had to offer, such as additional training, promotions, travel, and the ability to own a home. I was also leaving the active-duty Air Force family, which I loved and knew I would greatly miss. The Air National Guard, on the other hand, was a component of the Air Force I did not know much about. I had been planning to start my college education, yet for some reason, I sensed that leaving the active-duty Air Force might delay that goal.

In April 1987, I transferred into an Air National Guard Unit—the 261st Combat Communications Squadron (CBCS) in Van Nuys, California. This unit was projected to receive an Air Traffic Control Squadron mission, so they accepted me as a transfer. After our wedding, Gary and I lived in Illinois for a few months as he finished his Marine Corps assignment.

During this time, I flew to California to perform my required monthly drill duty. I was fortunate that my good friend Christine from basic military training had grown up in California and her parents happened to live in Van Nuys. Although they didn't know me, she arranged for me to stay with them on my drill weekends. I came to look at them as surrogate parents, and they seemed genuinely happy to have me as their surrogate daughter.

Because I'd been approved into the ANG under the Palace Chase program, I had to serve double the amount of time left on my Air Force active-duty contract. At the time, I had a year and a half of active service remaining out of my three-year enlistment, so I would need to serve three more years in the ANG. That was fine with me because I definitely wanted to continue to serve.

However, transferring to the ANG was a huge culture change. On active duty, I had been used to a certain level of decorum. We learned to address noncommissioned officers, senior noncommissioned officers, and commissioned officers properly and with respect. My uniforms were always heavily starched, and my boots were spit-shined. Due to my training, I followed these rules, customs, and courtesies to the fullest. I believed in high standards and in going above what was expected. To me, it was important for an Airman to always do their best to make a good impression and show leadership that they were conscientious and accountable in all things—dress and appearance, standards, training, personal deportment, attitude, and more. Quite frankly, I was a gung ho Airman.

In Van Nuys, California, there was a casualness to the Air Guard that I had not expected. A good number of the airmen called one another by their first names, which was unheard of on active duty. Dress and appearance standards were fairly lax, and some Airmen did not even polish their boots, let along starch their uniforms or ensure that their hats were crisp, not crumpled. Wigs were authorized for wear in 1987, and some male Guard members actually wore them. Initially, it was a shock to see some men get out of their car and put their long hair up into a wig. Most hair and mustaches were not within regulation—at least not according to what I had seen on active duty. It was difficult for me to understand why many Airmen did not seem to strive to be the very best Airmen they could be. This was a culture I knew I would have to try to understand.

My squadron in the Air Guard initiated a program called "Super Troop of the Month." The leadership looked for Airmen who went above and beyond in dress and appearance and military bearing. I won the award consecutively for several months. After a few months, a noncommissioned officer told me he was going to roll me in the dirt and step on my boots. I guess he was tired of the same person winning, but it didn't change the way I presented myself. At first, his comments angered me, but then I let them motivate me even more to consistently maintain the highest levels of professionalism, dress, and deportment. I was always squared away. Eventually, other Airmen began to win Super Troop of the Month, and I was pleased to think that perhaps my dress and appearance had motivated them to be better.

The cultural difference was not the only surprise I experienced in California. Early in the morning on a drill weekend, when I was staying with Mr. and Mrs. Garcia in Van Nuys, I suddenly woke up because the house was shaking. *What is happening?* I thought, confused. I ran to the master bedroom, and all I remember is Christine's parents yelling at me to get in the doorway. Naturally, earthquakes were something they were used to, but this Minnesota gal had never experienced such a phenomenon. Once the shaking stopped, they checked to make sure I was okay. Admittedly, it took a little while for me to calm down and go back to sleep.

As I waited for an ATC mission, I earned a secondary Air Force Specialty Code as a ground radio operator. About a year and a half after joining the California Air Guard, I came to realize that the 261st Combat Communications Squadron was never going to get an ATC mission. Against all advice from my supervisor and colleagues, I transferred to the 147th CBCS in San Diego as a ground radio operator. I became proficient in ground radio operations, where I got to talk on the radio or key the mic, and I even learned Morse code.

While considering this transfer, some had cautioned me that the commander was a challenge. However, as I weighed things out, the potential benefits far outweighed the perceived challenges. Most important was the unit's location—it was much closer to Camp Pendleton. I thought to myself, *I'm a good Airman, I do my job, and I'm not a troublemaker. What can possibly go wrong?* After much thought, I listened to my intuition and transferred.

I soon realized that the "rumor mill" was just that: a bunch of rumors. It seemed to me that those who didn't have a good experience with the Commander most likely had difficulty following the rules and meeting his expectations. I was pleased that the Commander, Lieutenant Colonel George Bowen, and I developed a solid professional relationship. Years later, he, too, transferred to Hawaii, and he often stopped by my office to visit.

I enjoyed my duty with the 147th, and while there, I had the opportunity to go on two exercises. One was to Red Beach, Marine Corps Base Camp Pendleton, and the other to Simi Valley. During one of the exercises, we did nighttime operations where aggressors tried to infiltrate our perimeter. All Guard members and aggressors were in gear outfitted with a multiple integrated laser engagement system or MILES. The MILES gear had sensors that beeped if you were hit by the laser beam of another weapon.

I was paired with a new Second Lieutenant in our foxhole. Being a gung ho Airman, I purchased camo paint for my face. Carefully following the example of how to apply the camo pattern, I was ready for nighttime operations. As the evening and exercise progressed, the lieutenant decided to leave our foxhole to check the perimeter. Upon his return, I dutifully asked him for the password of the day. It was obvious he'd forgotten it, but I challenged him two more times, just as I was trained. When the lieutenant could not provide the password and continued toward my position, I believed him to be an aggressor and fired my weapon. Immediately, his sensors went off. Needless to say, he was not pleased with me. I had done what I was trained to do, though—one shot, one kill, at night. Hooah!

❧

The biggest surprise of all occurred less than two months after arriving in California. Gary and I learned we were going to become parents. This had not been part of the plan. I had my life mapped out, and having a baby fourteen months after getting married was most definitely not a part of it. I was going to continue serving in the California ANG and planned to one day go to the FAA and become a civilian air traffic controller. Having a baby would certainly change those plans.

It took time for me to come to terms with having a child at that point in our lives, but ultimately, I did come to accept God's plan. The turning point came one day when I was about three months along. Gary was away in the field, so I went to the mall alone. I forced myself to go into the baby sections of some of the stores, and I wandered the aisles and looked at all the baby items. As I did, I finally connected with the reality that, yes, indeed, I was going to have a baby, and Gary and I were going to be parents. Life was going to look different, but I knew we would figure it out.

Shortly after that epiphany, I had an experience that further deepened my conviction that all would be well. Our child was a mere speck in my belly when, after enjoying a beautiful day at the beach, I heard the words, "Run! Rockslide!" I looked up, and sure enough, rocks were about to rain on our heads. Gary ran one way, perpendicular to the slide (the right way—must have been that Marine training) while I, thinking I was superwoman, turned and ran toward the beach. With no time to think, I tried to outrun the falling rocks. I tried to jump over a berm of rocks and ended up falling and sliding headfirst down them. Superwoman I was not!

Soon after the dust settled, I continued to lay there. I looked around for Gary and quickly took inventory of my injuries—I was scratched, bloodied, banged up, and had a fat lip. When the beach patrol arrived, Gary was by my side, and I was crying. The medic poured a disinfectant on me, and soon I was covered in brownish liquid that stung. The only good thing that came out of this was finding out the baby was okay—and getting a ride up the cliff from the beach patrol.

Getting pregnant so soon after our wedding added an additional twist to our lives. As a part-time Drill Status Guardsman, I served one weekend a month and attended two weeks of annual training.

The rest of the time, I worked at a full-time job in the civilian sector as an assistant manager at a thrift and loan. I enjoyed the work and got to do a wide array of transactions within the loan and banking industry. With the exception of deposits, withdrawals, debits, and credits, which I'd done in my banking job in Little Falls, my other duties were all new. My primary responsibilities were approving auto loans, conducting background searches and employment verification for potential clients, and overseeing all the collections and repossessions of vehicles for our branch.

Each month, our goal was to beat the other branches and come in with the lowest number of delinquent loans. As always, wanting to do my best and come in first place, I was determined to ensure that our branch won. On many occasions, I went door to door to collect payments. I can remember one time when I had to go to National City to collect a loan payment. The client lived in a low-income neighborhood with run-down homes and rumored drug dealers. I may have been pregnant, but I felt safe as I carried a baseball bat along with me—maybe I wasn't using my best judgment at the time.

On another occasion, I drove to Chula Vista and walked in to the company where our client worked. She was several months behind on her loan payment, and I would not leave until she brought me either cash or the car keys. I had tried to collect from her on several occasions already, but this time, I was determined to win. I was done trying to help her. After I waited patiently for several hours, she finally gave up and brought me the keys.

Pretty soon, I was known as "the repo queen." One Christmas Eve, I recruited Gary and my eleven-year-old stepson, Nathan, to go on a stakeout with me. I had been trying to track down a client who was months behind on her car payments and suspected she would be at her mother's house on Christmas Eve. Sure enough, after a short recon, we located the vehicle exactly where I thought it would be. Nathan stay in the car with a flashlight. Gary and I let the air out of the tires, and I called the repossession company to hook up the vehicle and tow it away. To this day, Nathan loves to tell the story of how we repossessed a car on Christmas Eve, and he was the lookout.

One morning, I went to the bank to make our daily deposit. As I faced the teller with checks and money spread on the counter, a man jumped up right next to me, pointed a gun in my face, and told me to hit the floor. It was a bank robbery! Seven months pregnant, I literally hit the floor. I was scared to death and worried that the robber would steal my wedding ring, so I carefully slipped it off and put it in my mouth. Then I thought, *What if he makes us talk?* So I took the ring out of my mouth and put it down my blouse. Fortunately, the robber departed, and no one got hurt. Bank personnel immediately closed the doors and secured the building.

I called Gary, frantic, and before I knew it, he was in the bank. He stayed with me as the FBI interviewed me, which was unusual, since typically no one is allowed into a bank after a robbery. Maybe the FBI let him in because he was in his Marine Corps uniform, or maybe they just saw a very emotional pregnant woman. Our daughter wasn't even born yet, and already, she had been in a rockslide, an earthquake, and now a bank robbery!

# CHAPTER 13

# The Second-Worst Day of My Life

Our daughter, Ashley, was born on April 24, 1988, at Naval Hospital Camp Pendleton. A couple of days after bringing her home from the hospital, I noticed a small spot on the top of her head. The following day, the spot was about the size of a dime, and when we woke on day five, it was about the size of a quarter. I quickly got her dressed and took her to the doctor. He immediately admitted her to the hospital.

The site where the fetal heart monitor had been attached in utero to her head had become infected. The doctor told me there was a strong possibility the infection had traveled to her spine, and they needed to do a spinal tap immediately. This was serious and potentially life-threatening. Instantly, I felt an overwhelming fear that she might die. I also felt like a horrible mother for waiting five days before seeking medical attention—I'd been trying not to overreact.

Barely able to speak, I called Gary. All I could get out was, "Come to the hospital now!" He arrived within minutes, and frightened for our daughter, we held each other tightly. The doctor had Gary hold Ashley as he performed the spinal tap. I felt helpless and desperate as I watched our newborn baby scream in extreme pain.

The doctor could see that I was falling apart, so he gently suggested I step outside the room. I noticed a pay phone at the end of the hallway and immediately wanted to call my mom. Mothers can make everything better, or so I hoped. We talked briefly and prayed together. Gary emerged from the room a short time later, looking pale. Having to hold our daughter as she screamed while the doctor performed the spinal tap had been difficult for him as well.

The test result finally came back: Ashley had no infection in her spine. God had answered our prayers, but she was still a very sick little girl with wires and tubes seemingly coming out of everywhere. Gary and I sat with her all afternoon, and I stayed all night while Gary went home to be with his three older children. I felt completely helpless, though—whenever I tried to feed her, she threw up and continued to scream. I had given birth just five days before, and now I couldn't do anything for my baby. I was a total wreck. Completely exhausted, I cried right along with Ashley.

It was late when I called Gary and said, "Come." He arrived quickly and took over the watch so I could go home for a while. After a few hours of sleep, everything looked different, and I had pulled myself together. I went back to the hospital and stayed right by Ashley's side, holding her small hand. Through the grace of God, our baby daughter recovered.

# CHAPTER 14

# First Deployment as a Military Spouse

When Gary was assigned to the First Battalion, First Marine Regiment, First Marine Division, his unit had just returned from deployment and begun a new eighteen-month cycle. They spent the first six months rebuilding the unit to its authorized strength then had six months of predeployment training schedule. His unit was getting ready for a six-month deployment throughout the Western Pacific and parts of Asia (WESTPAC). This meant physical training, long rucksack marches, many overnight exercises, and longer hours each day. The battalion was trained as special operations capable, so they were often gone to different bases for specialized training.

Frankly, I wish they had trained and remained off-site because Gary's in-and-out schedule caused quite a disruption to our family routine. Coming and going, often staying home only long enough to do laundry, threw everyone's schedules and our family life off-kilter. Of course, I understood the need for months of training and preparation prior to deployment, but many times, all I could think was, *Just go already*! I fully appreciated the magnitude of his responsibilities and the significance of the upcoming deployment, but I also had a baby who needed a predictable routine and three other children who stayed with us two weekends a month.

During the predeployment and deployment phases, Gary was the S-3 (Operations Officer) for his unit. As the S-3, he was responsible for developing, scheduling, coordinating, and evaluating predeployment and deployment training exercises, personnel and equipment readiness, and coordinating with subordinate and adjacent units and higher headquarters, including foreign countries, preparing for all potential "real-world events" (combat operations). Prior to deployment, his battalion was redesignated a Battalion Landing Team and became part of the Fifteenth Marine Expeditionary Unit (MEU), Special Operations Capable, which expanded the scope of his responsibilities.[5]

A family readiness group assisted families experiencing difficulties during the deployment. Any time one of the spouses (typically a female spouse of a junior Marine) needed financial or emotional help, they were to contact a "key spouse." Due to Gary's position, I was one of those key spouses. I explained to my boss at the thrift and loan that for the duration of the deployment, I would need to take an occasional call and assist whoever needed help, but he was not at all supportive. He was a civilian who had very little understanding of the military and no desire to learn.

It was very frustrating to have a boss who also could not understand why I needed to take off two weeks for annual training as an Air National Guard member. He made me feel guilty for being gone and for making him assign my work to others. I dreaded those days when I had to call in to explain I had a sick child and couldn't come to work. My boss's mother-in-law took his kids to and from school, to their doctor appointments, and tended to them when they were sick, so of course, he couldn't relate to my difficult situation. Ashley had a lot of ear infections, and it seemed like I was at the doctor every other week—sometimes twice in a week. It was a hard time for our family, and then to have a boss like that made it even more unbearable. On a positive note, I have to admit that this particular boss taught me a lot about how not to treat your team.[6]

That six-month deployment, and even the time leading up to it, was one of the most challenging periods of my life. I was working full-time, had a drill-status Air National Guard commitment once a month, had a small child, cared for my three stepchildren every other weekend, and was responsible for the maintenance and operations of the house, yard, and car. With my family 1,400 miles away and no support system in California, it was a hectic, demanding, and challenging period. Looking back at how and when I slept—from about midnight until 5:00 a.m.—I'm not sure how I functioned.

Knowing these types of challenges are part of every military spouse's life, I had to find a way to persevere. I called my youngest sister, Shannon, and asked her to stay with me for a few months. Having her with me made life much more bearable. She took care of Ashley when I had household chores, meetings, or errands, and she was great company.

Deployments back in the late 1980s and early 1990s were so different from what they are today. Long before the days of e-mail, Skype, Facebook, smartphones, and texting, communication was far more difficult and sparse. In 1990, if we were lucky, every six weeks when the ship pulled into a port, we received a phone call—and that was only if you happened to be at home to receive the call on the landline. A few times when I wasn't home, Gary called and had to leave a voice message on our recorder. Missing him dearly, I would play the recorded message over and over just to hear his voice. I was angry at myself for not being home when he called since I knew it would be at least another month before he could call again. Gary and I wrote daily letters and numbered them. We also made sure that Ashley had pictures of her daddy to look at so she could remember his face.

Early in the deployment, I received an audit notice from the IRS. Initially, I panicked. The IRS was a big, bad, scary entity, and I knew nothing about our taxes or how to handle an audit—in the two years we'd been married, Gary had always done our taxes. I didn't even know where to look for our tax records. With the looming audit date on the IRS letter, I began to search for our tax records, going through file cabinets, drawers, and every box in storage. The search took precious time away from other responsibilities, and I was frustrated and fuming.

When Gary finally did call, I learned he had taken our previous years' taxes with him on deployment so he could work on the current taxes. Obviously, this was very thoughtful of him, but all I could think about was how much time I had wasted searching for nothing. The stress of managing everything single-handedly got directed at Gary. He was looking forward to a kind and loving conversation with his wife, but unfortunately, I let my frustration get the better of me, and he got the brunt of it.

The tax paperwork that I needed was in the next day's mail from Gary, sent from some foreign land. The silver lining of this story is that the IRS ended up owing us a refund.

So that our baby girl could stay connected to her daddy, I used a cassette player to record Gary reading storybooks. Each night, I placed Daddy's picture on the end table, put Ashley on my lap, opened the storybook, and hit play. It was Daddy's voice that she heard and his face she saw. We hoped that in six months when he returned, Ashley would recognize her daddy and not be afraid. If she was awake when Gary called, I also put her on the phone with him and prayed she would remember him.

# CHAPTER 15

# Another Scary Day

One day during Gary's WESTPAC deployment, I was home with Ashley because she had pink eye. I laid her down for a nap and knew I had a couple of hours to do the yard work, laundry, and as many of the other chores as I could fit in. While I was trimming the bushes in the front of the house, a sedan pulled up. A man in a three-piece suit with a briefcase got out and headed in my direction. My heart was pounding, and I felt as though I could not breathe. At that moment, I believed he was coming to tell me that my husband had been killed on deployment.

I was obviously not thinking clearly in that instant, as I know a chaplain would have been accompanying a senior Marine Corps officer if he were making a death notification. But for a brief moment, I was scared stiff. With my heart racing and chest tight with anxiety, I put up my hand and exclaimed, "Stop!" I was not prepared to hear the news I believed he was going to tell me. Fear consumed me as I stood still with my heart pounding so hard I was sure it would jump out of my chest.

Immediately, the man stopped and reached into his pocket. He pulled out a badge and said he was conducting a special background investigation on my husband. My knees went weak and almost buckled. The investigator explained that he could not get in touch with any of Gary's references. I explained that he was on a deployment and most of the names on the reference list were most likely on deployment as well. He apologized for scaring me and left.

I went into the house and picked up our daughter and held her for dear life. That was not an experience I would ever want to repeat. To this day, just telling that story or thinking of that moment causes an extreme emotional reaction. Mentally, I had thought through his death many times. What would I do, who would I call, where would he be buried, what about Nikki, Nate, Neili, and Ashley? Where would we live? I had many mental checklists for the "what-ifs." Planning ahead and having a checklist of what to do helped me cope with the possibility that Gary might not return.

At some point in Gary's deployment, he called to tell me that he had orders to go to Okinawa, Japan. I was not very excited about this. Being so far away with a small child and having Nikki, Nate, and Neili remain in California, how would we keep all four children connected? Like any military family, though, I knew we'd just figure it out and make the best of it. Shortly after that, Gary called back and said he had received new orders—to Hawaii! Yeah, right, I thought. At first, I didn't believe him. After it sank in, this Minnesota girl was superexcited about going to the land of sun, surf, and sand.

Better yet, I was able to quickly find an air traffic control flight that had an opening and would accept my transfer. I was elated about getting back into ATC as a Drill Status Guardsman. And although we would be separated from Gary's children, we'd be able to keep all four siblings connected because we'd still be in the United States. Even though we wouldn't be on the mainland, it would be easier to keep them close through phone calls, summer vacations, and Christmas visits.

Looking back, I believe the Marine Corps did a very good job of preparing families for the deployment. I recall attending a family-separation briefing day with Gary. They gave us resources and even had a briefing on relationships, where we received a sheet that explained the various stages of separation. I don't recall today what those stages were, but at the time, we could look at the sheet and say, "This is the stage we're in now." It helped us tremendously to know that what we were experiencing was normal.

Sometimes, however, because the current stage we were in was extremely difficult, we could hardly wait to enter the next stage. The first few stages of separation were particularly challenging—and they were very emotional. Especially as we prepared for the deployment, I had to pull into myself and away from Gary to get ready for what lay ahead. Once we were in the deployment stage and he was gone, I needed to adjust to being the sole decision-maker. The reunion stages, which required a different type of adjustment, were usually easier to manage—and a lot more exciting, especially the honey-moon stage.

When Gary returned from his six-month deployment, all four kids and I met him at the pier, along with my sister Shannon. The kids all ran to him. I was grateful and relieved that Ashley obviously recognized her daddy and wasn't the least bit afraid to go to him and be scooped up into his arms. The most poignant moment was when Ashley took her little twenty-seven-month-old hands and put them on his face, as if to make sure he was real and really there. Since the time he left when she was twenty months old, I had made sure she heard Gary's voice reading her stories and saw his face in the picture every night. It was heartwarming to see that she went right to him. As a mom, I felt like I had accomplished my mission.

AB Jelinski, Basic Military Training, 1984

BMT, with AB Garcia, 1984

ATC tech school radar block, 1985

Offutt AFB tower training

Wedding day, Sobieski, Minnesota, 1987

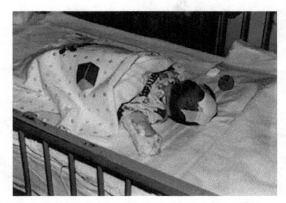

Baby Ashley hospitalized at five days old

Hall family, Camp Pendleton, 1989

California Air National Guard duty.

Cammied up in MILES Gear, CAANG

CW2 (ret.) Wilfred Jelinski and A1C Denise Jelinski

# Part Three

## Living In Paradise

# CHAPTER 16

# Hawaii
# The Aloha State

Shortly after Gary returned from his Western Pacific tour, the Marine Corps gave him a new assignment: he would be working at Camp Smith, Hawaii, in the G3 Command Operations Center. He would also have duties in the Counterdrug Program and as the officer in charge of the Special Category Message Program, a program that required one of the highest security clearances within the Department of Defense. We landed on Oahu in August 1990, shortly after Operation Desert Shield, the first Gulf War, had begun. Gary was an extremely unhappy Marine at the time, as all the Marines in the units he had trained with during the WESTPAC tour were turning around and heading to the Gulf.

The bond between military members can actually be stronger than the bond between family members. Gary had just spent three years of his life with these Marines. He trained and led them, deployed with them, and had the deepest respect for who they were as Marines. Gary understood their capabilities to go to war and defend our country. His military family was heading into harm's way, and instinctively, he wanted to be by their side, leading them.

For a Marine officer used to an active, high-speed operations job, sitting at a desk added to his frustration. Although I tried, there was nothing I could say or do to make Gary feel better about not deploying to the Gulf with his fellow Marines. At first, I tried to help him see the positive aspects of his new assignment—such as our family would be together for the first time in three years on a day-to-day basis. I had to trust that God had a different path for Gary, and for whatever reason, that path was in Hawaii. I eventually realized there was nothing I could do other than be supportive. He would have to come to grips with the change and disappointment in his own time.

⌘

We stayed at the Sheraton Waikiki for two months before we found housing, which sounds more exciting than it actually was. For the first two weeks, living in a hotel felt like being on vacation. Ashley and I went to the pool nearly every day and took long walks through downtown Waikiki. After a couple of weeks with a toddler, though, living in the hotel got old. Our daughter needed space to run and play, and we hadn't brought many toys with us. To this day, I can recite much of the script and sing along to all the songs of *The Little Mermaid* since we must have watched it at least three hundred times. Thank goodness for Ariel and Eric!

Finding a place to live on our budget was not easy. We only had one car, so we did our searching in the evenings. The base housing offered to us was unacceptable: the homes looked shabby, run-down, and dirty. We decided to rent a house since Gary's tour was only expected to last three years, and quite frankly, we were not in a financial position to even consider buying one.

We found a rental property in Aiea on Ulune Street, a noisy bus thoroughfare just down the hill from Camp Smith. My new ANG unit was at Naval Air Station (NAS) Barbers Point, about fifteen miles from the house. Although we knew it would be financially difficult, Gary and I agreed that for the first year, I would stay home with Ashley. I hadn't had the opportunity to spend a lot of uninterrupted time with her in California; by the time she was six weeks old, she was already in day care. Being a stay-at-home mom would provide stability for Ashley and give me the chance to spend some quality time with her.

જી

Life in Aiea settled into a comfortable routine. Gary went off to work, and I stayed home with Ashley. To save money, I washed and starched Gary's uniforms instead of sending them to the cleaners. (Quite frankly, I did a better job than the cleaners—I never put double creases in his trousers.) I also spent time clipping coupons and looking for cost-free activities for Ashley, such as going to the park, the beach, and climbing Diamond Head.

As soon as we moved into our new house, Gary and I began to reach out to neighbors and embrace the Hawaiian culture. Our neighbors, in turn, made us feel as though we'd come home—Carrick and Sandy Agbayani and their children, Mona and AJ, became dear and treasured friends and remain so today. Our children grew up together. There was nothing the Agbayani family wouldn't do for us, and vice versa. They introduced us to authentic local Hawaiian cuisine by making ono (delicious) food, and Carrick took Gary and Nathan pig hunting one summer. Hunting and fishing were essential activities for the Agbayani family, and they hunted wild boar pigs with dogs and big knives. From the stories Gary and Nathan brought home, I know it was quite an experience for both of them.

The Agbayanis included us in many gatherings and treated us like family. Mona and AJ's great-grandmother lived with them and quickly became grandma to Ashley too. Grandma Rose was a wonderful, sweet lady who enjoyed sitting outside and sewing. One of the blankets Ashley treasures most was handmade by Grandma Rose.

Ashley and AJ were close in age and spent a lot of time together. Listening to them playing outside was entertaining. Ashley, a little girl from the mainland, quickly picked up Hawaiian Creole English, the local language referred to as "pidgin." The deal in our home was that she could speak pidgin while she played outside, but she needed to speak proper English inside the house or at school. Ashley's young life in Aiea was quite diverse. She grew up in a melting pot of different cultures and ethnicities, and life near the ocean provided many beach adventures. She grew from a toddler and blossomed into a little school-age Hawaiian girl.

ॐ

As part of my ANG unit responsibilities, I attended drill weekends and performed annual training duties. I looked forward to them because I could continue to put on my Air Force uniform and serve my country. Being in the Air Guard allowed me to keep that piece of the Air Force I felt I'd left behind with my active-duty service. By this time, I knew that being in the military was a calling for me, and every time I went to drill, I reconnected with it.

I began air traffic control training at Wheeler Army Airfield, thanks to an agreement that allowed Air National Guardsmen to train in the Army facility. During that first year in Hawaii when I was home with Ashley, I typically performed three proficiency training days in the control tower each week. I had not previously had the opportunity to work with a brother service. Being around Soldiers and learning about Army culture was quite different from what I had been exposed to previously; for example, lower-ranking Soldiers were not treated with the same level of respect I'd experienced in the Air Force. What I came to appreciate was that in the Army, as in the Air Force, Soldiers were addressed by their rank. I was also grateful that the Army had an interest in my training, which ultimately helped with their manning schedule along with my goal to eventually receive a tower facility rating.

Each week, I performed special or proficiency training at Wheeler Tower toward my rating. Not only was this a great opportunity to train, but it also helped our family by bringing in an additional part-time salary. Living on one income meant that every penny was carefully budgeted. We usually made it work, and Gary and I both understood that our necessities and our responsibility to Gary's first family had to be top priority. We always wrote the support check for his children on time before anything else. We both wanted to support Gary's children financially and in every other way possible.

Our tight budget didn't allow for many nonessentials. As Easter approached in 1991, we had no savings and only eighty-eight dollars in our checking account to get us through to the next paycheck. I had eagerly looked forward to continuing my family's lifelong tradition of having a new dress and shoes to wear to church on Easter. Even more importantly, I wanted Ashley to have a new dress and shoes. As a mother, I felt like such a failure that I couldn't buy our daughter a new outfit. I tried to hide my feelings, but the situation was upsetting.

One day, Gary surprised me with a card. In it were forty dollars and a note that told me to take Ashley shopping for an Easter dress and shoes. I shed some tears, grateful to be able to buy Ashley a new outfit but especially touched that Gary had been saving a few dollars here and there, knowing how important this tradition was to me.

We stayed connected with Gary's children mainly through Sunday night phone calls and Gary's visits to see them in California. Each summer, the kids came to stay with us for about six weeks, and they spent every other Christmas with us. We did fun things on the weekends, like visits to the Honolulu Zoo, Sea Life Park, and various beaches. We also watched movies and took weekly hikes up Diamond Head and the Aiea Loop.

Going from one child to four was a big change, and we all needed an adjustment period when we became a family of six. Our tiny three-bedroom, one-and-a-half-bath home included a lanai, a roofed veranda that gave us an extra "bedroom," but there was no private place where any of us could retreat. Just like I'd experienced while growing up, we had to learn patience as the six of us shared one shower.

Gary and I still paid child support while the kids stayed with us, and we had to stretch our food budget to feed double the amount of people. Although the kids never knew it, we got creative with coupons and found ways to design nutritious meals that cost less. Mealtime preparation took longer since cooking for six required more effort and additional inventiveness. I reflected back on my childhood and thought how easy it would have been to make sugar and butter sandwiches. However, knowing there was no nutritional value in butter, sugar, or white bread, it wasn't an option.

Understandably, the decibel level in our household increased, so Gary and I did all we could to make sure the kids had plenty of outside activities and games. It seemed that just as soon as we found our groove as a family of six, it was time for the children to leave. It was always difficult for Ashley to have to say goodbye to her brother and sisters; she was too young to fully understand the concept of a blended family.

As the children got older and became teenagers with attitudes and hormones, the dynamics changed. Gary and I did our best to model respect and family values. I never attempted to replace the kids' mom—they called me Denise—but I made it clear that my word and rules were the same as their father's. One afternoon, Gary's youngest daughter talked back to her dad disrespectfully. I looked her in the eyes and said, "I don't speak to your father like that, and you certainly are not going to." That was the end of it. I never had to say anything more than the usual "knock it off" to get everyone back on track.

The children attended mass with us, and Sundays were extra special. On "family day" Sundays, Gary was home the entire day, and our focus was totally on the children.

꒰꒱

After I stayed home for a year, Gary and I decided I would go back to work in the summer of 1991. As luck would have it, our financial planner in California had also moved to Hawaii, and she was looking for an office manager at United Services Planning Association and Independent Research Agency (USPA 8c IRA), now called First Command. When we lived in California, Kathy Skillington had helped us start a sensible retirement program through USPA 8c IRA with a meager fifty dollars per month. After reconnecting with her in Hawaii and undergoing our annual financial review, Kathy helped us put a debt consolidation program in place. Doing so took a heavy burden off our shoulders and made more of our monthly income available to us.

At the same time I was gearing up to look for a job, Kathy coincidentally told me she needed office help. We agreed I would work six hours a day so I could still spend plenty of time at home with Ashley. Being an office manager gave me my first opportunity to work on computers—although many organizations and businesses were using computers in the 1980s, I'd had limited exposure to them when I worked at the thrift and loan. Being able to access and work with different programs and information on computers certainly became a huge learning experience.

During this same time, the Hawaii National Guard (HING) began offering computer software classes. Looking for opportunities to grow and improve my skills, I enrolled in and attended every possible software program class. Along with classes in the core functions of computers, I took every Microsoft Office Suite class available. Everything I learned helped me in the Air Guard as well as in my civilian job.

My primary responsibilities at USPA and IRA were to gather financial information for clients and potential clients, prepare financial documents, and communicate with insurance and investment companies. I was fully responsible for managing the financial seminars Kathy and her fellow financial planners offered about every six weeks. I found people to invite, sent out invitations, called the invitees to follow up and encourage them to attend, and created the guest list. Kathy put out monetary incentives for me to earn, and with every seminar, I earned them. Because Kathy and I always had the most guests, other agents and their assistants continually asked us how we got as many people as we did to the seminars. I believe my success resulted from my persistence and follow-up in encouraging people to learn how they could deliberately plan for their future. I became passionate about the importance of financial planning, and working with Kathy strengthened my resolve to pay off our debt and achieve financial independence as well.

Things were also going well at the air traffic control flight (ATCF). At an annual awards banquet in 1992, I was named the

Hawaii Air National Guard (HIANG) Outstanding Air Traffic Controller of the Year. In a subsequent year, I was recognized as the Noncommissioned Officer (NCO) of the Year for the Flight and Group. These awards recognized what it took to be the best. At the time, the awards were based on meeting and exceeding all standards, completing one's professional military education and all required training on time, passing proficiency training tests, maintaining a good attitude, and standing head and shoulders above the rest.

Professional Military Education (PME) was essential to achieve the highest levels of excellence in any capacity or to take on additional leadership responsibilities or be promoted. As soon as I was eligible, I enrolled to complete my next level of PME, so I would be better prepared for future opportunities. I equated it to having more tools in my toolbox.

# CHAPTER 17

# Worldwide Marriage Encounter

We had been in Hawaii for about a year when our marriage started unraveling. The stress caused by the myriad changes prior to our move and the detachment that had developed between us leading up to and during Gary's deployment had left an indelible mark on us as a couple.

I had felt like a single mom during the eighteen months of Gary's training and deployment. I learned to rely solely on myself, so Gary's intermittent stays at home disrupted the schedule and routine I'd established in his absence. Once he was home from deployment in July 1990, we had about a month to get ourselves packed and ready to move to Hawaii. Not only was I used to taking care of things myself, but now I also had to deal with Gary's unhappiness about his new assignment. I went into my self-reliant survival mode. All those months of feeling like a single person caused a buildup of resentment, anger, and frustration, as well as a loss of connection with Gary. When I wanted to feel like a newlywed, I instead felt like I took a back seat to everything else in his life.

Fortunately, our faith and having a community to share it with were still top priorities for both of us. We found a wonderful church near our home in Hawaii, and St. Elizabeth became a second home for the three of us. The parish was alive, inviting, and charismatic.

It also had a private Catholic School for grades K through 8, and Ashley eventually attended seventh and eighth grades there. Gary and I became Eucharistic ministers and lectors and took on many other roles to support our church community. People from all over the island came to worship at St. Elizabeth Church.

One Sunday while attending mass, we listened to a couple talk about Worldwide Marriage Encounter (WWME). Because we were still struggling in our young marriage and trying to find the intimacy and connection we'd once had, the message really caught our attention. WWME is a weekend program presented by a Catholic priest and three couples, designed for married couples with a solid marriage who want to make their relationship better. Financial strains, poor communication, a young daughter, and Gary's unhappiness about not being able to deploy all continued to take a toll on our marriage. I was not one to share my feelings, so I kept a lot of emotional "junk" wrapped up in little boxes and stored deep in my thoughts.

Gary and I agreed that a WWME weekend was something we needed to do. Our only concern was leaving Ashley, but some couples in our church community volunteered to watch attending couples' children. While this made us a little nervous, we trusted in God that everything would be okay.

On a Friday night in October 1991, we made our way to the St. Stephen Diocesan Center. During that weekend, no cell phones, radios, or TVs were allowed—or anything else that might distract a couple from working on their marriage. We were introduced to the art of "dialoguing," a foreign concept to most of us in attendance. The priest and presenting couple would introduce a topic, share their experiences, give us a question, and then provide us time to independently write to our spouse about how it made us feel. This scared the heck out of me. *What?* I thought. *Identify my feelings? Write and discuss my feelings? This is going to be interesting and very uncomfortable for me.* Not for Gary, though, because he easily shared his feelings and had a way with a pen and words.

I struggled to write about how I felt. Not only did I not like having to share my feelings in any form, but I also didn't really know how to share them. As a kid, the messages I received included, "Stop that crying, or I'll give you something to cry about." If I cried because I was in physical pain, for instance, my mom and my older sister made comments that implied it couldn't be *that bad* and I needed to stop whining. Basic training reinforced the idea of "no emotions" even further. When we were allowed to call home for the first time, tears ran down my cheeks as I talked to my mom. Being away from home and in a new environment where I didn't know what to expect, I couldn't hold back my emotions. As I hung up the phone and the TI noticed my tears, she shouted, "Jelinski! Stop that crying. I don't ever want to see that again!"

The topics we discussed that weekend at St. Stephen cause conflict for many married couples: finances, communication, sex, raising kids, discipline, hiding our true selves behind the masks we wear, and many more. Saturday proved to be a gut-wrenching day, especially as the presenting couples shared intimate stories that made me cringe. I couldn't imagine in my wildest dreams confessing experiences laced with shame and guilt—I'd been raised to think of such topics as things you keep hidden to protect the family name. As they spoke, I kept thinking that these experiences were private between a husband and wife and were meant to remain buried—maybe even from each other.

As the day progressed, however, I could tell everyone was opening up and sharing more, including Gary and me. I felt more loving toward Gary and hopeful that we could have a happy marriage. I still did not enjoy sharing feelings, but I did what an obedient student does: her homework as directed! By midafternoon Sunday, it was visibly noticeable that almost every couple had grown closer through their dialogue. Couples were sitting physically closer, looked at one another more lovingly, and openly shared some of their experiences and breakthroughs. Gary and I, too, shared openly with the group on issues that were quite personal—ones I never dreamed of sharing with people I hardly knew—but the WWME environment was a safe place where trust and confidentiality existed.

The weekend ended late Sunday afternoon with everyone celebrating mass together. As we walked out of the chapel, we were greeted by a large WWME community of people who'd previously attended a weekend, along with many of their children. They held signs, candles, leis, and brought food for a community dinner. The couple that watched Ashley brought her to the dinner, and we were overwhelmed to be met with this loving and supportive community who'd been holding us in prayer throughout the weekend.

That night, Gary and I were asked to become a presenting couple for WWME. For me, it was a painful process because we had to handwrite all our talks on assigned topics—and then another couple would edit them and push me to go "deeper." This was before we had a home computer, so the writing part was doubly painful. One topic we needed to delve into was finances. From my perspective, Gary never fully grasped my need to be debt-free and have my own money—not "our" money or "family" money but "my" money. Not to spend but to have. I knew that discussing this sensitive topic in a loving manner was important—not because there would be a resolution but because he would at least hear me and understand my feelings.

It took hard work for me to expose fears about being broke. Growing up, our family always had what we needed, but we knew finances were tight and there could never be any "extras." Along came marriage number one, where my ex took out loans and spent our money before paying bills. After the divorce, I had to take care of myself with little means, but I did it. With my marriage to Gary, we started out with three kids, and a baby came soon after that. We never seemed to get ahead financially, and at times, we got further behind. I knew I'd signed up for this life, so I sucked it up, but I felt angry, frustrated, and hopeless most of the time. I never talked about it—until we became a part of WWME. I knew that sharing our experiences would help other WWME couples do the same, but it was excruciating to reveal what I'd walled up inside. It was like taking a sledgehammer to an iron wall and attempting to chip away at it.

One tough experience we needed to work through was the time I established a "secret" savings account. Without telling Gary, I put some bonus money I had earned into a separate savings account. It made me feel secure having something set aside for a rainy day. The money sat in the account and eventually grew to four thousand dollars. That was the year the IRS said, "You owe us six thousand dollars"—and we didn't have the money. For days, I struggled with the decision to tell Gary about the account. All hell broke loose when I finally told him I had four thousand dollars set aside in another account. Gary felt betrayed and lied to for doing this behind his back. I, on the other hand, was glad that at least we now had most of the money to pay the IRS without taking out a loan.

We spent many evenings "dialoguing" about this past issue and my ongoing need to have a nest egg as security. As difficult as this was, I stuck with the process because of what I'd learned from our Marriage Encounter weekend. I knew I had to tell my deep dark secrets to break down as much of my wall as possible, to release what I'd kept bottled up inside, to strengthen our marriage, and to help others.

Ultimately, the process helped us come to a mutual under-standing of Gary's feelings and my need for financial security, and we wholeheartedly believe that it saved our marriage. Marriage takes work, commitment, and a lot of love and communication. To this day, we continue to use many of the tools we learned in Marriage Encounter.

# CHAPTER 18

# A Yearlong Black Hole

The words "You're disqualified to serve in the Air National Guard" hit me like a ton of bricks. I never dreamed that a physical issue could potentially end my military career, but it almost did just that.

In 1995, the onset of endometriosis hit me fast and hard. It was excruciatingly painful to the point where I could not even sit for any extended period. I eventually had surgery to remove a cyst, fallopian tube, and scar tissue, but the pain lingered and continued—every day, all day. Some days were better than others, but I experienced discomfort and dealt with pain around the clock.

The worst pain came during a particular week each month, and I couldn't tolerate wearing anything but loose clothing. I kept those clothes in a separate section of my closet and only wore them to work during those times. I had informed my closest coworkers that when they saw me wearing those specific dresses, they needed to give me space and let me keep to myself. I definitely didn't want to socialize with anyone during that time. Eventually, I had to leave my civilian job since I could no longer sit and do my work. As a part-time Drill Status Guardsman, I continued to meet my requirements, but I had to be extremely careful about when I scheduled my tower proficiency time.

After a year of sheer misery, where Gary would often find me in excruciating pain unable to move, crying and lying in a ball on the floor, I decided to have a hysterectomy. I had put it off for an entire year because I was scared to death to undergo the procedure but desperately wanting quality of life won out. Ultimately, the surgery did completely alleviate the pain.

After my recovery, I had to be cleared by the HIANG flight surgeon to return to duty as an air traffic controller on flying status. I turned over all my medical records to the 154th Wing Medical Group for review. Imagine my surprise when my supervisor came to me and said endometriosis disease would disqualify me from further military service. I was beyond stunned and afraid my career was finished. All the hard work, the endless hours of studying, learning, and growing, everything I had planned for my future could all come to a screeching halt. It was one of the most personally devastating moments of my career, and I felt as if I had absolutely no control over the outcome.

The next drill weekend, I met with the flight doctor to understand why this was happening. Apparently, there was one word in the medical write-up from the doctor who had performed the surgery that would disqualify me. The flight doctor unsympathetically ended the brief meeting, as though he were ready to move on to the next appointment. As I left the meeting, I was screaming at him in my head, *This is my career!*

I immediately contacted my surgeon at the Tripler Army Medical Center and requested that my records and the write-up be reevaluated. Unfortunately, the documentation did not change—the report stood "as is." I, however, was not ready or willing to give up, not by a long shot! I went back to the medical group and met with a second flight doctor. I pleaded with him to take time with me, research the regulations, and show me how this could be a disqualifying event. Personally, I disdained ever having to plead for anything, but because my career was on the line, I was prepared to do whatever it took to get a fair review. I explained that I'd had surgery and was no longer in any pain or discomfort, so this decision made no sense to me.

I wish I could remember that doctor's name because I'd like to give him credit for being extremely thorough as well as receptive to finding a solution. He read through volumes of regulations, and in the end determined it *was* not a disqualifying condition. He took additional time to write up his report in such a way that my health would never again be questioned.

To this day, I tell people not to accept the first or second diagnosis or decision when it comes to their health or their career. It's possible for doctors and leaders to read and interpret regulations or policy differently from each other—there are gray areas where interpretation comes into play. It's, therefore, important to exhaust all avenues before accepting any prescribed outcome.

I would never advocate circumventing the system or doing anything unscrupulous or unethical. My advice is simply to take the time to ask and reask questions to ensure the right outcome. Thanks to my persistence, I dodged the proverbial bullet that could have ended my military career—before it ever took full flight.

꒰꒱

During this same time frame, Gary's ex-wife took him to court for additional child support, which created an extreme financial hardship for us. Up to this point, I had been managing our finances, maintaining a budget, and making our ends meet. We were financially responsible: saying no to frivolous spending, paying off the credit card debt, and doing our best to save. And now, through no fault of my own, we had huge lawyer bills and nearly double the child support to pay. It seemed my life revolved around working to pay child support.

I loved Gary's children too, but now our daughter was being hugely affected. We had to take her out of a private Montessori school and put her in public school. This was a tough decision to make as a mother. I felt like a failure—just as I had when I couldn't buy her a new dress and shoes. For several weeks, the emotional and financial hardship weighed heavily on me and affected my work. I often found myself wondering, *How*—how—*were we ever going to get through this and make ends meet?* At times, I caught myself on the verge of tears and fought to stifle my pain and fear. I even called our landlord to see if she would reduce our rent. We stopped our meager retirement investment and scrimped on anything and everything we could. I didn't know what we were going to do.

Toward the end of the child support court case, Gary's oldest child, Nikki, asked to live with us for her senior year of high school. We changed our third bedroom from an office to a bedroom and enrolled her in school. We explained the family rules to Nikki and knew there would be an adjustment period.

On the first day of school, I sounded just like a typical mom, "You're not wearing that to school!" I warned her. Nikki changed her clothes, and I dropped her off at school about a mile from our house. She would have to walk home since I would be working at the tower.

Nikki was outgoing and a cheerleader, so she quickly made friends in the first couple of weeks. One weekend, she asked to use the car to go out with friends. Gary and I agreed but set parameters of where she was permitted to go. Fortunately for me, but not so fortunate for Nikki, I knew my car well: after she came home, I noticed an excessive number of miles had accumulated on my odometer, and the gas tank was low. Nikki, however, insisted that she'd only traveled in the area we allowed. I knew she wasn't being truthful, but she stuck to her story, and Gary wanted me to drop it. I felt like I was caught in the middle.

Then the phone rang, and I answered it. The call was for Nikki.

"Who is calling, please?" I asked. The male caller gave me a name.

"How do you know Nikki?" I questioned him.

"I met her last night in Nanakuli," he responded.

*Oh, now this is going to be good*, I thought.

She was not allowed to go to Nanakuli. Finally, the truth came out, and Nikki was officially grounded. Being a typical teenager, she thought she could circumnavigate the rules. After this incident, however, Nikki understood our family rules and never again tried to "get away with it." From then on, we knew we could trust her.

As the days and weeks went on, our family life fell into a rhythm. Undeniably, though, there were changes in our household. I soon found out how much Gary regretted not having been there more for his children. He was determined to make up for lost time, no matter what. Gary has always been a loving husband and father, yet he felt guilty for not spending as much time with Nikki, Nathan, and Neili as he did with Ashley.

Many times, when Gary needed to make a parenting decision regarding Nikki, he didn't ask my opinion. In the past, we had always made family decisions together, and now I was being left out. It hurt. It didn't seem to matter what I said, what my opinion was, the cost to our relationship, or how I felt about the situation. Gary made most of the decisions as they pertained to Nikki, and I was left on the sidelines. I no longer felt like a partner in our marriage even though I worked to help pay the child support and buy groceries and other necessities. I felt alone, isolated, and completely voiceless.

We continued to attend our monthly Marriage Encounter gatherings, which gave us hope, encouragement, love, and support. Once we were back home, however, we couldn't seem to make any significant improvements in our decision-making practices.

I understood that none of this was Nikki's fault. I hoped and prayed she was oblivious to most of what was going on between Gary and me. We tried to shield her and Ashley from our discord. I put on a good face around Nikki; I was pleasant and genuinely interested in her school, outside activities, and friends. I enjoyed spending time with her and attended her cheer events, and I felt like she trusted me as her stepmother. She was a huge help with Ashley and babysat when Gary and I went to functions. When she began to date, I became a very protective mama bear. The young men had to have dinner with us and spend an evening in our home. I asked many questions about them, their families, and how they were raised to treat a young lady. After all, we were trusting Nikki's date with her life, and we needed to ensure he would take good care of her.

As we struggled with routine parenting decisions, my relationship with Gary continued to suffer, and I began to care less and less. I hardly ever voiced my opinion. I was quiet and reserved at home, and it seemed like Gary and I no longer had a real marriage—we were merely roommates, living together in the same house. I came home, made dinner, cleaned up, bathed and read to Ashley, and then immediately went to bed. There was nothing else to do. I felt empty, alone, and extremely sad.

The best part of the day was going to the tower. It was an escape from the darkness that consumed me at home. I didn't seem to care about anything other than going to work and taking care of our daughter. Sometimes Ashley was the only reason I got out of bed. With the environment in our home, what else was there? The deep dark sadness was an ever-consuming black hole, and I could not crawl out of it. *Why even try?* I thought. Other than being a mother, there was nothing to live for and certainly nothing positive to be happy about.

Many times, I approached Gary to explain how I was feeling. Sometimes things got better for a short while, but our marriage was not what it should have been, and I felt unimportant to him. The one blessing during those dark days was that Nikki became the big sister six-year-old Ashley had always wanted. The bond Ashley and Nikki built that year was loving, close, and strong and remains so today.

The saving grace for our marriage was that our WWME community continued to carry us. They were there for us and helped us work through many issues during this difficult time. They continued to encourage us to hang in there. Many times, I hid behind a mask just to get through a meeting—never sharing my deepest feelings of hopelessness, fear, and anger. The only person I let in was one woman in our group. Wanya and I were very close and shared our deepest confidences. She listened but never took sides or judged. Talking with her allowed me to release some of the heavy weight and burden of my feelings, but I still couldn't get out of the dark pit of despair.

I remember that during this time, my hair and clothing changed. I didn't pay as much attention to styling my hair, and I stopped caring about starched creases in my civilian slacks and shirts. Even my makeup was sad. This went on for months, and I hated my life. However, I never let the girls or anyone at my Air Guard unit know I was struggling. I put on a happy face at the tower and at drill. In all honesty, I enjoyed being there. It was the one place where I could make a difference, and it served as a daily reprieve from the grind at home.

After nearly a year, I got up one morning and made the decision that I was done being in the *black hole of death*. I was tired of being the big sad downer. I started with my outward appearance and took conscious actions to look physically different. I pulled myself up and out, changed my hairstyle, wore brighter makeup, and dressed like I cared about my appearance. Once again, I began to starch and press my civilian clothes, even putting creases back into my jeans. I was ready to fight—for happiness, a better relationship, and an equal say in what happened in our home. I was done feeling like a doormat. I decided my opinion and voice mattered, and I had just as much say in decisions as Gary did.

The black hole had lasted nearly a year, but I was determined it would be over as fast as it began. Knowing it was time to reengage with life, I took great lengths to put unresolved feelings in a box and bury them deep into the recesses of my mind so I could move forward. Although I still carried anger, resentment, and the fear of going into that black hole again, I made a daily conscious effort to stay afloat. It was a scary dark place, and remembering its depths still chokes me up today.

Sadly, I never felt like I could reach out to anyone other than Wanya for help. Although I felt I should seek counseling, air traffic controllers didn't do that back then. Unfortunately, due to the stigma attached to seeking mental health services—and possibly being classified as unfit to perform a job—many of us did not seek the help we needed during difficult times. Even today, I believe there are many people who don't seek help although they are encouraged to use the many resources available.

# CHAPTER 19

# Self-Development and Personal Growth

With a small child and as a spouse of an active-duty Marine living on an island with no family or close friends, it was extremely difficult to attend Professional Military Education (PME) courses in residence. Gary was gone off-island for temporary assigned duty too often for me to commit to attend school. PME would have taken me off-island for four to six weeks at a time, and there was no one who could keep Ashley for that long. My only recourse was to complete Airman Leadership School, Noncommissioned Officer Academy, and Senior Noncommissioned Officer Academy via correspondence.

As a young Airman at the time, I did not know or understand the value of attending PME in residence versus completing the courses via correspondence. Eventually, I learned a significant difference between the two: PME by correspondence couldn't provide the interaction between instructors, fellow students, Active, Guard, and Reserve members. There was no opportunity for questions, discussions, or presentations. Correspondence PME was a means to an end, but it was done in isolation.

At some point, I realized I needed more than what correspondence PME offered me in the way of personal and professional growth as an NCO. Consequently, I made a very conscious and deliberate decision to find a way to make up for what I would have received if I had been attending classes in person. To satisfy my desire for continuous self-improvement, I placed myself on a path of self-development and personal growth. I began to read books on leader-ship and management. I listened to tapes and CDs. I watched videos, read articles, and focused on becoming a stronger leader. Since I wasn't able to take full advantage of PME, such as the sharing of trials and tribulations as well as the positive changes happening within the Air Force, I sought other ways to become a better version of me.

My favorite author and motivational speaker is Dr. John C. Maxwell, and I found his leadership advice both common sense and practical. Some of his most influential books include *Developing the Leader Within You*, *The 21 Irrefutable Laws of Leadership*, *Leadership Gold*, *How Successful People Think*, *Tide 21 Most Powerful Minutes of a Leader's Day*, *Thinking for a Change*, *The 360 Leader*, *Winning with People*, *Be All You Can Be*, and *Today Matters*. Dr. Maxwell's words are still inspirational to me today.

During this time, Gary and I were invited to listen to a business presentation for a network marketing opportunity. We agreed beforehand that as soon as the presentation was over, we'd leave. Ever the skeptic, I was ready to walk out after it was finished. Gary, however, wanted to stay and hear more—which was completely out of character for him. *What?* I thought.

Eventually, Gary nudged me along, and we began to work our network marketing business together. I supported his decision to get involved and was willing to work a couple of weeknights and regularly attend meetings and seminars. Because of our business, I began to read additional leadership and inspirational books on self-belief, setting goals, and the power of a dream. We engaged with incredible leaders and, in addition to Dr. Maxwell, listened to people like Dr. Stephen Covey, Dr. Gary Smalley, Zig Ziglar, Florence Littauer, Charlie "Tremendous" Jones, Kurt Warner, Robert Kiyosaki, Dr. Laura Schlessinger, and many other leaders who shared their personal stories and experiences.

Our business grew to the point where we received a special invitation to be in a small group with Dr. Maxwell. It was a phenomenal opportunity that made a significant difference in how I thought and what I wanted to accomplish. Being around positive people who had goals and higher aspirations, and who showed me what was possible, was life-changing. They made me want to be a better person, wife, mother, and leader. Although we are no longer involved with this business today, Gary and I learned a great deal from our interactions and conversations with these various leaders.

Even Ashley's life was influenced during that time. She attended goal-setting and dream-building activities with us—and even a leadership camp when she was ten years old. As a result of being around such positive people and having the opportunity to attend functions, Ashley learned that through hard work, being and staying positive, and continuing to develop and grow, anything is possible. From those elementary school years and throughout high school, Ashley read and was exposed to leadership education.

There was a direct correlation between our network business and how well Gary did in his civilian job in sales after retiring from the Marine Corps. We both began to think differently—we only wanted to have positive thoughts and be around positive people with strong ethics and values. The interaction with leaders from around the world inspired us to keep on a path of continual growth and personal development.

One pivotal behavioral change was observing leadership examples. For instance, as a senior noncommissioned officer, I began to closely watch Hawaii Governor Linda Lingle. I listened to how she spoke and the words she used, and I paid attention to how she carried herself and how she engaged with people. I watched how our Adjutant General and the Hawaii National Guard Commanders conducted themselves professionally. I studied them to become a better leader myself, and I recognized through their interactions with people that I needed to get out of my comfort zone if my personal and professional growth were to continue.

Being somewhat of an introvert, I knew that I needed to engage more with people as opposed to staying in the background. At first, it was incredibly uncomfortable doing things like public speaking, emceeing events, and getting up in front of groups to conduct briefings, make conversation, and to simply be more visible. I began to force myself to interact and strike up conversations.

Through our business, I learned a concept that helped me a great deal. One particular business leader told how he dreaded talking to people, and so began to use the acronym "FORM" to help him in his interactions. I quickly adopted this tip, and it has helped me throughout both my civilian and military careers. The acronym stands for the following: F for family, O for occupation, R for recreation, and M for message or motivation. The first three letters focus on the other person—only the last letter applies to the one beginning the conversation. Whenever I engaged with a person I didn't know, the first thing I did was ask them about their family, then about their occupation and recreation, and finally left them with whatever message I wanted to get across. I continue to use the acronym in professional and social settings as a way to establish rapport with others.

# CHAPTER 20

# Baby, It's My Turn!

The end to my yearlong hiatus from working due to my health just happened to coincide with Gary's retirement. On April 1, 1996, Gary retired from the United States Marine Corps. I, however, still had considerable time left to serve.

I remember the two of us having a conversation about the future soon after he retired. I looked him straight in the eyes and said, "Okay, baby, now it's my turn." *Now* was the time for me to do all I had wanted to do in the Hawaii Air National Guard. I had always performed my annual training and fulfilled my drill responsibilities, but I wanted to go above and beyond: volunteer, deploy, and fully participate in exercises. I also wanted to take on higher levels of leadership and responsibility, as well as be ready for promotion opportunities.

Gary supported my desire to do more and pursue what I wanted to accomplish. He volunteered to become "the rock" at home and take on additional household and childcare responsibilities. Ashley knew that I would be gone more, but she was proud of what I was doing with the Air National Guard and encouraged me, just like Gary did. I was grateful for their support and cooperation because it gave me the latitude to pursue my dreams and goals. I was able to commit to additional responsibilities and pursue professional development at a different level than I had been able to do before, which meant I could now focus on further developing the responsibilities at a supervisor/managerial level.

I loved being able to say "yes" to opportunities instead of "No, sorry...I can't." Overtime, I had an opportunity to do a short tour at the Air National Guard Readiness Center in the Air Traffic Control division at Joint Base Andrews, Maryland. I also volunteered to augment a Missouri Air National Guard unit, preparing for an Operational Readiness Inspection and volunteered for a thirty-day Air Expeditionary Forces deployment to Italy. As an air traffic controller, I also had incredible opportunities to deploy on Joint Chiefs of Staff exercises in Korea and Japan, as well as in Hawaii. For the most part, these were all opportunities for new experiences in new places, including other continents. Due to the experiences in the Air National Guard Readiness Center, I learned how we could make improvements in our own unit in Hawaii. Over the course of a decade, I was fortunate to serve in different leadership positions in our squadron as well as be promoted, which ultimately led to becoming the mobility tower chief controller.

✦

For the following decade after I joined the 297th Air Traffic Control Flight (ATCF) in 1990, the unit underwent some significant changes. My first Drill Status Guardsman Commander retired, which made way for the detachment commander to become a full-time Commander. Our new Commander was a Captain, a prior enlisted man, and was soon promoted to Major. We also went from not conducting training in a fixed facility to coordinating and having the ability to train in US Army and Navy ATC facilities. Back then, ANG ATC units did not deploy often, but that changed in the late 1990s. Half our flight deployed on a Title-101 active-duty mission. However, the biggest change came in 1999 when the ATCF took on a full-time ATC mission while concurrently maintaining its deployable mobility mission. The unit also transitioned from a flight to a squadron.

Initially, the ATCF was only a mobility type of unit. We had a mobile tower, radar facility, and mobile navigational aid. Our mission was to deploy anywhere in the world, set up our equipment, and provide ATC services. Once we received orders to go, we had seventy-two hours to get packed and on our way. In a real-world deployment, we could be ordered to set up on a dirt strip in the middle of nowhere.

While home-stationed at Naval Air Station Barbers Point, drill weekends were devoted to preparation for potential state or federal unit activation. On those weekends, the tower controllers performed our proficiency training using a static display that depicted the Barbers Point airfield, including runways, taxiways, and local reporting points. We used model aircraft and physically maneuvered around the static display to practice phraseology, sequencing, and aircraft separation, just as we'd done in ATC school. During those drill weekends, the radar controllers trained separately with a simulator to practice controlling aircraft flying ground-controlled approaches and precision approach radar.

Controllers also had recurring training in topics such as separation standards, wake turbulence, hijacking procedures, lost communication, and phraseology. When we weren't doing our separate proficiency training, our unit did other ancillary training on drill weekends; for instance, cardiopulmonary resuscitation, self-aid and buddy care, .9 mm and M16 weapons qualification, annual physical fitness testing, and anti-terrorism force protection.

Because we were a small flight, with less than one hundred of us, we were a tightly knit group. The camaraderie was strong. When we worked together, we knew we had each other's backs. We also knew how to play together—after some of the drill weekends, we enjoyed barbecues in the unit's backyard. A handful of personnel stayed and enjoyed quite a few cold beverages after the barbecues with the commander. We would hear comments the next day about the after-hours party. Although I knew it was happening, I never participated. It was harmless fun, where the guys who had been there a long time "talked story" over adult beverages, but it was not something I was interested in. I wasn't a drinker, and all I wanted to do was get home to my family.

We also had an annual family day during the December drill weekend, including a Christmas party. Santa came, and the children received gifts, and we had door prizes, games, an abundance of food, and a whole lot of fun. Until Ashley got old enough to figure it out, I played Santa Claus. Using my best male voice, none of the children knew who I really was.

Our flight remained the same, and drill weekends were fairly routine until 1997 when the radar controllers and maintenance section deployed to Taszár Air Base in Hungary. All that remained of our flight home station were tower controllers, administration, and supply personnel. Because the full-time federal technician, a radar controller, had been deployed, I was asked to take his position in the ATC section. Although I'd never wanted to be the full-time ATC technician, it would only be a year, and I felt a sense of obligation to the section.

Due to my Marine Corps military spouse training, I recognized the need to look out for the families of those who had deployed. Family readiness programs did not exist in our unit, but spouses needed to have a point of contact for assistance or emergencies. I made sure the spouses had essential names and numbers. Additionally, I organized a couple of social functions to help them get out of the house and talk with other spouses of deployed members. When the deployed personnel returned, they showed their appreciation of my efforts to make their time away easier for their families by presenting me with a plaque. As time went on, family readiness groups became more and more important and were established within the entire Hawaii Air National Guard. They remain strong today.

During the deployment, I became aware that the commander's wife was quite ill with cancer. She asked me several times to relay a message to her husband to call home since I acted as the liaison between the home-station unit and the forward-deployed controllers. There was tension in her voice when she called. It was common knowledge in the unit that they were having marital difficulties, and it was also well-known that the commander drank too much. I was troubled that his drinking was tolerated and even condoned by some, and it was difficult for me to respect him. Nonetheless, I continued to do my job to the best of my ability under his leadership.

Upon their return from Taszár in 1998, several of the controllers retired, which allowed for upward mobility of our Airmen. The permanent full-time ATC technician, who had been deployed, left to work for the FAA, so I applied for his position. I had done the duties for a year and thought it wasn't as difficult as I'd once imagined. As the full-time ATC technician, some of my main responsibilities included office and personnel records management and overseeing controller training and records. I was also liaison to Headquarters, 201st Combat Communications Group, the Air National Guard Readiness Center Air Traffic Control division, and the mainland units, where our controllers went for five-skill level upgrade training. I managed all professional military education, training days and dollars, and coordinated with the 154th Wing Education and Finance offices. I was also responsible for all home-station workdays and management of all resources and equipment as they pertained to the air traffic control mobility section. Overall, the position required an immense amount of coordination, attention to detail, and organization, and I knew I was ready for it.

# CHAPTER 21

# A Dual Mission
# Leads to Conflict

During the following year, in 1999, another big change happened when NAS Barbers Point was closed under the Base Realignment and Closure Act (BRAC). Barbers Point became Kalaeloa Airport, a state-run airport, and the 297th ATCF was tasked with providing the air traffic control services. This meant we now had a dual mission—our original deployable mobility mission *and* a new full-time mission to provide ATC services for Kalaeloa Airport. The change also meant that the 297th ATCF controllers would have Air National Guard fixed facilities to train in, and eventually, upgrade training would be done at home station. During this same time, our flight also transitioned to a squadron with more positions and additional leadership opportunities. Eventually, I went from the assistant tower chief controller position to the mobility tower chief controller and superintendent.

Prior to BRAC and taking on the full-time mission at Kalaeloa Airport, our facilities were located on a singular compound, and our unit was fenced in. The main building housed the command staff, controllers, maintenance, supply, and administrative personnel. After formation and roll call, the entire unit gathered for commander's call when the commander briefed the entire unit, answered questions, and announced promotions or retirements. Commander's Call was a time for Drill Status Guardsman (DSG) to find out what had transpired during the previous month and what was coming in the future.

When classes were conducted, the room was split in two with a partition, and the controllers did bookwork and ATC training in a smaller space. The second building housed personnel equipment, protective gear, cots, tents, and personnel. We parked unit trucks, generators, tower equipment, and the navigational aid and mobile radar van in a large parking area by the second building.

My office was adjacent to the command support staff office. It was small but provided adequate space for small group meetings, a desk for the DSG ATC administrative person, a file cabinet, and my desk. When we first took over the operations at Kalaeloa Airport, there was no discussion about moving my office to the old Navy ATC tower facility. I was good with that since it was extremely rundown. The furniture was old and made of rusty gray metal. Every room needed paint, and the ATC tower was a total disaster with ripped-up carpet and broken chairs. Additionally, the male/female shared restroom was disgusting. I had no intention of moving my office to that dump! In the main building, where my office was located, we had separate clean restrooms with showers for men and women. It was a newer facility with nicely painted walls, carpet, and central air, as well as janitorial services, and I was comfortable and happy there.

After assuming responsibility for the Kalaeloa Airport ATC operations, things moved quickly. The commander met with FAA, state, HING, and Guard Bureau personnel. He started by hiring an ATC Manager and five Title-5 (civilian) controllers. The nationwide job announcements went out, and soon we received stacks of applications. The commander engaged me to help review the packages, prioritize applicants, and help in the arduous selection process by presiding on the hiring board. He and I began to work more closely together, and I smelled alcohol and saw glassy eyes on many occasions. No one ever said anything; we just moved forward with the task at hand. Once the Air Traffic Manager (ATM) was hired, much of the ATC responsibilities of vetting future hires and developing

Letters of Agreement, Memoranda, and local procedures fell on his shoulders.

The ATM and I had many private conversations, where he expressed his frustration with the commander's inability to respond in a timely manner. It was also difficult to communicate between the unit and the fixed facility. The unit and the ATC facility were about a mile apart from each other, so the ATM and the commander drove back and forth frequently. Initially, there was no e-mail connectivity, and it took many months for that issue to be resolved. All too often, the commander's door was closed, and the phone went unanswered. Additionally, over the years, I had come to understand that the stoic, unemotional Commander did not communicate very well. On drill weekends, he tersely gave us essential information but was never one to elaborate.

Once the civilian ATM and Title-5 controllers had been hired, next we needed to hire Title-32 controllers—current DSG controllers who were hired as full-time controllers. Title-32 controllers worked full-time in the ATC facilities, wore their uniform every day, and had a full-time mission of providing ATC services at Kalaeloa Airport, but they still had a commitment to the HIANG for drill weekends (Unit Training Assembly, or UTA) and two weeks of annual training. They were required to maintain their mobility or deployment responsibilities to their state and federal mission as an Air National Guard member.

Operations began in the control tower, and later, the radar facility was opened and staffed. Although I was a Title-32 controller, initially, I was not included as tower manning. I was not put on the daily schedule with the other Title-5 and Title-32 controllers, nor was I used as full-time manning. My office remained in the ATCS main facility, and I continued to manage the mobility piece of our mission, including all aspects of managing the DSG controllers. I also maintained my facility certification in the tower.

It didn't take long for the full-time and mobility missions and personnel to clash. The full-time civilian training and standardization controller was in charge of all full-time controller training and certifications and ensured correct documentation in all training records. However, I was responsible for all training and documentation on the mobility side. Having my office in a separate facility became a hindrance to communication and to resolving simple conflicts. Eventually, the commander approached me about moving to the fixed ATC facility, and I understood the bigger picture of consolidating all ATC under one roof.

It's not like I had a choice in the matter, though. The commander made the decision to move me, and I had to make the best of it. Although I hated the mere thought of being in that facility, I knew I would need to make it work. I claimed an office, removed the trash, cleaned, painted, and hung up pictures and window coverings. If I had to be there, it needed to at least be comfortable, and it had to be clean. Our amazing maintenance personnel worked their magic to get my window air-conditioning unit working so at least the temperature was bearable. Barbers Point on the Ewa side of Oahu is known to be the hottest part on the island.

For well over a year, we did not operate as a coalesced team. Staff or office controllers were viewed differently from those who manned the facility full-time. Some Title-5 controllers who were initially hired left, and others were hired to replace them. Kalaeloa Airport seemed to be a location that served as a "farm" for controllers to get into the DOD system and then transfer back to the mainland for what they considered a better position or location. Certainly, the cost of living in Hawaii factored into the decision of many who left, but disagreements and tension between management and the controllers made for a negative environment. It seemed to me that no one was very happy working at Kalaeloa.

In time, an air traffic control union was formed to protect the rights of the controllers. In the entire facility of full-time Title-32 and Title-5 controllers, only two didn't join the union, and I was one of them. The other was an active-duty controller. To me, the union was not a positive entity for our squadron. As military personnel, we were taught to always go above and beyond. Under union law, the full-time Title-32 controllers could not perform any mobility military duties while working their full-time schedule.

On top of that, the union president was what I called a pot-stirrer. It seemed as though he went out of his way to look for reasons to file grievances and was proud when he added one more to the list. I could not support this type of leader and did not want to be part of what the union represented. From my perspective, the union had not been put in place for the overall good of the organization—it simply created more division between management and some of the full-time controllers.

There aren't many people I can honestly say I don't like, but the union president was one of those people. He was sarcastic and a smart aleck. The union president, management, controllers, and I managed to maintain a level of professionalism, but over the course of a year, the work environment became hostile. A couple of civilian controllers often undermined what I tried to accomplish militarily as the superintendent of the ATC mobility section. Some of the civilian controllers would encourage the younger Airmen to get around things we were responsible for militarily.

When the union decreed that a Title-32, "uniform-wearing" controller, could not be asked to do anything that supported the mobility side of the house while they were on full-time ATC duty, I'd had enough of the absurdity. According to the union, the DSG controllers were there to key the mic and work traffic during their duty day—and that was all. Asking them to do anything outside their full-time duty job description "violated" union policies and their contract. Even if they had a two-hour break during their day, I could not ask them to do anything further that did not pertain to full-time operations. I could not even ask them to catch up on their ancillary or recurring military training.

To me, this was pure insanity. I thought we were all on the same team, trying to ensure that we met all criteria and goals for the full-time, state, and federal missions. Readiness and preparedness took time, initiative, and constant focus to ensure that all controllers completed their training and were always ready for "the call." Things needed to get done, and sometimes all of us just needed to do what was necessary to make it work. Unfortunately, due to the union and its contract, not everyone shared in that philosophy.

In fact, two civilian controllers, in particular, tried to undermine my authority. As the superintendent, I was responsible for all DSG controllers who came in during the week to make up a drill weekend or who were on special duty orders. A few controllers were on extended orders, meaning they came in Monday through Friday. There were times I had to reprimand or counsel some of those controllers for various reasons. On one occasion, I issued a Letter of Counseling (LOC) to a DSG controller for continued tardiness. I had spoken to him many times about this issue. It was well within my authority, and the documentation clearly justified it. One of the civilian controllers, however, helped the Airman fight the LOC. This meant additional work to justify my position—I had to attend meetings and provide the commander with documentation showing why I had issued the LOC.

The letter stood as issued, but justifying it consumed precious time. I could have been doing a multitude of other required tasks. It was a constant grind trying to do what was right, only to have some of the civilian controllers undercut my authority and prevent essential work from being accomplished.

The hostility grew, and it reached a point where I eventually filed a hostile workplace grievance against one particular civilian controller. I knew that doing so would make things much, much worse before they got better, but it was the right thing to do, and I needed to stand on principle. The commander and the ATM saw what was going on and supported me in filing it.

The grievance was substantiated after the investigation, but it was an ugly and embarrassing process for me. The controllers did not like being interviewed. I suspect they felt as though they had to choose a side, but I just wanted the truth to be told.

One Title-32 controller asked me why I did it. I couldn't say much at the time, since it was an ongoing investigation, but I knew what he meant. Part of the military culture was that you didn't air unit problems in public—you dealt with them privately. This situation, however, had reached a threshold where it was impossible to manage in-house. In fact, fixing a hostile work environment required bringing issues out into the open.

My goal was to make things better for the organization as a whole and for those who would come after me. I had to take a stand that this type of behavior was unacceptable and unprofessional; it could not be allowed to continue. After the investigation, it took time for things to get back to some semblance of normal around the controllers and in the facility. Would I do it again? Absolutely. To me, it was the right thing for the organization, and it sent the right message that crossing lines of authority would not be tolerated.

# CHAPTER 22

# Message Received

Before Kalaeloa Airport could be certified operationally ready in 1999, National Guard Bureau personnel from the Air National Guard Readiness Center (ANGRC) air traffic division came to Hawaii to evaluate and confirm that we were indeed ready. Two of them were well-known throughout the ATC community for being extremely thorough—tough but fair. Mr. Scott Duke, the consummate professional, had a strong personality and was known as Mr. ATC. He was a retired Air Force controller and in charge of all ANG ATC squadrons. He lived, breathed, and slept ATC. Mr. Bryan Burnham, also a retired Air Force controller, reminded me of Sheldon on *The Big Bang Theory*. He was a details kind of guy, smart with a quick wit.

As the Director of ANG ATC, Mr. Duke was in charge of the group and the evaluation. Mr. Burnham was the Training Manager—in charge of training and standardization. Both gentlemen could easily detect a smoke screen, improper training, or procedural errors. They were all business, and everyone who interacted with them wanted to have all their ducks in a row.

I didn't have a lot to do with the evaluation, as this was all about full-time operations and not the mobility mission. However, knowing evaluators would be in the house, I took painful measures to ensure all records were accurate and updated, mobility checklists were current, databases and publications were in order and current, and more. It turned out to have been a good move because the evaluators asked many questions about training, including who tracked and scheduled recurring and mobility training, who tracked controllers' training on the mainland and their training days, and so on.

The evaluators also asked me about how the mobility side and the full-time side interacted. I answered professionally and honestly, which raised some eyebrows. Without portraying anyone in a bad light, I answered their questions factually, which gave them a deeper understanding of what was actually happening at Kalaeloa.

Within the ANGRC ATC directorate and other ANG directorates, Airmen from the field or states have opportunities to go to the ANGRC for a short tour of duty. Not long after we took over the full-time mission at Kalaeloa, Mr. Burnham asked me to perform a thirty-day tour with Mr. Duke at the Guard Bureau in the ATC division. I believe this opportunity came along because of the way I'd conducted myself during their evaluation: I understood the DSG and full-time mission and was professional in the way I provided the information they sought. I believe they also understood my dedication to ATC.

My commander approved the tour, and off I went. It was an amazing learning experience. I brought back administrative ideas and examples of how to improve our operations. Initially, my renewed sense of purpose, passion, and energy was not well received by the civilian training manager. During a staff meeting with the commander, I was explaining what needed to be included in a certain report when the training manager became highly disrespectful.

"Then tell us what needs to go in it, Ms. Smarty Pants," he said sarcastically.

I saw red and looked at him right in the eyes.

"Don't you ever speak to me like that again," I said sharply. I would not tolerate impertinence.

At that point, the commander shut down the dialogue and moved on. The training manager and I later had heated words but resolved it in the end.

༄

I had been a master sergeant for a handful of years and was waiting for the commander to talk with me about being promoted. As the superintendent, there was no one ahead of me in my chain of command; the line went from me to the commander. I had completed all the requirements years earlier, volunteered in the HIANG and in the community, did the tour at the ANGRC, and performed my job well. The commander never had to worry whether or not I was taking care of business. I managed all ATC requirements and activities as they pertained to the mobility mission and the DSG controllers. I don't ever recall a time when the commander questioned me about something getting done, yet I often wondered why he never spoke to me about promotion or his expectations.

It was a different Air National Guard back then. With no chief air traffic control officer (CATCO)—the person in charge of the ATC section—and no formal feedback or mentorship program, there was no one I could look up to for guidance. I continued to be a good Airman and do what I believed was right, but the lack of feedback was frustrating. One time, I sent the commander an e-mail asking for his comments, but he never answered it.

*Message received*, I thought. Getting feedback was not going to happen in our unit.

Recognizing the need to regroup as a team and step up our game, I organized a leadership day for all controllers. The experience turned out to be positive and productive. We engaged in goal setting as individuals and as a section and listened to leadership tapes by Dr. John Maxwell. We talked about what we wanted to achieve, what type of section and unit we wanted to have, and what we needed to do to get there. I remember feeling at the end of that day like I had gotten to know the controllers on a deeper level as they shared their individual journeys. With mission statements in hand, signed agreements of personal goals and expectations, and a commitment to the agreed-upon steps, we started down a new path together as a united section.

Time passed, and as I looked at my counterparts in the ANG ATC units across the mainland, I saw that most of them had become senior master sergeants. It was starting to annoy me that the commander had never initiated a conversation about my future. I needed to know why he wasn't recommending me for promotion. I thought there must be something I wasn't doing, so finally one day, in late 1999, I asked to meet with him.

I asked him about his expectations for me. All his feedback was good; the only thing I lacked, he said, was a radar facility rating. He believed the superintendent should be dual-rated in both the tower and radar facilities. That was it!

As much as I appreciated finally learning this information, I couldn't help but feel frustrated that he'd never communicated his expectations to me earlier. I had been an SNCO since November 1995 and began reporting directly to him in 1998. I didn't know where I'd find the additional time to achieve the second rating, but I set my sights on figuring it out and getting it done. There were always higher priorities, though, and I probably became discouraged, realizing how long it would take to achieve a radar rating. I had a difficult enough time getting hours in the tower to maintain my facility rating, let alone acquire a second rating.

Some months later, I was talking with a colleague from a mainland unit. He asked why I was still a master sergeant, and I explained the commander's requirement to have a radar rating. We talked about other mainland ANG ATC superintendents who did not have a dual rating and that there was no ANG requirement to have one. That conversation stuck with me for a long time. I felt like I was busting my hump, singularly managing the demands of the section, while the Title-32 controllers continued to be bound by a union contract to only key the mic and work traffic.

It wasn't that I was promotion hungry—I just believed I had accomplished what was required to be *considered* for promotion. I was the superintendent and tower chief controller—not the radar chief controller. I should not have needed a radar rating to be promoted. Thus, a few months later, I developed a list of accomplishments, additional responsibilities I had undertaken, and organization and community service participation. Then I asked to speak with the commander over lunch. I wanted the conversation to be private, with no possibility of interruptions or eavesdropping by other unit members, so we ate off-site.

I began to explain what I wanted to talk with him about, but before I got out the first bullet point, he cut to the chase.

"You deserve to be promoted," he said. "I'll submit the paperwork."

I was flabbergasted! I was also angry.

*Why? Why? Why?* I thought, exasperated. *If you believed, I deserved advancement, why didn't you put me in for promotion before now?*

Of course, I didn't say that out loud. Frankly, I didn't have anything more to talk about. I had prepared my list and what I planned to discuss, and it was all shot to hell with his abrupt statement. We made small talk, lunch was over, and he subsequently submitted the paperwork for promotion.

Prior to my promotion board in November 2000, I studied, read, memorized, thought of questions, and prepared answers. I checked and double-checked my uniform and was well prepared to meet the promotion board. That morning, I woke up sick as a dog. Not one to ever miss drill, I took aspirin, and with a pounding headache and churning stomach, I went to drill. Not feeling any better that afternoon, I drove to the promotion board site at our state headquarters. I remember nothing about the board. On the way back to the unit, I had a hard time driving because of my pounding head. I stopped, called the commander, and told him the board went well. I then asked to be excused for the remainder of the day because I was ill. He approved my request, so I drove home and went to bed.

The next day, the commander informed me that I had passed my promotion board. His congratulations fell flat, however, because of the way it had all rolled out.

# CHAPTER 23

# Beyond Kalaeloa

In 2000, an ANG call for augmentees[7] caught my eye. The 241st ATCS in St. Joseph, Missouri, was undergoing an operational readiness exercise (ORE) at Dugway Proving Grounds, Utah, in preparation for their inspection the following year, and they needed augmentees to assist and backfill positions. I knew the 241st ATCS tower chief and had great respect for him, as did the entire ANG ATC community. Since the 297th was due for an operational readiness inspection (ORI) within the next two years, I believed this would be an excellent opportunity to watch, take notes, and gather critical data that would help our unit in our upcoming inspection. The commander concurred, and I volunteered.

The quarters at Dugway were old run-down barracks in the Great Salt Lake Desert; dust and sand covered almost everything. I was on the third floor with other female controllers. We each made our areas livable and adjusted to our new surroundings. The next day, we went out to the field to begin setup operations. Because I was there as an augmentee controller, not a leader, I was placed on a crew in a nonsupervisory role. The 241st controllers needed to take the leadership roles.

After we set up the tower and equipment, we needed to make improvements around the facility. I volunteered to make a hardened alternate facility with sandbags. This facility would be the alternate tower location during times of evacuation or high winds—all part of the exercise. A male controller and I made an awesome alternate facility that even had shelves for phones. The Inspector General (IG) was quite impressed with our creativity. I especially liked this job because it was physical. It was dirty but provided a good workout as we tossed sandbags around for hours.

As the exercise began in the tower, the IG directly started asking me many of the questions intended for the crew supervisor, who was in charge of the crew and facility at the time. At some point, she asked, "You are the supervisor, right?" I explained that I was an augmentee from another unit. Then the tables turned to the crew supervisor.

We conducted our operations well and followed the tower checklists. Many times, I assisted the supervisor with locating information and took the lead during portions of an exercise that was specifically designed for the tower. Throughout the exercise, I took photos of things I believed would help my unit during our exercise and inspection—decontamination procedures, signs that assisted members at the decontamination point and casualty collection point, signs that identified simulated blackout procedures or the need to shut down air-conditioning/ventilation during a chemical attack, hazardous waste receptacles, hardening facilities, and various other procedures. My unit was not accustomed to doing many of the decontamination procedures to the level the 241st did. For instance, we had never wrapped a vehicle in plastic to protect it from a chemical attack—and we didn't have the materials and resources to do so. Their signs and procedures seemed to be well thought out, and their procedures were standard across the unit and spelled out clearly—I could not say the same for our level of standardization.

During the exercise, high desert winds kicked up, forcing us to secure loose items. We lowered and secured antennas, masts, and any other equipment that could blow away. Just as I stepped outside a port-a-potty, it blew over. *How disgusting that would have been to be inside when it toppled!* I thought.

I thoroughly enjoyed participating in the exercise and was recognized as a superior performer by a member of the IG team, who presented me with an IG challenge coin. It was a great experience, and I felt good assisting another unit as well as bringing back a plethora of information for our unit. Upon returning to my home station, one of the first things I did was to request an electronic copy of all the 241st checklists. The 241st tower chief was happy to share his work, and I was pleased to pass it on to the section supervisors in my unit. Their checklists were well done, thorough, and more current than anything we had. I was grateful for a new starting point. For some reason, one item really stood out in my mind: their facility hardening plan to protect the tower, radar, and tactical air navigation (TACAN) facilities from simulated bomb attacks. We didn't have one. I made a mental note to make this plan an action item.

✧

Early in 2001, the commander decided that our unit would deploy to Wendover, Utah, for an operational readiness exercise in June, to prepare our unit for the upcoming inspection. The entire unit would deploy, including command staff, administrative personnel, controllers, maintenance, power production, HVAC, and supply. We had to take everything we needed to sustain the unit for an entire week. That meant all equipment, tools, spare parts, manuals, flips, charts, laptops, mobile radios, and much more.

The logistics were overwhelming; even the preplanning for this exercise became daunting. I had zero experience as the superintendent in deploying the entire unit, let alone my section, for an exercise of this magnitude. This was different from doing an exercise at home station and deploying across the runway on the airfield, which we had done several times. When it came to developing Letters of Agreement, 360-degree overhead pattern procedures, coordination letters, and other ATC–related memoranda, I felt like I was in over my head. This was not simulated; this was going to be real world with live traffic.

The Letters of Agreement were duties a CATCO would have been responsible for. We no longer had a CATCO, so the responsibility fell to me as the superintendent. At a minimum, I believed the Commander should have assisted in the development of these critical procedures. I was the tower chief controller and package chief for the radar and tower controllers and all maintenance personnel. My hands were full ensuring the tower, radar, and TACAN packages had their checklists, procedures, individual training records, and medical certifications. I also had to make sure all regulations, instructions, and equipment were up-to-date and that our unit was ready to deploy. I acquired through Hickam AFB all aeronautical documents for the Wendover, Utah airport, including flips, charts, maps, and any relevant airport information. All recurring, proficiency, and mobility training had to be completed and annotated. There was much to be done and checked twice to ensure completion.

Ultimately, the deployed location coordination letters were what gave me the most angst. Many times, I sent drafts to the Commander for him to review and got no response. I left voice mail and e-mail messages for him to call me, again with no response. It became extremely frustrating, and I felt as though my back was up against a sharp corner. After numerous attempts to communicate with the Commander, I called his admin section, who said the Commander's door was closed.

From my perspective, the lack of communication and guidance from the Commander was inexcusable. His seeming lack of concern about matters attached to deadlines left me even more exasperated. In my opinion, this was not leadership. I had already come to understand that he was not an effective communicator, but this went way beyond "poor communication." Other technicians were asking me questions about their sections, but I couldn't give them answers.

Despite the lack of guidance, we all pressed forward and did the best we could. Several technicians were aware that the commander's now ex-wife had a reoccurrence of her cancer and that things were going downhill in his personal life. No doubt this was an extremely difficult time for him and his ex-wife since they had two children. I think this is why we made excuses for his lack of communication and slow decision-making, as well as for the mornings when he appeared to drag himself into the office.

I empathized with him, recalling a situation years before when I had found a lump in my breast. It was late fall when the doctor said I needed a biopsy. I was scared to death of the outcome and only shared the situation with Gary. I was a wreck for weeks and had to keep my mind busy; otherwise, I'd find myself crying in the office. I decided to let the Commander know what was going on since I would need some time off. A short time later, he responded and invited me to lunch to talk. It was a kind gesture on his part and one of the first times I sensed that he cared.

A good deal of time had passed since my scare, and now I found myself reaching out to him and asking if I could help in any way. Clearly, this was an extremely difficult time for him, yet being the consummate samurai, his responses were always the same: "I'm doing okay" or "She's doing all right."

I tried to be compassionate, but the responsibility to get everything done was weighing on me. I couldn't ask the full-time Title-5 or Title-32 controllers for assistance, as this was a mobility issue and not related to the fixed facility. Fortunately, several Drill Status Guardsmen were also FAA controllers, and they helped me craft the 360 Overhead Pattern letter.

As time got closer, the Commander took several of us on a site survey to Wendover to look at the airport, billeting, dining options, and emergency facilities, and to coordinate with airport personnel. Additionally, we drove to Hill AFB to meet with F-16 pilots, since they would be our customers at Wendover, and coordinated approaches and procedures with them. I felt fortunate to have a copy of procedures they had previously flown and used at the airport; I was able to review all procedures and compare them to what we had written, which enabled us to make our letters stronger with added detail.

After our meetings at Hill AFB, we drove three hours back to Wendover to check on additional facilities, including the location of the hospital. We also looked into hotel accommodations, meal availability, churches, and laundry, exercise, and gym facilities—everything we would need for our deployment to Wendover.

There was one challenge for us in Wendover: the city straddles the Utah–Nevada border, and gambling is legal in the Nevada hotels. We knew we would need to ensure that those facilities were off-limits areas for our Airmen by briefing them on the rules and consequences of violating the policy letter. As it turned out, and through good SNCO leadership, there were no infractions.

We learned that an evaluator would be present throughout the exercise to review our checklists, procedures, and individual training records. I knew Senior Master Sergeant Larry Paskert fairly well; he was old-school and a good man. He knew ATC rules and procedures. He and I had met at ATC conferences and spoken several times on the telephone, and I was comfortable knowing his eyes would be looking over my shoulder.

With orders in hand, the unit members reported and departed Oahu as planned. We arrived in Wendover, off-loaded the equipment, and bused personnel to their hotels. I briefed the controllers and maintenance personnel on the schedule, the fictitious name of our deployed location, threat-condition level, and logistical information, including setup procedures for the following morning, and reporting instructions for when and where personnel would meet. All went as planned. Unit members were split up and stayed in two different hotels.

I happened to be staying in the same hotel as the Commander and some of the other technicians. After we were released for the day, I went to work out. Several of the technicians and the Commander sat by the pool and enjoyed some cold drinks while discussing various matters. I returned to find them still at the pool. As I walked by, a couple of the controllers grabbed me by the arm and threw me in the pool. Knowing it was all in good fun, they even let me take off my shoes first. After some jovial conversation and still dripping, I went to my room to prepare for the next day.

The following morning, I was ready to execute the plan of the day when a fellow technician said, "That's not how we're doing it." *What?* I couldn't believe what I was hearing. When I learned that the Commander had made some last-minute modifications the night before at the pool, I was livid. As the Package Chief, I had the majority of the personnel under my responsibility, and to find out procedures were changed around the pool made me furious. Knowing there was nothing I could do to change things, however, I sucked it up, adjusted fire, and pressed forward.

I was dual-hatted as the overall package chief and tower chief controller. The package chief had oversight for the tower, radar, and TACAN personnel (controllers and maintenance). Each section, or package—which included the tower, radar, and TACAN—set up their respective equipment. Once we were set up, the individual packages operated somewhat autonomously. The Commander had overall responsibility of all his people and oversight of his command staff. While we operated as separate packages, we understood we were one team with one mission, and it was imperative to coordinate with one another.

Once we set up the tower equipment, we reviewed checklists. Before calling the facility operational, the TSN administered the local-area knowledge exam to all controllers, and tower facility certifications were completed. Everything seemed to be going well. Once every package was operationally ready, we began operations at our fictitious deployed location, a.k.a. Wendover Airport.

As the tower chief controller, I had personally ensured the tower controllers' records were up-to-date and that all training had been completed and signed off. I worked hand in glove with the TSN to ensure that testing materials were developed and procedures outlined. Shortly after going operationally ready, Senior Master Sergeant Paskert approached me about the radar controllers' records. Although I had asked the DSG radar chief controller several times about the completeness of those records, I had not personally looked at them; he had assured me the records were inspection-ready. Senior Master Sergeant Paskert painted a very different picture.

"If this had been our actual inspection, the inspector would have shut the radar facility down," he said, shaking his head. "Not only were the records incomplete, there were no facility certifications for your deployed location entered into the records."

The old adage "trust but verify" came back to haunt me in a fierce way. All the planning, preparing, reviewing items in triplicate…and now incomplete training records were going to be our demise? I was furious!

Senior Master Sergeant Paskert could see what had happened, and he had a solution.

"You need to go over to the radar facility and tear into the radar chief controller," he recommended.

There was an implicit expectation that I would do as he suggested. I had never lit into anyone, but I did just that. It wasn't a cordial conversation, and the radar chief controller knew I was fuming. Although we were not currently working live traffic, I took this personally. We were to perform as if everything was "real world." The training record debacle reflected negatively on me as the package chief, and I didn't like it one bit.

The radar chief controller and I were colleagues, friends actually, and now I had just chastised him. I certainly did not feel good about our interaction, and deep down, I felt as though I should apologize. Knowing we were being scrutinized and evaluated, I tried to shrug it off and pressed on with the rest of the day. The radar chief controller called later to confirm that the records had been updated, and all facility certifications had been entered appropriately. The conversation was curt but professional.

In all honesty, I felt ashamed of myself because I'd allowed Senior Master Sergeant Paskert to influence my behavior. I had never treated the radar chief controller like that before. I felt as if I had lost his respect and most likely his friendship. It bothered me a great deal. On the other hand, some controllers apparently could not make the leap from exercise mode to real-world operations. Because we were working with live traffic, this was not a fictitious exercise—it was real world. We used this deployment as an operational readiness exercise to prepare for the ORI, but we were doing it with real aircraft in the pattern. I would have handled the conversation with the radar chief controller differently had Senior Master Sergeant Paskert not "suggested" I tear into him, but I was admittedly angry that the radar controllers' records had not been inspection-ready.

We returned to Oahu from Wendover, feeling like we had accomplished what we set out to do. Overall, everyone performed well, and operations went smoothly after the initial records issue. Even my relationship with the radar chief controller continued to be professional and friendly. The exercise and deployment seemed to bring the unit closer together and fostered higher comradery among us. This had been a great experience and set the foundation for what was to come in 2002 with our impending ORI.

⌘

Getting to know my counterparts in the ANG ATC units on the mainland proved to be highly beneficial. Not only did I meet and get to know great Airmen, but I also developed lasting friendships. For me, the sharing of information was crucial. I always felt like in Hawaii we were a step behind what the other units were doing. Perhaps it was because we were the only unit that belonged to Pacific Air Forces (PACAF). Relationships in the Guard are important—sometimes it's who you know or knowing who to contact for specific information. Then there are those times when others think of you.

One day, I received a call from a colleague in another unit. He had a line number for an Air Expeditionary Forces (AEF) thirty-day deployment in Aviano, Italy. He was unable to take the assignment and asked if I wanted it.

"Absolutely yes!" I immediately responded.

I approached the commander about the AEF and explained what I'd be doing. As an air traffic control liaison officer, I would be working for the Director of Operations. We were to inquire and receive reports from surrounding ATC facilities pertaining to runway and navigational aid statuses, airport closures, outages, equipment updates, and manning requirements. We would also gather and publish the daily weather for various local areas. My Commander approved me to go on the deployment, and I was excited about the opportunity.

The thirty-day deployment to Italy was one of the best assignments I ever had. While I made the most of all my deployments, this was different. This was Italy! We worked ten-hour days providing the required information to the local facilities and to higher headquarters. The work was fairly slow and routine, but we stayed busy.

During the AEF in Aviano, we were allowed to sign out and leave the base on the weekends, but we had to be in groups of two. It was easy to partner with other Airmen to go off base, and I visited Venice and other towns around the area. Several of the Airmen who worked in my area signed up for a daylong Morale, Welfare, and Recreation (MWR) bus tour to Neuschwanstein Castle and Dachau concentration camp in Germany. The drive through Austria and Germany was breathtaking. Having never been in a castle before, throughout the tour, I tried to visualize how the inhabitants lived at the time within the walls of such an immense and fascinating structure. For instance, it struck me how cold it must have been in parts of the castle where windows remained open throughout the winter. As we toured Dachau, the cruelty and death that occurred during WWII were incomprehensible to me.

Every time an Airman needed a travel partner to Venice, I was in. Besides enjoying the culture, architecture, history, and beauty of Venice, I bought souvenirs and Italian jewelry to take home. I purchased a dozen lavender porcelain roses for my mother, and she still has them in her living room today.

When I left Italy, I told myself, "This is a country I'd like to come back to for vacation." For now, however, it was back to Hawaii and the impending ORI preparation.

# CHAPTER 24

# ORI Mode

We had used the 241st ATCS checklists several times, yet the radar chief controller and I felt the need to continue to tweak the deployment checklists. We revamped the tower, radar, and administrative publications and binders to look more professional. We went through reams of paper updating AF Instructions (AFI), regulations, and policy letters.

As the only Pacific Air Forces (PACAF) gained ATC unit, we waited for inspection criteria and guidance from PACAF. The Commander asked our higher headquarters to intervene with PACAF, and we were consistently told the criteria was coming and to stand by. It was extremely frustrating, trying to prepare for a major inspection with no grading or inspection criteria.

The mainland units belonged to a different Major Command, Air Combat Command (ACC). ACC had an instruction manual outlining their ATC inspection criteria, but because it was from a different command, we continued to sit idly by for the PACAF inspection criteria. Days of waiting turned into weeks and months, and soon the inspection was upon us. Fed up with the bureaucracy, I relied on what I had learned as an augmentee with the 241st ATCS.

The team of technicians in my unit pulled together, figured out what needed to be done, and took appropriate action to the best of our abilities. I informed my section that I'd made a decision to use ACC's inspection criteria; I figured it couldn't be that different. We never did receive inspection criteria from PACAF, and I was thankful that I'd listened to my gut.

Several months before the inspection, I went to see the Commander and had a heart-to-heart discussion with him. I was done. As the superintendent of the ATC section and as a Senior Master Sergeant, I had been at the squadron for about twelve years. During that time, I had served as a DSG, a temporary technician, and a full-time federal technician. At the end of 2000, I began to feel like it was time for me to move forward. I believed I had developed the controllers in their leadership capabilities to the best of my ability, and it was time for me to move on so they could assume additional responsibilities to lead in their own right. I also believed that I, too, had to move forward if I was to grow and further my leadership skills. I wanted to work with leaders who would challenge me to the next level.

It wasn't just that, though—the lack of support from leadership and the Title-32 controllers created an extremely difficult situation, and I'd had enough. I felt as though the union contract had me hamstrung. The Title-32 controllers were "hands-off" assets during the week, creating a continual source of frustration. I'd been working many frequent nights and Saturdays doing ORI preparation because my workday was consumed with routine duties. As I looked around, no one else was working alongside me, and important questions and concerns continued to go unanswered by leadership. Assigned duties for when the Title-32 controllers were on DSG duty went largely undone. It was like pulling teeth to get many of the controllers to do more than their individual responsibilities. With the lack of support from leadership and ongoing challenges between full-time and mobility operations, I firmly believed it was time for me to move on. I was hungry for professional growth.

It's been said that "people don't quit their job—they quit their boss." This turned out to be true for me. I told the Commander I was in through the ORI, but after that, I would be looking for a new position. I had too much pride and professionalism to leave or jump ship before a major inspection. I would never do that to the unit or to those for whom I was responsible. A part of me also wanted validation of my performance from the ORI. After all, I'd worked hard, despite the lack of cooperation and support, to get us ready.

As the weeks went by, the full-time technicians and I planned for birthing quarters, meals, transportation, emergency facilities, and any other requirements needed in the field. I was in contact with our former CATCO, Captain Anthony Lancaster, who had returned to the HIANG and was now serving in a Combat Airspace Management position in our Group Headquarters. He and I had continued to converse from time to time. Captain Lancaster had a calm demeanor and was always a voice of reason and maturity. He understood the complexity and dynamics of the mobility and fixed operations. Together, we had gone through the transition of the 297th taking on a full-time operation and had shared similar experiences and frustrations. I completely trusted that anything I discussed with him would be held in confidence.

One evening, I mentioned to him that after the inspection, I would be leaving the unit and my full-time technician job and would be looking for a DSG position. Captain Lancaster expressed surprise that someone would give up a senior full-time position without having something else lined up. For me, though, it wasn't about the position, money, or retirement. My decision had everything to do with wanting to be appreciated, valued, and considered an integral part of a team. I was hungry for support, communication, respect, and the opportunity for professional and personal growth. Captain Lancaster understood when I said I could no longer work for the Commander. Unbeknownst to me, he became my biggest advocate to the 201st Group commander and my subsequent lateral transfer into combat airspace management in the fall of 2002.

The preoperational readiness inspection was a difficult time for our squadron. Our Commander continued to deal with personal challenges in his life. It was a demanding and challenging time for me as the superintendent, which required me to wear many hats. As I continued to manage the day-to-day operations of the ATC section,

I was also responsible for the CATCO, package chief, and tower chief controller duties, which went back to the lines drawn between the mobility and the fixed-facility missions. With the exception of the recently assigned mobility radar chief controller, who was also a full-time Title-32 controller and took his duties seriously, I felt like I carried the weight of the myriad tasks on our list.

Because the ORI had nothing to do with full-time fixed operations, full-time Title-32 and Title-5 controllers were "hands off." Although I was fully committed to preparing for the ORI and did everything possible to ensure our success, the preparation came at a great sacrifice and cost to me personally and to my family. I had been stretched as far as I could and frankly felt like I had bled for the squadron. Thankfully, Gary and Ashley were continually supportive.

At one point, I told them, "Just help me get through this inspection, and then things will go back to normal."

Days before the start of the ORI, the Commander's ex-wife passed away. There were rumors that the ORI might be canceled, and we lived in uncertainty for what seemed like an eternity. Finally, we got word that the inspection would go on as planned. Another master sergeant was assigned as the tower chief controller (TCC). I would operate as the CATCO during the day, and the commander would take the night shift as the nighttime CATCO.

# CHAPTER 25

# Keeping a Promise

In Hawaii, eighth-grade graduation is a really big deal. Naturally, with all the challenges I'd managed as we prepared for the upcoming inspection, Ashley's graduation fell on the evening prior to the start of the ORI.

As a rule, I rarely make promises. To me, a promise is concrete—your word is your bond, and there is no wiggle room for error. Throughout her lifetime, I've made two promises to our daughter. The first was that when she was ten years old, we would take her to California to Disneyland, SeaWorld, Universal Studios, San Diego Zoo, and Medieval Times and that her brother and sisters would be with us. Gary and I saved and planned for a full year, purchasing all the tickets, saving meal and souvenir money for the trip and even money to develop all the rolls of film. Everything was paid for in advance since I don't believe it's a vacation if you have to come home and spend a year paying for it.

The second promise was that I would be at her eighth-grade graduation "on time." Leading up to the ORI, I suspect she didn't trust or believe that I would be on time for her graduation. I promised Ashley that I would stop working at 4:30 p.m., change clothes, and be there. Even with that commitment, I don't think she believed me. At 4:29 p.m., the office phone rang. I hesitated to answer it. Uncertain whether I should pick up the phone, I abruptly said, "Air Traffic." This was not how I ordinarily answered the phone, but

I knew that I had one minute before I had to change to keep my promise.

It just so happened that it was my Group Commander. I cringed. He'd heard that I planned to leave the squadron after the ORI. The Colonel went on to say, "Do a good job during the ORI, and after it's over, I will authorize a lateral move to bring you to the Group Headquarters as the full-time combat airspace manager (CAM)/ ATC liaison officer."

I was overwhelmed. This was going to be a huge strategic risk for me, but I was all in. I quickly thanked him, and we hung up. Even after taking this career-changing call, I was able to keep my promise and arrived on time to Ashley's graduation ceremony.

⌇

In the National Guard, it's all about "slots," or what position you're assigned to. In the air traffic control squadron, I was an E-8 assigned to an E-9 position. That meant that, while not guaranteed, had I continued to be a good Airman and do all the things required of me, I most likely would have been promoted to Chief Master Sergeant. However, there was no possibility of promotion at HQ201st Combat Communications Group, as the highest enlisted Combat Airspace position was a Senior Master Sergeant. I was grateful for the opportunity to transfer—it didn't matter that I would not be promoted. I was excited to learn something new and face new challenges. Of course, most enlisted Airmen aspire to become a Chief Master Sergeant, but sometimes the timing, opportunity, or path to Chief do not exist. For me, it was about service and the greater good of the organization. It was also time for me to leave the 297th Air Traffic Control Squadron.

Execution day for the ORI came. Setup went extremely well—the tower was up quickly, as were the command support tents. The radar facility takes much longer to be operationally ready because there are lot of cables to run and more complex equipment to set up. The navigational aid went up and came online with no issues. I worked through the day and most of the evening since the Commander was with his family. I recall going to my quarters to catch a couple of

175

hours of sleep when there was a knock at the door. As part of a scenario to test our adaptability, the inspector general (IG) team had taken out the tower chief controller, and we needed to rework the manning schedule. As the CATCO, that was now my responsibility.

With an hour or so of sleep, I couldn't even think straight. I sat with the controller who'd awakened me and asked him to work the manning schedule with me—I didn't want my tired state to be the reason for an error. Later that day, when I was back on duty, one of the IG inspectors came into the command tent.

"Can I see your hardening plan?" he asked.

It was a proud moment when I responded with a question of my own.

"Hardening plan for the tower, radar, or TACAN?" I replied.

"Tower only," the inspector said with a slight grin.

After he left, we quickly radioed the radar and TACAN and told them to be prepared with their hardening plans. Senior Airman James Luna-Hill did us proud. He was a quirky controller who had developed and calculated the requirements for the hardening plans for all three facilities. He had listed down to the number of sandbags how many were required for each facility to harden it against potential explosions. It seems like an insignificant item, but it was an inspectable one. Without the hardening plans, our grade would have been affected.

Our DSG members and technicians in all sections worked hard and performed exceptionally well. The effort paid off: we received an "Excellent" rating. The inspection was finally over, and we had come through with flying colors. We all breathed a sigh of relief and enjoyed the moments that followed. The air was electric with pride and enthusiasm in a job well done.

# CHAPTER 26

# Starting a New Chapter

Shortly after the ORI, I transferred to the Headquarters, 201st Combat Communications Group into the combat airspace manager position. I quickly contacted the air traffic control division at the Air National Guard Readiness Center (ANGRC) and inquired about combat airspace school. Unfortunately, the school was unit-funded, and my unit did not have the funds to send me.

After several discussions, though, the ANGRC ATC division agreed to fund my airspace school provided I agreed to deploy to Operation Iraq Freedom (OIF) or Operation Enduring Freedom (OEF) as an Airspace Manager.

*Deploy?* I thought. *Heck yes! When can I go?*

Prior to transferring to the 201st, I wrote decoration packages for three individuals for their performance during the ORI. The Commander said he was going to write an AF Commendation Medal package for me and another individual, but as the deadline approached, the administration/personalist contacted me. He told me the commander had not written either of our packages.

*Not again*, I thought, irritated.

Once more, the Commander was not in the office when I tried to contact him. I wasn't going to do anything about my package, but I strongly believed the other individual deserved to be recognized.

"I'll write the package for the other individual," I told the personalist. "Don't worry about my award."

If the Commander did not think I was worthy of an award, then so be it. I was not going to write one for myself, and I certainly was not going to track him down and ask about it.

In the end, all packages were submitted on time, except mine. It hurt deeply, but I tried to let it go, knowing in my heart what I had done and how I had contributed to our Excellent rating. I would not send further e-mails or leave phone messages. I'd had it. I packed up my office and left for the 201st.

As time passed, while awaiting the start of airspace school, the question still haunted me. I wanted to know why the Commander never submitted the award package on my behalf. I needed to hear him say it—whatever it was. I tried to push those thoughts away; I told myself I needed to leave all this behind me and start fresh.

After a few months, it was time to attend airspace school. Much like ATC school, I had to study hard to learn the combat airspace material. Most of the airspace students were pilots who understood the lingo, acronyms, and airspace procedures. There were only a few of us in the class who weren't pilots. Throughout the course, students often got together for dinner and to enjoy the area nightlife. I felt like I was in the fishbowl at Keesler AFB all over again. No, I could not come out for fun—I had to study!

I had not been at the Headquarters 201st Group long when I learned that the 297th ATCS Commander was being reassigned to my unit. Initially, I could not believe it. I was dismayed, but I did not share my thoughts or feelings with anyone. There was no point—it was a command decision. I merely hoped and prayed that I would not fall under his supervision. My plan was to remain professional and courteous and to steer clear of his office. While I continued to shake my head in dismay, on some level, I knew it was a good move for him. He had some rough years behind him, and maybe now he would be able to catch his breath and regroup.

While going through the office mail one day, I came across the awards and decorations order that announced the awarding of individual decorations. As I read the list, I was elated to see members of the 297th recognized for their contributions. It was a proud moment, reflecting back on their performance pre- and post-ORI.

On the other hand, the glaring absence of my name on that list was embarrassing. After all these months, I felt another stab of disappointment. I fully understood we were a unit that was rarely recognized—it was our culture. I'd been in the ANG fifteen years and had received two AF Achievement Medals. One was from my time on active duty and the other was awarded by the ANGRC.

I walked over to my former Commander's office and stood at the doorway.

"Sir, do you have a moment?" I asked.

He looked up from his desk and motioned me in.

"Sit down," he said, looking at me expectantly.

I sat down and carefully measured my words.

"Sir, the list of decorations for the ORI came out," I said evenly. "My name isn't on it."

He didn't immediately say anything, so I forged ahead.

"I don't know if I did something to change your mind or didn't do something, but I would like to know why I'm unworthy of a decoration."

He looked at me blankly.

"Your name's on the list."

I shook my head firmly.

"No, sir, it's not," I said. "I'd like to know why."

"Well, I wrote the package," he said defensively. "It must've gotten lost."

"Permission to speak freely, sir?"

"Say what's on your mind," he responded.

I sat forward on the edge of my chair and told him about my conversation with the personalist.

"My package was never submitted, sir," I said. I was respectful but direct.

"I'll look into it," he said. "And I'll write a Meritorious Service Medal package that includes your previous years of service. The ORI will be part of that."

I stood up and tried to keep my face impassive.

"With all due respect, sir, don't bother."

I turned around and walked out of his office and back to mine. I sat in my chair and stared out the window.

*There*, I thought. *I asked and he said it.*

I had looked the Commander straight in the eyes and asked him to explain his lack of action. Although the sting of not seeing my name on the list hadn't subsided, I had the personal satisfaction of having asked him.

Now it was time to move forward and forget about it.

༭

After graduating from airspace school, I went to the Thirteenth Air Force, Air Operations Center (AOC) on Hickam AFB, where I met with the combat airspace section and developed a partnership with the active-duty Air Force combat airspace managers. They were in the process of building their combat plans and combat operations airspace teams, and we began to collaborate on training, support of daily operations, and exercises.

As a Title-32 federal technician, I could only use the Thirteenth AF AOC facility to hone my airspace skills. The AOC used the Theater Battle Management Core System (TBMCS), a secret system, to build all the airspace for daily operations and for exercises. This capability did not exist at the 201st, so partnering with the Thirteenth AF AOC allowed me to utilize the system and keep my skills sharp. It also provided them with an extra person they could use for manning during exercises and daily operations. After some time, the Thirteenth AOC Airspace section came to view the HIANG as "continuity," bridging the gap between Airmen PCS-ing (permanent change of station) in and out. We were the Guard, the hometown team that didn't PCS, and we had a different type of deployment schedule than our active-duty counterparts. We were consistently at our home base and available when active-duty members either PCS'd or deployed.

After some time, I got my AEF deployment to Al Udeid Air Base in Qatar to work in the Combined Air Operations Center from January through April 2007. I was stoked because I had volunteered to deploy several times as a controller, but nothing had ever come to fruition. My airspace section at the HQ 201st Combat Communications Group (CCG) had an additional E-7 slot. The person filling that slot soon retired, and we brought another controller over from the 297th ATCS to fill the position.

Master Sergeant Hidetaka "John" Murakami and I had served together for many years as fellow controllers. He was not only a controller but also a flight attendant *and* airline pilot. This was an opportunity to bring a plethora of experience to the HQ, as well as an opportunity for Master Sergeant Murakami to become a combat airspace manager. The ANGRC also funded his training with the agreement that he, too, would deploy. Because there were a limited number of airspace deployment slots, we agreed to split my slot so both Master Sergeant Murakami and I could fulfill and honor our agreement with the ANGRC. I would now deploy January through early March 2007, and Master Sergeant Murakami would take the second half of the deployment. While disappointed at having to split my deployment, I understood it was a win-win for the Headquarters 201st CCG and Master Sergeant Murakami.

Over the years, I had many short deployments for exercises as a controller and combat airspace manager. In addition to domestic locations, I had the opportunity to participate in Team Spirit twice in the early 1990s and Ulchi Focus Lens in the mid-2000s, both in Korea.

As an Airman, it was interesting and exciting to deploy on board a Navy ship. I deployed on the USS *Blue Ridge* for Exercise Keen Edge and to Yokosuka and Yokota Air Base, Japan, for Joint Chiefs of Staff exercises. During these deployments, I learned more about the culture of the other services and developed a profound respect for what each service brought to the fight. I have often said that no one service is better than the other. Each brings different skill sets and capabilities to accomplish the overall mission. We have leaders and true professionals in every service, each focused on the same goal: defending and protecting the United States of America.

While at the 201st CCG, several NCOs approached me about my former Commander. They were uncomfortable with his appearance and demeanor. When he came to them regarding work-related business, they said they could smell alcohol. They also commented on the empty beer cans in the back of his truck parked outside. Our building was a headquarters with DVs, active duty, and other dignitaries who went in and out for various meetings and events.

The first time or two that an NCO approached me about the Commander, I tried to shrug it off. Quite frankly, I didn't want to deal with this situation again. About the third time it happened, one of the NCOs came to my office, pleading for help. As the ranking SNCO at the headquarters, I felt it was now my responsibility to do something. I spoke with the Group Commander, whom I believed knew full well what was happening. Now that it was brought to his attention, though, he would have to take action, and he said he would.

I hated being the one having this conversation with the Group Commander, but I knew it was the right thing for me to do—it was my responsibility to help the NCOs. At the end of the day, no matter what, I continued to hope that the Commander would find his way to peace and enjoy a meaningful and happy life.

# CHAPTER 27

# Command Chief

About a year after transferring to the HQ 201st Combat Communications Group, an announcement for the Hawaii State Command Chief Master Sergeant (CCM) (E-9) position was posted. It was the summer of 2003, and I was a Senior Master Sergeant. In the Air National Guard, a State CCM is the most senior Chief Master Sergeant within each respective state, territory, or the District of Columbia and serves at the discretion of the Adjutant General. After reading the job announcement and seeing that *promotable* Senior Master Sergeants could apply, I decided to submit a package.

During a discussion with a very senior General Officer, however, I learned that as a full-time federal technician, I could not be a CCM. I respectfully asked where I could find that information or guidance, and he said he would get back to me.

Other states had full-time technicians as their state CCM, so I needed to know the basis of the General's comments and what he was referencing. I had learned to question remarks such as these—just because something has always been done a certain way doesn't mean it's right. After a couple of weeks, I had not heard anything back, so I e-mailed the General Officer. I respectfully restated our brief conversation and asked for the guidance that he referenced. His e-mail response was encouraging:

> While incompatible with your full-time techni-
> cian position, there is a waiver process.

That was all I needed to hear. He cited the human resource reference, and I delved in to read the details.

After getting the required approval from my commander to apply, I quickly crafted a memo to the Hawaii National Guard Adjutant General (HITAG), Major General Robert G. R Lee.[8] He approved my waiver request to apply for the state CCM position.

I understood that, traditionally, a currently serving Chief Master Sergeant would be selected for such an important leadership position. At the Chief Master Sergeant level, relationships with the organization's senior leaders and key personnel typically have been long developed, and that is critically important at a senior level of leadership. Still, some rare individuals (Senior Master Sergeants) possess the same desirable attributes but don't have a direct path to making Chief Master Sergeant. Although I believed the deck was stacked against me, I knew I was ready and could do the job. I made the decision to press forward and applied for the position, then went into my "preparation mode."

I spent countless hours studying the Wing organizational struc-ture, airframes, chain of command, and key leaders. I believed in the old axiom, "Failing to prepare is preparing to fail." I went through the interview process and did my absolute very best. I felt confident that I'd performed well at the board and provided solid responses to all questions.

A few days after the interview, the HITAG, Major General Lee, called me and said, "I selected a Chief Master Sergeant for the position." I was a bit taken aback. I knew my interview had gone extremely well and my record spoke for itself. In nineteen years of service, I had only finished second in a board selection once before. I felt as if the wind had been knocked out of my sails. It hurt, and I was disappointed. No doubt my voice reflected that. Major General Lee was encouraging but said, "It just wasn't your time."

I spent several days quietly mulling over my nonselection. I thought long and hard and questioned what I could have done differently. In the end, it boiled down to staying the course, continuing to do what I was doing, and being a good Airman. Because I believe in always trying to find the silver lining in everything and that something good comes out of every situation, I pressed on. I did not pray to get the job, but rather that God's will would be done. I did all I could do to remain competitive, but I trusted the path the Lord had for me. I still did not fully understand why "it was not my time," but sometimes we just don't know why life turns out the way it does. The important thing is that I never gave up, never stopped doing my best, never quit believing in my abilities. My trust in the Lord and belief in myself continued to guide me, even in the hardest of times.

৯৲

Several months later, an announcement came out for the 154th Wing, Command Chief Master Sergeant position (WG CCM). The WG CCM is the most senior of all Chief Master Sergeants within each respective Wing. As with the State CCM, an experienced Chief Master Sergeant is normally selected within the Wing. However, once again, as a Senior Master Sergeant, there was the possibility I might be selected for this position.

The announcement read "current Chief Master Sergeants or *promotable* Senior Master Sergeants are eligible to apply." I was the latter. After verifying that my waiver letter was still good, and after receiving the approval of my Commander, I submitted my application package. All I had to do now was wait for the interview.

What was significant about this potential opportunity was that I was a member of the HQ201st Combat Communications Group, and the position was for the 154th WG CCM. The 154th WG and 201st CCG are both part of the HIANG and located on Hickam AFB (now Joint Base Pearl Harbor-Hickam). Both organizations had geographically separated units on other islands and on Oahu. It had been my observation that there was a distinct separation between the Wing and the 201st Combat Communications Group personnel. A good number of Airmen didn't fully know or understand their brother organization or the Airmen assigned to it. HIANG Airmen were assigned by either technician or military position to the HQHIANG, the 154th WG, or the 201st CCG.

Within the HIANG, these two organizations were parallel organizations, where the Combat Communications Group did not fall under the 154th WG in the chain of command. The 201st CCG fell directly under the Hawaii Air National Guard Commander, as did the 154th WG. However, the 154th WG supported the 201st CCG in many aspects. For example, the CCG did not have a medical unit, so CCG personnel went to the 154th WG Medical Group for physicals, shots, and pre- and postdeployment requirements. When a CCG Airman had pay issues, they went to the Wing's finance office, as the 201st CCG did not have a finance office. All identification cards were issued by the Wing's Mission Support Group. The CCG Education Managers were able to service most educational needs, but there were times CCG Airmen had to go to the 154th WG Base Education office. On a drill weekend, the Wing had a fully operational dining facility (DFAC), whereas the CCG did not. All HIANG Airmen ate lunch at the WG DFAC. Other than the above examples, for the most part, the 201st CCG Airmen did not interact with the Wing, and Wing Airmen had little reason to come to the 201st CCG for anything.

When I had asked my Commander for his approval to apply for this position, he was very discouraging.

"There's no way you'll be selected because you don't belong to the Wing," he said candidly.

While surprised that he actually came out and said that to me, I knew there was truth in his words. Still, I wanted to try anyway. I believed I was fully qualified, capable, and willing. I wanted to serve in the WG CCM position, and, more importantly, I didn't have a separation mentality. I believed we were all part of a larger organization, the HIANG, each contributing to its overall mission. I also believed that if I never tried, I'd ultimately disqualify myself from future opportunities. I had nothing to lose by submitting my application package. There would be another board to face, but I understood that the Wing Commander would make the final selection.

❧

It came time for the interview board. As I recall, there were six or seven Chief Master Sergeants and one Senior Master Sergeant being interviewed. That one Senior Master Sergeant was me. I was well prepared. I had practiced and polished my introduction, anticipated and prepared responses to questions, and developed a strong closing statement. When the Wing Commander asked if I had any closing comments, I thought, *Great! Yes, I do*!

I gave my brief remarks and, in closing, looked him square in the eyes and said, "Sir, leadership is leadership. It's transferrable from unit to unit and includes going from the 201st CCG to the 154th WG. Given the opportunity, I will do my very best for the organization and our enlisted corps. Thank you."

I stood, shook the hands of the Commander and the board members, thanked them, and left. When the interview was over, I felt that I had presented myself well. I had done my very best and was confident in my answers, skills, and abilities. Now all I had to do was wait for the results of the board.

The phone call from the 154th WG Commander came while I was at home. As Gary and I were getting ready to attend a concert at the Neal Blaisdell Concert Hall on the evening after the board, the Wing Commander, Colonel Peter Pawling, called and said that he'd selected me to be his WG CCM.

I was shocked, but this time in a very happy way. Not being a member of the Wing or a Chief Master Sergeant, I had almost convinced myself that I would not be selected. Other than being honored and humbled and saying, "Yes, sir," over and over, I don't remember much more of the conversation. It took a while for it to actually sink in that Senior Master Sergeant Jelinski-Hall, a member of the 201st CCG, had been selected to be the next 154th WG

CCM. This was the first time that someone from outside the Wing had been selected to serve in this leadership position.

The fact that Colonel Pawling—now Major General (ret)—placed his trust and confidence in my ability is still humbling. Looking back, had he not given me the opportunity to serve as his WG CCM, my entire career would have looked completely different. I honestly did not think of it at the time, but two "glass ceilings" had just been shattered. The first non-Wing Command Chief Master Sergeant for the 154th WG had just been selected…and she was a woman.

Later, I came to realize that my selection was also another "first." The normal progression in the Air Force (Active Duty, Guard, or Reserve) is to get experience as a Chief Master Sergeant before getting selected to a Command Chief position. I had gone from a Senior Master Sergeant to Command Chief in a single day. I never set out to break glass ceilings or to "set firsts"; I wanted to lead by example and be the best Airman I could be in service to my country. I am still extremely humbled by the trust Colonel Pawling placed in me. It made me more determined than ever to put everything I had into serving the men and women of the Wing to the very best of my abilities.

Years later, I came to learn that Colonel Pawling selected me over the strong advice and counsel not to from some of his Group and Squadron Commanders. The biggest concerns came from select Chiefs who had been in the Wing for a long time; they believed it was not good to select someone from outside the Wing. I had much to prove as an outsider and as a Senior Master Sergeant. Not one to shrink away from a challenge, I immediately began to dig in.

꒰꒱

Being selected for the WG CCM position meant that as a full-time federal technician, I reported directly to the HQ 201st Combat Communications Group Commander, Monday through Friday. Militarily assigned, as the WG CCM on drill weekends and during annual training, I reported directly to the 154th WG Commander.

Going back to the unspoken separation between the two organizations, there were many times when serving two Commanders was a balancing act. There were occasions of conflict, but I tried hard to bridge the gap between the 201st CCG and the 154th WG.

For instance, on one occasion, newly promoted Brigadier General Pawling asked me to relay information to the 201st CCG Commander. In response to his message, the Group Commander got stern with me and stated, "If General Pawling wants me to know something, he can tell me himself." I believe he felt slighted by not receiving a phone call directly from a colleague and having to learn about information through me—an enlisted member.

Other times, such as during 201st CCG staff meetings, when I had information about something the Wing was doing that could have affected the group, I shared it. The information was not always met with gratitude. More often than not, it seemed that leadership was threatened by the fact that I had the information, and they did not. Still, I felt it was my duty to share the information for the good of both organizations. Ensuring that I was fair and represented both organizations was important to me.

As a 201st technician, simultaneously holding the WG CCM position, I knew I needed to keep the statuses and positions separate. There had to be clear lines to avoid any conflict or appearance of impropriety. When the WG commander held his staff meetings or other types of meetings, to avoid any conflict of interest, I would take leave from my technician position to attend the meetings. Fortunately, both headquarters were within the same compound. This provided the opportunity for me to stop in the WG CCM office on a regular basis, either before or after my federal technician work hours or during lunchtime. Although the WG CCM duties were supposed to occur only on drill weekends or during annual training, to be effective in this position and stay abreast of Wing matters required many additional hours.

I found it interesting that when I spoke to Airmen within the Wing, many didn't know anything about the 201st CCG, and they wondered who occupied that building across the street. Since the CCG didn't provide a great deal of support to the WG, there was no reason to cross the street to find out who or what was there. Overtime, through dialogue and education, our Wing Airmen came to understand the mission of the 201st CCG, which was to provide combat communications during times of state emergencies, full-time air traffic control services, and to support the federal mission when mobilized. I believe this understanding helped bring the two organizations closer together.

The State Command Chief had oversight of the 201st CCG enlisted corps and those in geographically separated units (GSU); however, when I spoke about enlisted matters, it was with *one voice* to all, including the CCG and those on neighboring islands. I believed strongly that if it was relevant to enlisted members in the Wing, it was *equally* as relevant to enlisted members in the 201st CCG and those in GSUs. Many enlisted matters that I worked on as the WG CCM also affected the enlisted members of the CCG, including the First Sergeant Council, the awards and decorations program, and the enlisted performance feedback program, as well as the handling of issues, dialogue, and compliance. It was, therefore, important to me as an SNCO and a technician at the 201st CCG to be as inclusive as I could be.

# CHAPTER 28

# 154th Wing
# Command Chief

As the WG CCM, my schedule was like any other Command Chief Master Sergeant's. I made myself available to all Airmen, stopped in different shops or sections to talk with enlisted personnel—sometimes planned and at other times unannounced. I was engaged with the First Sergeant Council, enlisted promotions, counseling, mentorship, reorganizing, igniting the TOP-3 Council comprised of SNCOs, seeing off or welcoming home deploying Guard members, making hospital visits, attending numerous meetings, dealing with suicides, accidents, and a myriad of other matters. There was never a shortage of things to do, but I enjoyed every minute. During my tenure, the Wing underwent OREs, a Health Services Inspection (HSI), and an ORI.

Being one of the Air Force's largest, most complex wings, we had three Total Force Integration (TFI) or Associate (Active and Guard) units. We were busy. With three flying missions,[9] the Wing was constantly launching or recovering aircraft. Ensuring partnerships with the active-duty Wing, Thirteenth Air Force, and Pacific Air Force was hugely important.

We carefully and methodically cultivated and worked on those relationships. On a regular basis, we built bridges and provided different types of Guard 101 briefings. This was extremely important, as there are differences between the Active, Guard, and Reserve components, which means there are some differences between the rules that apply to each of the three. Because we were methodical about the training and education so that the entire TFI had a better understanding of the nuances between the active duty and the ANG, the end result, from the top down, was that everyone had a deeper understanding, respect, and appreciation for the Guard, acknowledging that the Guard brings critical civilian and military skills to the mission.

Some of my first observations in my CCM position revealed the need to make significant improvements to some of the central programs. For example, it became apparent that the Wing had a First Sergeant Council with many vacancies. Additionally, there were noncompliant accountability standards for the Family Care Program, the awards and decorations program was in disarray, there was consistent noncompliance with the Enlisted Performance Feedback Program, and there was no vehicle for SNCOs to provide recommendations or bring up concerns that affected the enlisted corps. In some areas, personal and professional deportment standards needed to be addressed.

I set my priorities and started with the area that would have the most impact on the organization and specifically on the enlisted corps. It was important to show the Wing enlisted corps that I was there for them to work hard and to do whatever I could to help promote and improve the enlisted corps as a whole. As the WG CCM, one of my primary duties was that of the Functional Manager for the First Sergeant Council (FSC). My role with the FSC included providing leadership, direction, and guidance to the council, overseeing recruitment of new First Sergeants and accountability of First Sergeant programs, and ensuring that dress and appearance and professional relationship standards were enforced. The FSC was made up of all HIANG First Sergeants (154th WG and 201st CCG). As I recall, at the time I was selected as the WG CCM, only three or four First Sergeant Positions were filled. Most of the positions were vacant, and shortly after I assumed the position, two or three more First Sergeants chose to retire.

From my perspective, it would be a Herculean job to ensure that we recruited and trained the right individuals to fill the First Sergeant vacancies. We needed high-caliber and high-energy SNCOs to join the FSC. The positions needed to be filled with outstanding, dedicated Airmen with strong leadership skills who wanted to take care of other Airmen. My job was to ensure that we found such Airmen.

I was aware of a certain mindset within some of the leadership across the HIANG, and it needed to change. In past years, there were times when a Technical Sergeant would be assigned and promoted into the First Sergeant position for their last three years of service. It wasn't necessarily that they were the right person, most qualified, or had a burning desire to serve the enlisted corps; some of these NCOs were assigned as the First Sergeant merely as a means of promoting them before they retired. This was contrary to what needed to be done to build a strong FSC.

There was also resistance against the WG CCM having oversight and management of the First Sergeant selection process. In the past, commanders selected who they thought were best to serve in this position but hadn't necessarily complied with the AF Instruction governing the First Sergeant program.

As efforts began to recruit and build a stronger FSC, I discovered that our organization was extremely fortunate to have Master Sergeant Kelly J. Wilkinson, who herself was a relatively new First Sergeant and president of the FSC. Master Sergeant Wilkinson was a hard charger, someone who took on a lot of responsibility and did things right. Always the consummate professional, she believed in the mission and had passion to do the job. She was the type of person who wanted to make a difference for the enlisted corps, the organization, and the HIANG families. More importantly, she, too, had a vision to develop a highly effective and professional FSC that cared about their people, instilled accountability, maintained standards, and kept the bar held high.

Being new to the position and not having been a First Sergeant, I looked to Master Sergeant Wilkinson for her guidance and for the history of the HIANG FSC. As the FSC president, she assisted me in establishing a new team. In many ways, she initially mentored me when it came to the intricacies of First Sergeant matters, rules, and programs. I trusted her to tell me like it was and to correct me if I misspoke. We collaborated a great deal to identify how to create a new culture within the FSC. Without question, the journey to establishing a proactive and hard-charging FSC team would have been extremely challenging if not for the assistance of Master Sergeant Wilkinson, now a retired Chief Master Sergeant. She was and is today a trusted colleague, confidante, and, more importantly, my friend.

This was not the first time, nor would it be the last, that I received valuable counsel from someone junior. Early in my career, I learned that not all the "good ideas" came from someone at the top. Real leaders realize the value of input from throughout an organization.

Even if the input is not used, making an individual feel validated and an important part of the team is a critical part of building unit/organizational cohesiveness.

With the exception of Master Sergeant Wilkinson, it seemed that the former members of the council were not willing to rise to the level of standards and commitment we needed to make the FSC the leadership team it needed to become. For example, members of the Security Forces Squadron (SFS) are authorized to wear the Security Forces (SF) beret. The beret is earned through hard work and dedication to one's job, and those who wear the beret are extremely proud of it. As an air traffic controller, I understood the importance of this—as the wearing of an ATC badge is equally significant. If an SFS member volunteered and was chosen to become a First Sergeant, they had to take off the beret when they earned a First Sergeant diamond on their chevron and instead wear a regular AF uniform hat. It's one or the other, and as the new WG CCM, I had to adhere to and enforce the Air Force Instruction as written. This was not popular, but it had to be done, so the current SFS First Sergeant chose to retire instead of take off the SF beret. He was not willing to adhere to the AF Instruction, comply with the standards, and follow the rules. To me, he had three choices: remove the beret and wear a regular uniform hat, be reassigned to another position, or retire from the First Sergeant position. He chose the latter.

With the support of the Wing and Group Commanders, my office received funding to bring the Air National Guard First Sergeant Area Functional Manager to Hawaii to help strengthen our FSC, the programs the council managed, and assist with the recruiting process. Additionally, the Area Functional Manager would be able to help us make changes to improve the programs the FSC managed. At the time, Chief Master Sergeant W. Allen Usry was the ANG First Sergeant Area Functional Manager.

Upon his arrival, we immediately got to work. Transported in a HING C-12 plane, we flew to briefings on Oahu, Kauai, Maui, and the Big Island. It was a whirlwind weekend. Chief Usry, a former Marine, told great stories. He was inspirational and highly motivating. After his talks, even I wanted to become a First Sergeant! We definitely got our money's worth with the pace and schedule we had him on. At one point, Chief Usry asked if we had time for lunch, and my response was, "No!" We were on a tight schedule, our briefings had run late, and I did not see the need to make time for lunch. Fortunately, one of our Airmen provided the Chief with a plate lunch, local-style Hawaiian.

It was not long after Chief Usry's visit that we recruited the highest caliber of First Sergeant candidates. We were ready to fill all vacant positions. Once selected for a First Sergeant position within the unit, the recruits had to attend a three-week First Sergeant Academy, where they would learn about First Sergeant duties, roles, responsibilities, legal matters, how to establish their respective Family Care Programs, and undergo and pass physical fitness and academic testing. Although they had been selected, an Airman could not become a First Sergeant until they'd successfully completed the academy. As the functional manager, I tested them on their fitness prior to their departure. Although 75 was a passing score, I required a score in the mideighties. I wanted to ensure they had a buffer to accommodate for fatigue, temperature, and altitude changes.

Over a short period, we sent many future first sergeants off to the First Sergeant Academy for training, and upon their return, they set up their respective unit programs. To my satisfaction, our team was established and committed to the work ahead. There was a lot to do to be in compliance with the AF instruction that governed the First Sergeant Program.

As a result of our efforts, other HIANG Airmen began to look at being a First Sergeant differently. It was no longer looked at as a position to get promoted into, serve for two to three years, and then retire. We recruited young, bright, energetic Airmen who wanted to make a difference. Chief Usry kick-started the excitement about being a First Sergeant and the desire within the organization grew from there. Many one-on-one recruiting discussions and conversations with Commanders took place. The intent was to take one of their best and brightest, provide for a career-broadening experience, and then return or send that Airman back to their unit to better improve their organization.

As with all our Airmen, I was very proud of the FSC we established. I believe their strength and involvement inspired other councils and Airmen to be better and want to do more. There is absolutely no doubt that their hard work and dedication greatly benefitted the entire HIANG officer and enlisted corps and their families. To me, they will always represent what a motivated and professional First Sergeant *team* should look like. They were the very best!

I considered it a privilege to be a trusted agent within the Wing leadership and to be able to attend M5 meetings. This was a meeting held by the Wing Commander and included only the Group Commanders from the Mission Support, Operations, Maintenance, and Medical Groups. WG CCMs are considered the Wing Commander's right-hand person and are typically included in all group leadership meetings. We discussed many sensitive and confidential matters during these meetings as they pertained to Wing business. It was a safe environment where the Wing Commander, Group Commanders, and I were able to speak freely and openly about issues. After a short time, I felt the Commanders came to rely on, value, and trust my opinion and candor.

Throughout the process of building the FSC, having the support of the M5 team was critically important as personnel were reassigned to different squadrons. The M5 backed my plan to assign First Sergeant personnel to squadrons other than the one they came from. Not all Squadron Commanders embraced having a different First Sergeant assigned to their squadron, but leadership knew that restructuring the FSC made the organization stronger. There was also a significant financial cost to get the new members of the FSC trained, so the support of the M5 was essential to allocate the required funds for training days and dollars.

During a drill weekend, the M5 and I would visit units as a team. I developed a unit visitation schedule and coordinated with the respective organizations. It was important that the Airmen saw leadership united and visible. We each spoke a few minutes and then fielded questions from the Guard members. Brigadier General Pawling had a quick sense of humor, so it was always a bit entertaining as well. We fed off each other, and I believe we enjoyed the time visiting as much as the Airmen did.

It was important that the Airmen had access to Wing leadership and that they could look into our eyes when we said, "We are here for you, care about you and your families, and are working hard to make improvements within the Wing." This time also provided an opportunity to put eyes on our Airmen as well. Many times, one could see or pick up on subtleties through "eyes-on" leadership. We could visibly observe dress and appearance standards and professionalism, as well as proper military etiquette. For example, if someone didn't call the room to attention when Brigadier General Pawling entered and left the room, that told me there was a lack of understanding of proper protocol, which I would then take up with the Unit First Sergeant or senior leadership.

Additionally, it allowed us to take a pulse of how our Airmen were doing. All the computers, cell phones, and advances in technology can never replace eyes-on, one-on-one leadership. Reading body language, listening to vocal tones, and looking into someone's eyes can only be effectively done in person. Trust is built this way. It is the best leadership practice there is—period.

# CHAPTER 29

# Decorations Tell
# Your Story

National Guard members belong to a specific state during peacetime and do not rotate or move every few years like our active-duty counterparts. As such, and generally speaking, recognition in the form of decorations tends to be somewhat lacking in the National Guard. Some states and units do a phenomenal job recognizing their people while others...not so much.

Decorations and awards were not important to me throughout most of my career. Serving was not about getting an award or a military decoration or medal. I believe pride of service and of a job well done comes from within, and that was always the motivation for my actions. That said, it bothered me that some people, later in my career, unfairly judged me because of my lack of decorations.

At my WG CCM promotion ceremony, I met then Captain David Lowery (now a Lieutenant Colonel and PhD), an active-duty member from the Fifteenth Air Base Wing (ABW). The 154th WG commander, Colonel Pawling, had invited the Fifteenth ABW commander to attend. His aide, Captain Lowery, accompanied him. At the conclusion of the ceremony, Captain Lowery and I talked for a little while. At one point, he looked down at my ribbon rack and stated that he had never seen a Chief, let alone a Senior Master

Sergeant, promoted to Command Chief while only having an Air Force Achievement Medal with one device as their highest decoration.

It stung a bit to hear Captain Lowery's comment, but I was proud of my Air Force Achievement Medals. Having just met him, I did not elaborate on my past, and perhaps my silence created an opening for his assumptions. He'd been around the HIANG long enough to have a solid understanding of the culture and some of the inadequacies of our programs. Overall, HIANG Airmen were not being appropriately recognized for their dedicated service, achievements, and significant contributions to the federal and state mission. That is not to say that no one got recognized, but we were sorely lacking in that area, and leadership knew it.

Having an active-duty Captain question my lack of decorations was eye-opening, but when it happened again with a colleague, it really grabbed my attention. I was at a Command Chief conference when a fellow active-duty Command Chief Master Sergeant walked up to me and asked, "How did you screw up and still manage to become a Command Chief?"

I was taken aback and didn't understand what he meant until he pointed to my ribbon rack. I assured him I was not a screwup but that I had belonged to an organization that did not recognize their people. I also explained that as a new CCM, I was committed to changing that culture. That was the first time I ever felt embarrassed because of my lack of ribbons.

A few months later at another conference, I was questioned again about my lack of decorations. This time, it was by an ANG Command Chief. Being a Guardsman, he understood the culture in some organizations and states. We had a lengthy discussion about the situation, and once again, I was left feeling less than equal to my counterparts and colleagues—and a bit embarrassed. Overall, most Guard CCMs, and certainly all active-duty CCMs, had an appropriate level of decorations for their rank, contributions, and time in service. I later found out from that same ANG Chief that he took it upon himself to address my 201st CCG Commander at that conference and attempted to shame him about failing to recognize his people. That was not something I had wanted to have happen, but I chose not to say anything further about it to my Commander. I was not going to address decorations with my leadership, believing that if they deemed me worthy of a decoration, they would write and submit a package.

It wasn't until those two situations occurred that I began to take note of others' ribbons and decorations and became very self-conscious about my ribbon rack. It was glaring to me that the active-duty Chiefs had significantly more and higher level decorations than many of their Air National Guard counterparts, but I understood why or how this was the norm. Active-duty members typically move every three or so years. Upon departure from one base to another, their service, performance, and contributions most often warrant an award. National Guard and Reserves don't move like the active services, and consequently, their service, performance, and contributions are routinely overlooked or taken for granted.

As I continued my observations, I saw there was even a noticeable difference in awards between Air Force Reserve and Air National Guard Chiefs. This was not something I was envious of, but the Chief was right: decorations do tell your story. A lack of decorations can tell yet another story, which may not be accurate. Some may believe a lack of decorations means poor performance, mediocrity, or a troubled past, but it can also just mean unfortunate lack of recognition.

I had grown up in a HIANG culture, where there was no expectation of receiving awards or decorations, so this was the norm for me. Thinking back, I'd accepted a lack of recognition as the way things were because this had been the way it was growing up. In my family, you did what you were supposed to do, and there was little fanfare or acknowledgment for doing it. I'd left the 297th ATCS as a Senior Master Sergeant, having been the Superintendent, Squadron, and Group NCO of the Year; Squadron, 201st CCG, and HIANG Air Traffic Controller of the Year; and later, the HIANG SNCO of the Year, recognized by the Inspector General during the 241st ATCS ORE, and privately, during our "Excellent" ORE, I received two Air Force Achievement Medals for my active-duty service and Air National Guard Readiness Center support. I knew what I had done to earn my Air Force Achievement Medals and was very proud of them. During the twelve years in the 297th ATCS, I did receive longevity devices and a state ribbon for deploying to Hurricane Iniki in 1992 on the island of Kauai. Whether or not I earned or deserved other decorations was not for me to say. It was up to my supervisors to make that determination, and that simply was not the culture of the 297th.

It was my good fortune that Captain Lowery volunteered to look at our decorations procedures and collaborate with me to fix our awards program. Although I didn't fully know what the problem was with the program, I jumped at the opportunity to partner with him. It was a very gracious offer, and I anticipated we had much work to do to make the HIANG Awards and Decorations Program work and do right for our Airmen.

Overall, we were not doing what I thought was a good job in recognizing our people, but the question was why. I quickly came to learn that some deserving Airmen had not been recognized for many years, decades even—and some had never been acknowledged. It was not unusual to discover a Master Sergeant with fourteen, sixteen, or more years who had never received an Air Force Achievement Medal. Packages were submitted but not properly tracked, and many were lost in the process.

Quite frankly, Airmen referred to the awards and decorations program as a "black hole": things went in but never came out. Since the packages seemed to go into an abyss and disappear, the attitude became "Why bother writing one?" This was the number one topic of feedback I received from Airmen as I went from unit to unit, attended meetings, and asked questions: fix the awards program! The bigger picture was even more important. Often, we were quick to react to poor performance, but not to excellence. Recognition had a direct impact on individuals as well as on organizational morale.

We recruited a group of subject-matter experts and established an awards and decorations action team. Over the course of several months, the HIANG Awards and Decoration Instruction was rewritten, tested, retested, and approved. We streamlined and simplified the process and delegated the approval authority at an appropriate level. Committed Airmen dedicated time to ensure the program's success.

The next hurdle was to convince officers and enlisted members to reconstruct and resubmit packages retroactively for the many years of service and performance that had gone unrecognized. This took a great deal of convincing, and there was enormous skepticism. After nearly a year of hard work, our Airmen began to be recognized for the exceptional work they had previously done and were currently doing. It was not long after getting this program up and running that the US Air Force changed the entire Awards Program for all components (Active, Guard, and Reserve), which made it even simpler to submit an awards package.

I found it humbling that after twenty-one years of service, it was an active-duty captain who took the time to write an awards package for my Air Force Commendation Medal. I had now been a command chief for nineteen months. Shortly after receiving the Air Force Commendation Medal, I received my first Meritorious Service Medal for my time at the 297th ATCS. My former Commander had followed through with writing the package as he said he would. Standing in front of Airmen and being pinned with my Meritorious Service Medal was a bittersweet pill to swallow—my former Commander was not present. Still, knowing that from this point on our Airmen would be appropriately recognized for their outstanding performance made it all worthwhile.

Above all else, it became essential to me that senior leadership take care of their people throughout their careers. To do that, supervisors needed to routinely review their records and consider appropriate level and deserving and meaningful awards and decorations. Service members and civilian employees—in all components and at all levels of government—sacrifice, deploy, volunteer, and do extraordinary things every day. Being recognized for excellence and a job well done matters. I came to understand that what we wear on our uniform or display in our offices tells a story of service, sacrifice, and personal and unit accomplishments. People may say it's not important to them, but we need to do it anyway. Later on in their career, it will matter. We don't ever want officers or enlisted leaders to make judgments about our people because as leaders we didn't do our part. Appropriate and deserving recognition is important for everyone!

# CHAPTER 30

# We Need a Road Map

Working for the betterment of the enlisted corps was not always met with unbridled enthusiasm when it meant additional work or the "C" word: change! Believing that thoughtful and directed change is good, another important enlisted matter that needed attention during my time as WG CCM was the ANG Enlisted Performance Feedback Program.

In 2004, the ANG–directed Enlisted Performance Feedback Program was pretty much nonexistent in our organization. Unlike today, with the implementation of the mandatory Enlisted Performance Report, at that time, the Air National Guard did not require every enlisted Airman to receive any kind of annual performance feedback. Some supervisors and sections provided drill status guardsmen with annual feedback, but there was no consistency across the HIANG. The Active, Guard, Reserve, and full-time federal technicians received an annual performance report, or technician appraisal report, but DSG Airmen did not, nor was it required.

Through the efforts of the ANG Command Chief's Office, the Air National Guard Readiness Center implemented a simple yet important program, where all enlisted members were required to give and receive annual performance feedback. This was a huge culture change and was met with much resistance. The leadership heard all the reasons why it would be too hard to implement. The fact is, we owed this to our Airmen. How can Airmen improve if they don't know their shortfalls? How do they know what they may be doing wrong or right or even how they fit into the organization? How do supervisors help their Airmen reach and achieve their goals if they don't know what they are? Feedback was critically important and necessary as part of that process. As the WG CCM, this program fell under my purview, and it was critically important that we got it right and took immediate action.

I explained the program to the Wing and Group Commanders and laid out a plan for the Wing to be in compliance. I held First Sergeants accountable for their respective units. To track compliance, we developed a simple Excel spreadsheet for each unit and one for the overall HIANG. The sheet had the name of the unit, Commander's name, First Sergeant's name, and percentage of enlisted feedback completed. The organization was broken down into groups. The First Sergeants were required to report the percentage complete to me by the Friday after the Unit Training Assembly (UTA). I then briefed that information at the weekly Wing supervisor meeting. The slide went up on the screen so the Wing Commander and every Commander/supervisor could see where their respective unit stood. By highlighting the numbers, the Wing leadership placed extra emphasis on the importance of completing the feedback sessions.

The Air National Guard leadership across the nation saw and understood the need for change, which was why the program was implemented from the highest level of ANG leadership. The impetus was the ANG Enlisted Field Advisory Council, an all-enlisted council that represented the enlisted corps from across all states, territories, and the District of Columbia.

Initially, it was difficult to get some supervisors on board with the program. While most understood the importance of giving and receiving feedback, there was pushback on the extra time to prepare the paperwork and conduct the feedback sessions between supervisors and subordinates. We discussed how to set up the Enlisted Performance Feedback Program to alleviate the workload on one individual or section supervisor. In theory, no one individual should write the performance appraisals for an entire section. By setting up a system where each level of supervision was responsible for the appraisals for their direct reports, we taught others to lead and provide feedback, and they, in turn, learned how to write and be a more effective supervisor. While this system was optimal, supervisors had some flexibility in accomplishing the performance feedback for their people. For instance, some units conducted the feedback during one particular UTA, and others did it by birth month, service anniversary month, or alphabetically.

With the support from Wing leadership, Commanders, and strong SNCOs, our enlisted Airmen began receiving important feedback, supervisors were talking with their subordinates, and our enlisted corps was getting stronger. You can't know how you're doing if no one ever tells you, you can't make course corrections if you don't know you're off-course, and you can't do a good job unless you know what a good job is. The feedback session also provided an opportunity to ask about professional military education, civilian education, and family and work-life balance. Additionally, it offered an opportunity to ask if our Airmen were having any hardships in their life or with their relationships. And as a natural progression, it was also the perfect time to review their awards and decorations.

# CHAPTER 31

# Higher Education

As the WG CCM, I made the rounds to different units and sections and spoke with our Airmen about a wide array of subjects. One of those topics included the Community College of the Air Force (CCAF) two-year associate degree. This was a very humbling topic for me to broach. Here I was, the WG CCM talking to our Airmen about the importance of acquiring their CCAF degree, and I had not yet completed mine. Initially, I felt like a hypocrite as I spoke to the WG-enlisted corps about education. As a Chief, it was hard to stand before junior enlisted and have that conversation.

It actually helped to use myself as an example and talk about the fear of failure and the possibility of not doing well enough to get my degree. By standing in front of Airmen and admitting that I had not completed my CCAF, I was able to speak with authenticity about the importance of higher education. Ultimately, though, I decided that I needed to walk my talk. I owned up to my lack of education, took the bullet, and resolved to get it done. It was time to fix this!

The HIANG Base Education Office had a huge responsibility coordinating all the Basic Military Training (BMT), technical schools, Professional Military Education, and special school training, as well as helping our Airmen with tuition assistance matters and the completion of the CCAF degree. To get started in the right direction initiating my CCAF program, the HIANG Base Education Office was my first stop. I swallowed my pride and met with our education personnel. They provided me with my military records that showed the credits I had earned through my training and PME courses.

Due to my early educational foundation, which had not been strong, attending college scared me. I was truly afraid I wouldn't pass, which would embarrass me even more than not having pursued a degree. That old "fear of failure" reared its ugly head again. After I had made the decision that it was time to start, I knew the next step was to visit the Base Education Center on Hickam AFB. I was anxious as I sat in the waiting area because I didn't want anyone to see me there.

One of the education advisors sat at her desk in the middle of the waiting room. The rest of the advisors had private offices. I kept praying and reciting, *Please don't let me get that lady in the center of the room.* I didn't want to be out front and be embarrassed by the questions I needed to ask. Of course, in walked several Active and Guard Airmen whom I knew.

"Hi, Chief!" they said enthusiastically.

"Hello!" I responded warmly, giving them a big smile.

*Please don't let me get that lady in the center of the room.*

Naturally, I got the advisor in the center of the waiting room. She assumed by my rank that I knew all about education, the process of enrollment, and so on. I told her to treat me like a young Airman who had never taken a class and to walk me through the entire process. We had a language barrier since she was well versed in all aspects of higher education, including college lingo, and I was not. Embarrassed, I managed to navigate through the unfamiliar waters of higher education. I chose Wayland Baptist University as my college. I wanted to take the easiest class first since I was anxious about taking any college classes, so I asked her for a recommendation.

Ethics it was—followed by American History I 8c II and then Speech. I thoroughly enjoyed the history classes and learned a lot. Speech was my all-time favorite course—and one of the best classes I have ever taken. I learned many techniques about public speaking that helped me a great deal in subsequent positions within the National Guard. As a side note, when I saw the name of my speech professor, I said to myself, "There can only be one person with that name." It happened to be my dear friend Mr. Modesto Cordero.

When I walked into his classroom the first night, I walked up to him privately and said, "I don't know you, and you don't know me. Please treat me as if we don't know each other or have any personal friendship." I needed him to understand that I was there as a student, and I expected him to treat me as such, grading me on my performance just like all the other students. Although I'm certain he never would have treated me differently, I wanted to assure him that I expected nothing less than his honest feedback. I'm proud to say that no student in that speech class knew of our friendship. At the end of the class, I paid him the highest of compliments because he was a phenomenal professor, and I learned a great deal from him.

I purposely left intermediate algebra for last and was especially nervous about taking a math class, let alone an algebra class. In my heart, I knew I should have never passed high school algebra. In high school, although I tried hard, asked questions, went up to the board, and asked my teacher for additional help, it never sank in. I think Mr. Bauman, my high school teacher, felt sorry for me and passed me with a C for effort since I never quit trying.

Here it was, nearly thirty years later, and I had to take an intermediate algebra class. The fear of failure weighed heavy on my shoulders; I was so afraid I wouldn't pass. The counsel from the education advisor was to take a refresher math class first. However, that did not fit within my goals or time line to finish before my deployment to Central Command. I decided to jump right in, as I was not going to let a math class keep me from attaining my CCAF degree. I could not expect my Airmen to do something that I was not willing to do. I needed to finish this!

The only way I could successfully complete the algebra class would be with my family's support. I sat Gary and Ashley down in the kitchen one night and told them about the class and my concerns.

"I won't be able to cook, clean, do laundry, shop for groceries, or do yard work for ten weeks," I explained. "I've really got to buckle down and focus on this without distractions. Can you guys handle all the house responsibilities for that long?"

They looked at my serious face, then at each other. I was relieved when they started laughing.

"What's new?" Ashley asked, grinning.

"Of course, we will," Gary said, putting his arm around me. "We've got this. Go get your degree!"

Prior to the start of class, I hired an active-duty Senior Airman. He agreed to be my tutor—I don't believe he knew what he was getting himself into!

As I walked into the classroom, I had a huge surprise. My professor was my daughter's high school science teacher. *This is not going to be good*, I thought. It was humbling at best. All I remembered about high school algebra was that there were $x$'s, $y$'s, parentheses, and something to the second power. The professor tried to put our anxieties to rest by explaining that there were extra-credit opportunities. We received extra credit for going to the blackboard, participating in class discussions, and doing extra homework. You can bet that even if I didn't know the answer, I went to the board anyway—I was not going to miss any opportunities to receive extra points. I didn't always have the right answer—and quite honestly, I usually didn't—but, by golly, I was going to get the extra credit!

I saw my classmates using a scientific calculator to calculate their problems. I had no idea how to use a scientific calculator—I did every problem in longhand. With the exception of class night, every weeknight and for several hours on the weekends for ten weeks, my tutor and I spent our time together in the Hickam AFB library. We were regulars, and at one point, the library assistant put a reserved sign on our table for us. I used to joke that I had rented that table space in the library. More times than not, we closed the library at 9:00 p.m., as we were the last ones to leave. Many nights, we walked over to the Hickam AFB gymnasium because it stayed open longer and we could get in at least another hour of studying.

I dreaded class night with every fiber of my being. It was humiliating and frustrating *to the tenth power*. Practically every night after class, I cried and beat myself up all the way home out of sheer frustration. I was so angry at myself and discouraged. Why couldn't I understand the algebra problems? I just didn't get it! Tests were an absolute nightmare, and I was always the last one to turn in her paper and leave.

At the end of the course, with every possible extra-credit point, I got an 89.4. Talk about a celebration! That tutor cost me more than the class, but without his assistance, I would not have passed intermediate algebra. I will be forever grateful for my tutor's time, patience, and stick-to-it-iveness.

Finally, I was able to stand in front of the Wing Airmen and talk about the importance of the CCAF degree, having now completed mine. I shared my experience and frustration with whomever would listen and hoped it served to inspire others to enroll and just begin, one class at a time. Part of my message was to never let the fear of failure stop them from achieving their goals. The only failure is to stop trying!

There were times while I was going to school when Airmen would say to me, "If you have time as the WG CCM to take a class, I, too, can make the time to take a class." I often told the Airmen, "We will walk this journey together and get it done." In leading by example, others followed.

Many years later, I interviewed a chief who'd missed out on a great opportunity because he had one class left to earn his CCAF. Which one? Math, of course! I encouraged him to enroll and just get it done so that he would not miss out on future opportunities. Moreover, I knew it would be good for his Airmen to see him completing his degree. I have spoken with a multitude of service members over the years about the importance of education. It's a "must do"—a significant tipping point in anyone's career.

# CHAPTER 32

# The Air Force
# Fitness Program

During my nearly twenty-nine years of service, the annual Air Force Fitness Program (AFFP) went through a lot of changes. When a program is changed significantly, people need to be made aware of those changes. They need to be briefed, and sometimes briefed again, to ensure that the changes are understood. When an organization of about 2,500 Airmen all need to get on board with a change, it takes time to "turn that ship." Some get it and are on board immediately while others understand they need to adhere and make the change slowly. Others will drag their feet, hoping the change doesn't catch up with them, or they resist or buck the system. Clearly, when significantly modifying a program, the entire culture of the organization needs to change with it.

When a large organization only meets once a month, however, it takes extra time to integrate changes and affect the culture.

Leadership at all levels must embrace and *lead* change for others to follow. That was evident when the updated Fitness Program (FP) was introduced as a result of recent studies, which showed that the current AF fitness test was not a true measure of our Airmen's overall health and fitness. Significant changes had been made to the annual test. The new fitness test assessment, which was more challenging than the previous assessment, consisted of four categories:

cardio (run), abdominal circumference, push-ups, and sit-ups. Each category by age was assigned points, and all had minimum standards to meet. Airmen had to pass all categories to pass the annual fitness assessment.

As safety and the health of the force were paramount, the Wing Commander, Group commanders, and I had many conversations about the implementation of the FP. Several Airmen in previous years had died during their annual fitness test. Being safety-first-focused and wanting to help our Airmen be successful, the Wing commander generated a policy letter, providing the organization with one year to prepare and ease into the new standards.

Initially, Wing leadership heard grumbling about the changes to the FP, but the bottom line was that this was the new standard, and we all needed to get on board. Leadership at all levels made the FP a high priority and continuous talking point on drill weekends. Commanders, Chiefs, and First Sergeants engaged with their people to explain the updated FP, standards, accountability, and how the Wing was going to implement the program. Some Airmen and sections began training together while other fitness gurus volunteered to help train those who were struggling. This took a lot of leadership and dialogue with our Airmen and an understanding that we are *one* Air Force with three components that must all adhere to the same standards. With the collaboration of the Commanders, Senior NCOs, First Sergeants, the safety office, and the medical community, we got there.

After the Wing Commander gave our Airmen a year to get in shape, practice, and prepare, they were tested. They either passed or failed. If they failed, they met with Medical Group personnel and were placed in a remedial program for improvement. For those Airmen who got a score of "Excellent," we implemented a recognition program to highlight their achievement. It was designed to inspire others to also achieve Excellent scores.

Subsequent to the changes to the FP came the introduction of physical fitness uniforms. This was new to the entire force, as the AF did not previously have physical fitness uniforms. Later, and to help our Airmen meet the standard with the appropriate wear of the physical fitness uniform, we made posters showing two Airmen wearing the fitness uniform properly. We believed it was important that we lead this initiative from the front by demonstrating the proper wear of the uniform. The posters were positioned in high-traffic areas, including the Medical and Mission Support Group and in the dining facility. It was interesting to observe Airmen in those areas begin to correct one another on the proper wear of the uniform. In the end, the posters served their purpose, and our Airmen excelled in improving their overall level of fitness.

I could not ask my Airmen to do their best if I did not do the same. This was not easy, as I had to work daily on push-ups and other exercises to develop my upper-body strength. Often, this meant doing push-ups in front of the TV at night. Running was also something that didn't come easily for me, so I created a mantra that I recited to psych myself up: "Running is my life. I love to run. Running is my life. I love to run…" It was important for me to always score in the "Excellent" category.

# CHAPTER 33

# Threats of Rape

Serving as the WG CCM was the most rewarding position I'd held in my career; I loved what I did and felt like the Wing leadership team was making a difference. I had the opportunity to work with the senior leadership of the 154th WG and develop partnerships with PACAF and with Fifteenth ABW leadership. Above all, I had the opportunity to work with others to implement programs and effect policies and procedures to strengthen our enlisted corps and the overall Wing. The Wing leadership was making positive changes, our missions were solid, and our Airmen were doing great things at the state and federal levels.

One day out of the blue, I received a phone call on my official cellular Blackberry. When answering my official phone, I typically said, "Good morning/afternoon. Chief Jelinski-Hall." The male voice on the other end was downright frightening and intentionally distorted so I wouldn't be able to recognize it. The man sounded gruff, used vulgar language, and talked about raping me. It was clear I was being threatened. I was so caught off guard that I actually listened for a few seconds. I kept silent, then hung up.

The call shook me up, but I rationalized that it must have been a mistake—a random caller with no particular number in mind. Although I tried to shake it off as not really a serious concern, throughout that day, I continued to feel unsettled because of the man's words. I couldn't stop thinking about the call.

Initially, I didn't tell anyone about the incident. Then a few days later, it happened again. It was the same voice and the same vulgar language on the other end of the phone. This time, I hung up more quickly. I sat back and thought, *This guy has my phone number, and again, he's talking about raping me.* After calling my number twice, I assumed he knew my name. The hair stood up on the back of my neck, and it scared me deep down to my core. I didn't know what to do, but I continued to keep it to myself. I was more careful and became more aware of my surroundings, including where I parked, but refused to let this caller alter who I was or what I did.

I received the third call while I was at home with Ashley, by now a teenager. The man never wasted time in starting his rant. This time was no different. He began with filthy language and described how he wanted to rape me. This was the first time I spoke to the man. I was strong and firm and told him to never call this number again. I then hung up the phone.

"Who was that?" Ashley asked, looking up from her homework.

"Just a telemarketer," I answered dismissively, trying to keep my voice light. "I'm so tired of them calling my business phone!"

Ashley bought my response and resumed her homework.

I went to the bathroom and bawled. Now I was deeply scared. It finally hit me that this was serious. This was *not* a random caller, and this person was clearly targeting me. Who was this man, and why was he doing this to me? Had I made some type of correction he didn't like? I always prided myself in making corrections on a professional level, so I quickly dismissed that thought. Was this someone who knew me from the fitness center or from evening college classes? I could not put my finger on any reason or anything I had done or said to warrant such behavior.

My WG CCM phone number was public, so I realized it could have been anyone, even someone within the organization. I dismissed that thought immediately because I could not comprehend an Airman doing something this awful. Perhaps this third call struck me even harder because my daughter was sitting by me. *If this guy has my number, does he also know who our daughter is? Or where she goes to school or the sports she participates in?* Thinking about the gravity of these possibilities, I knew I couldn't stay silent anymore. I needed to protect our daughter.

I finally told Gary what was happening, and needless to say, he was as angry as I had ever seen him. Actually, he was beyond furious and wanted to hurt the guy. Each time the man had called, I tried *69 to get a number, but it never worked. We decided not to tell Ashley what was happening because we didn't want to frighten her. However, we did keep track of her comings and goings and placed extra controls on her whereabouts, instructing her to call us when she left or arrived at a location.

I believed it was finally time to inform my leadership as well. I sent an e-mail to the WG and my full-time Group commanders that detailed what had been happening. It was factual and to the point. Although shaken inside, I refused to let anyone see that side of me. I would not let this man get the better of me. Looking back now, he *did* get to me—I just didn't allow myself to acknowledge or show it. True to form, I buried my emotions and put on a good front. Gary was extra protective and tried hard to convince me to call and check in with him more often, but I balked at that and continued to put on a hardened exterior and pressed forward.

The fourth call came as a voice mail. This man wanted to rape me, or at least that's what he threatened, and I believed him. That day, I instructed Ashley to drive straight home from school. I made it sound like I just wanted to come home early and spend time with her, which was true, but I also needed to know she was safe. I went home, and when Gary arrived, I had him listen to the recording. He was livid, yet helpless. I saved the recording and the next morning went to the Office of Special Investigations (OSI) on Hickam AFB. The OSI agent listened, but there was nothing they could do. He suggested I have our Communications Flight make a recording of the message in the event the situation escalated. This was not a comforting conversation. Escalate? I had not allowed myself to think about this situation escalating or to what level.

I did as suggested and went to the Communications Flight. A female SNCO took my device and listened to the recording to ensure quality and that the entire message was captured. I felt dirty and humiliated that I had to subject her to what was happening and have her listen to the vulgar recording. I was her Command Chief and felt like I was supposed to protect her from this type of disgusting behavior and from someone who was obviously a sick, disturbed person. I suspected that after she did her job and listened to the entire message, she'd be affected as well—you simply can't erase something like that from your memory.

The message and file recording were sent to the Wing Commander and my full-time 201st Commander. Brigadier General Pawling called me a short time after he received my message, disgusted by what he had heard. We talked about what more could be done, but we both knew there was nothing, unless something else happened.

Time passed, and fortunately, that was the end of the phone calls. Just as they'd suddenly begun, they just as quickly ceased. Why they ever started and why they abruptly stopped, I'll never know. I was just relieved and grateful it all ended and that I could occasionally glance over my shoulder rather than constantly watch my back. It took some time for me to put all the emotion in another little box and place it on a shelf in the deep recesses of my memory. I had become very good at doing that.

I never wanted to show weakness or fear to anyone, especially in the male-dominant environment in which I worked. I never wanted to be viewed as a weak or emotional woman even though I knew intellectually that it would have been normal for anyone going through something like this to have deep feelings and strong reactions. In reality, though, I wasn't prepared to think of "what could have happened" if things had escalated. The seriousness of the potential personal threat didn't really hit until I put my daughter's face on it—that's when the gravity of the situation really freaked me out. But no one ever knew. I just continued to stuff it down and kept my eyes on her whereabouts. Life had to go on.

# CHAPTER 34

# The Gaylor
# Groupie T-Shirt

One of the high points of my Wing Command Chief Master Sergeant tenure was hosting the HIANG SNCO Conference. We held the conference off-site so as to keep SNCOs from getting called to their office or stopping at their office during lunch and not returning. I wanted to do something really special and unique—something that would energize the SNCO corps.

I had heard retired Chief Master Sergeant of the Air Force (CMSAF) no. 5, Robert Gaylor, speak at an event and decided to invite him to our conference. He had a strong leadership message, was engaging, and really energized the crowd. I contacted him, and he agreed to be our keynote speaker for the HIANG SNCO conference. The invitation to attend the conference was also extended to the Fifteenth ABW, Guam, and Alaska ANG Command Chiefs.

When I invited Chief Gaylor to be our guest, I had no idea what that would entail. *Take care of his airfare, billeting, monetary donation, and provide whatever he requests*, I thought. One day, while in my office reading e-mail, I opened a message from the PACAF CCM. Command Chief Anthony "Tony" Bishop had sent me an attachment for hosting a former CMSAF. When I opened and read the attachment, I thought, *Oh my goodness…what have I gotten myself into?* It was a pages-long, very detailed checklist, including items such as pickup time, name of driver, name of escort, drop-off location and time, who will meet Chief Gaylor at the curb, questions to be discussed during the ride/transition, prep-cards for the Chief on the individuals meeting him, etc.

Each day and each movement from the start of the trip to the end of it required this level of detailed information. While not difficult, gathering the necessary information consumed a great deal of time. As with any event, there were also last-minute changes. I felt responsible to take on this task as I was the one who invited the Chief to our conference. In the end, having Chief Gaylor attend was hugely successful—he was well received by all.

As our guest speaker, Chief Gaylor told funny stories that drove home leadership messages that were both educational and entertaining. A natural storyteller, Chief Gaylor had a unique way of telling a story. Two of the stories people really enjoyed were "Hot Fries" and "High Tech versus High Touch." In "Hot Fries," Chief Gaylor told about witnessing an eleven-year-old boy grab a freshly prepared delivery and take off running down the street at full speed. When he returned breathless, Chief Gaylor asked him why he'd run so fast. The boy replied, "People want hot fries." Not only was this boy meeting the customer's needs, but he was also seeing their needs through the customer's eyes and delivering even more than they expected. That was just the way he did his job. At such a young age, this boy understood what people desire—a sense of caring from those who provide services. By telling this story, Chief Gaylor communicated to the SNCOs, without sermonizing, the importance of overdelivering and consistently doing their very best.

Chief Gaylor's stories were pure entertainment, bringing belly laughter and tears to people's eyes; however, what delivered the greatest impact were the leadership messages woven into each story, driving home the message that to be most effective, three things must come together: opportunity, aptitude, and attitude. When those three things collide, individuals will be successful.

One of my most favorite Chief Gaylor stories is "The Groupie T-Shirt," the history of which he e-mailed me:

> I spoke at a banquet at Tinker AFB in 2001. During the intermission before I spoke, a Master

Sergeant said to me, "I've heard you speak four times." Being a joker, I told him to keep track because after five times, he would be awarded a Gaylor Groupie T-shirt (a takeoff on the Grateful Dead). He laughed. So I opened my talk that night by repeating the offer. "After hearing me speak five times, you get a T-shirt," I announced. Of course, I had no T-shirts—I was simply seeking a laugh. I continued opening banquet talks by relating that same story. Little did I know that I was creating somewhat of a monster.

After about a year, people began saying to me, "Where's my T-shirt?" or "When do I get my T-shirt?" Turns out that people were keeping track of the number of times they had heard me speak. My wife, Selma, said, "You had better do one of two things. Either quit saying that or get some shirts." I spoke with my friend, retired Chief Norm Hoffman, who sold caps and shirts, and he advised me that forty-eight shirts would cost $221. I thought the price was worth the fun I would get by giving away the shirts. At first, I was a bit too generous and gave out T-shirts to escorts, drivers, etc. But when I realized the reaction to them, I tightened up the criteria. If I gave one to everyone who's heard me speak more than five times, I would be giving out thousands.

One guy asked me how he could get a T-shirt. In my usual joking manner, I told him, "I have to like you." That was sort of mean-spirited, but it seems that it's become the main criteria—that, and making a high-touch connection.

My favorite Groupie T-shirt story happened after giving a shirt to a chief's wife some years ago. He told me recently that one evening he began to feel that tonight might be the night for a little exciting action in the bedroom. He said after considerable grooming, he entered the bedroom where his wife was wearing the Gaylor Groupie T-shirt. He continued, "You have no idea how quickly I became deflated looking at your picture on the shirt."

I've gotten a lot of mileage out of the shirts. One interesting aside…just about everyone I've ever given a shirt to has been promoted, moved to a higher position, or succeeded in some manner. I feel that I am a great judge of people who demonstrate potential and integrity. Right now, on my list of Groupies, and I know everyone, there are over 135 individuals who have been given the shirt. I'm very pleased and proud that you are no. 99.

To this day, I cherish my groupie no. 99 T-shirt, given to me directly by the CMSAF no. 5, Robert Gaylor, at the end of the HIANG SNCO conference.

# CHAPTER 35

# Closing the Wing Chapter

My time with the Airmen of the 154th WG was more than I could have ever asked for. Having the opportunity to work with Wing leadership and for the enlisted corps was up to this moment the high point of my entire career. The Wing leadership team, including the Group and squadron commanders and SNCOs, operated like a well-oiled machine. We trusted one another. I believe that, if needed, there was nothing we wouldn't have done for one another. I held a deep regard and profound respect for the officers and enlisted members of the 154th Wing and for what they did daily in support of the state and federal missions. When there was a disaster, our Airmen didn't wait for the governor to activate them—they just showed up at their respective units ready to help. Moments like that showed me the metal of our Airmen—what they were made of, where their loyalties lay, and the respect they had for the citizens of our state and of their fellow Airmen. I was proud to serve alongside such amazing men and women.

I also had an incredible and supportive boss whom I could talk with about anything. It was a professional relationship I deeply appreciated and still greatly value today. Brigadier General Pawling believed in me and had confidence in my abilities. He gave me, an outsider, the opportunity to serve at a higher level when most leaders would not have selected me. I felt like the work we did as a command team truly mattered and that it had a significant and meaningful impact on the organization, our Airmen, and their families. As Brigadier General Pawling once said to me, "It was comfortable being part of the leadership team and a phenomenal organization in which to serve."

Having embraced the responsibility for the entire Wing enlisted corps, I had developed strong professional and personal relationships and had gotten to know the Airmen at all levels. The Chiefs, Top-3, and First Sergeant Councils were rock solid and doing good things in and outside the HIANG and for our Airmen. I often thought to myself, *It doesn't get any better than this. I cannot imagine the day when my time at the Wing will be over.*

We practiced "eyes-on leadership," and it made a difference for our Air Force, the state of Hawaii, and the HIANG. We did this by leaning forward, holding people accountable to standards, and being visibly present and available for our Airmen. The 154th Wing is one of the largest and most complex Wings in the entire USAF. The total-force (Active, Guard, and Reserve) units are a reflection of leadership, teamwork, a shared purpose, and an understanding of each respective culture. It has been said that the newest state-of-the-art equipment does not make an organization—the people do. The men and women in the HIANG exhibited the *aloha* spirit in everything they did. I am grateful to have served alongside the finest Airmen in the nation. Silver lining? You bet it was!

The silver lining I'd believed in when I was passed over for the State CCM position in time became apparent. It became clear to me that I'd not been meant to get the State CCM job. The WG CCM job turned out to be the best thing that could have ever happened for my career and for me personally. Serving at the Wing level provided a much better understanding of the overall Wing, its structure, and the people. Working enlisted issues was a blessing—the single most important thing about this job was getting to know the Wing Airmen from the top down and bottom up.

As a member of the 201st CCG, I had not had many opportunities to interact with a great deal of Airmen from the Wing. It didn't take long before I established a solid professional rapport with key leadership, officers, and enlisted members. Serving at the Wing level provided a much stronger foundation for what was yet to come.

That day came sooner than expected, and after three years, the State CCM position came open. While my heart was at the Wing, I knew there was also an expectation to submit a package and, if selected, move to the next level of leadership. It would be a bitter-sweet pill to swallow. I considered the Airmen of the Wing to be my Airmen, and much like a mother, I wondered how I could leave—this was my *ohana*, my family. While I wouldn't be leaving the state or the HIANG, it would be difficult to leave behind all that we had started and accomplished together. If I did move into the state position, I knew I would be eternally grateful for my time at the 154th Wing and would always carry a piece of that time in my heart.

# CHAPTER 36

# Hawaii Air National Guard

In the late fall of 2006, the HIANG State Command Chief position came open. This position was senior to the WG CCM position I currently held. Generally speaking, in the ANG, it is a natural progression to go from the Wing Command Chief level to the State level, but there is certainly no guarantee.

In any state, the selection of a State Command Chief is a competitive process. Although I knew the CCM job quite well, I was diligent and focused in my preparation. Going into my usual interview preparation process, and true to form, I overprepared by rehearsing my opening and closing remarks, as well as formulating answers to the potential questions I anticipated. I stood in front of the mirror and practiced eye contact and hand gestures and synchronized my physical movements to emphasize key points. I envisioned the entire room setup, including the panel table and my entrance into the room, to ensure that my facing movements were precise and crisp. Although I would be facing an entire panel, which included four individuals, I knew it would be up to the Hawaii Adjutant General to make the final selection.

During scrupulous inspection of my uniform in preparation for the board, something happened that I could never have anticipated. Call it Murphy's Law, or what we often refer to as "stuff happens," usually when we least expect it. The question is, How do we react to these situations when they occur? While I'd come to realize that when stuff happens, we have to quickly adapt, find the positive, adjust the plan, and then move forward, those words were about to take on a whole new meaning.

On my way to the interview, so as to not have any wrinkles in my uniform, I hand-carried my service dress uniform to the Hawaii State Headquarters and dressed there for the interview. My ribbon rack was magnetic, so, if needed, it could be easily adjusted. When I put on my service jacket, I caught the corner of my ribbon rack, and it fell to the floor. It wasn't a big deal to slap the ribbon rack back on and align and center it. At the time, my ribbons were a perfect square. Hurriedly, I placed them back on my jacket and went to the waiting room, where I interacted with several Senior Officers and Senior NCOs as I awaited my turn.

During my interview, it seemed that the TAG, Major General Lee, was looking at my ribbons. I wondered why and felt uncomfortable about it. After the interview, I went back to change and caught a glimpse of myself in the mirror. To my horror, I immediately saw my blunder and clearly understood why the TAG had been focused on my ribbons. I had placed my square ribbon rack on my uniform *upside down*. Mortified, I stood frozen in place.

*No, no, no!* I thought frantically. *Should I go back in to the board? Do I say something, apologize, fess up? What do I do now?*

After quickly running through the various scenarios in my mind, I thought, *No, there is no excuse. It's over, and you blew it!* I hung my head in shame and left the building thinking, *Game over!* I beat myself up for the remainder of that day, saying to myself, *With all the preparation I did, how could I let something so foolish keep me from achieving such an important step in my career?*

Within minutes, even though I knew the interview went exceptionally well, I convinced myself I would not be selected as the next State Command Chief. My blunder was inexcusable. Then my mind turned to why none of the officers or SNCOs had said anything. I wondered if they'd even noticed.

Later that afternoon, I received a call from the TAG. I silently breathed in as I waited for him to say that he'd selected another chief—because of my ribbon faux pas. However, to my surprise, the TAG told me he'd selected me to be the HIANG State Command Chief Master Sergeant. I was shocked, speechless, and flabbergasted that in spite of what I felt was a gross oversight on my part, he had chosen me.

Even after he told me I'd been selected and congratulated me, I couldn't let go of the ribbon debacle. I needed to know if he'd noticed and whether or not that had become a point of discussion in the selection process, yet I kept my mouth shut. It was eating me up inside, but somehow, I knew I shouldn't broach the subject with him.

After thanking him for this opportunity, I felt compelled to remind the TAG that after the New Year, I would not be there to serve in my new position for about two and a half months. I had previously committed to deploy to Central Command in Qatar in my full-time technician capacity. I assured him that the Wing Command Chief would take good care of the HIANG enlisted corps in my absence.

That same day, while speaking with the outgoing State CCM who had been part of the interview panel, I asked him if anyone said anything about my ribbons at the interview board. I just had to know since I was still kicking myself over this huge mistake. He said he had no idea what I was talking about, so I explained. Years later, Major General Lee told me he hadn't paid much attention to my ribbons. He said my comments and composure carried the day.

Although my oversight did not preclude me from being selected, it continued to haunt me. I realized I could continue to beat myself up over this incident. As I'd done in the past, however, I gave myself three days to rip myself apart and then prayed to God to take it from me so I could let it go. I had done all the right things to prepare and stuff happened—an unfortunate circumstance had occurred. Such is life. Admittedly, it was difficult for me to let go of my mistakes, errors, or omissions, much less forgive myself for them. In spite of that, I continued to work hard and reminded myself over and over that stuff happens and sometimes people make mistakes.

Being the consummate professional and taking pride in always having my uniform squared away, this experience ultimately humbled me and gave me a different perspective and outlook when I needed to address an Airman or Soldier to make a uniform correction. I had always approached them with dignity and respect when making corrections, but as a result of my faux pas, I had more compassion and understanding for others' missteps and oversights.

# CHAPTER 37

# Al Udeid Air Base, Qatar

In the mid-2000s, if an ANG Command Chief deployed in their technician position like I did as a Combat Airspace Manager, they had to take off the Command Chief stripes and deploy as a Chief Master Sergeant. In January 2007, I took off the Command Chief stripes and deployed to the Combined Air Operations Center (CAOC) at Al Udeid Air Base, Qatar, as a full-time technician. It was easy for me to change out my stripes because I was finally going to deploy and make a real contribution to the war on terrorism, and that far outweighed what stripes I wore. I also knew that what I would learn while deployed would make me a better airspace manager and a better leader.

After a long flight to Qatar, I was picked up and dropped off at my temporary room, a transitory dorm/trailer. A couple of days later, I was reassigned to a permanent room. The new airspace crew, which included two officers and two enlisted, had a few days of turnover time with the outgoing airspace crew. Fortunately, I knew two of the combat airspace managers who were rotating back to the States and their base of assignment. One was a former commander at the 297th ATCS and one was an airspace manager from the Thirteenth Air Force, Air Operations Center at Hickam AFB, with whom I'd worked extensively. The Master Sergeant and I had participated in exercises together and had a solid professional relationship. We knew each other's capabilities and communicated on the same level. I believe that because we knew each other, my transition was smoother and easier.

The Officer in Charge developed a schedule that allowed for physical fitness and any appointments we had. The four of us quickly settled into a routine. I worked in Combat Plans, planning the airspace for the next twenty-four-hour period rather than the combat operations section, which often dealt with moment-to-moment airspace changes. The work was rewarding; I felt like I was contributing on a higher level to the wartime efforts and was proud to serve in the area of responsibility. The combat plans airspace section developed the daily airspace control order for real-world operations and missions over the battlefields of Afghanistan, Iraq, and the Horn of Africa. Watching the air battle in real time that streamed into the CAOC gave me a feeling of mixed emotions, knowing that our efforts were directly helping to protect the fives of US and coalition service members while, at the same time, rooting out the enemy.

࿐

During my time in the Combined Air Operations Center, I was part of the team that flew to the Persian Gulf on a US Navy jet, a C-2 Greyhound, and landed on the aircraft carrier USS *John C. Stennis* (CVN 74). Our mission was to brief the admiral and his aircrew of the incoming carrier battle group on the airspace over Iraq, Afghanistan, and the Horn of Africa. I knew it would be a professional growth experience for me, as I had done little work with my counterparts in the Navy, but I'll admit I was a bit anxious about "taking the hook" and "catapulting" off the carrier. For small aircraft and jets to land on a carrier, an aircraft drops a tail hook, which then catches one of four arresting wires on the carrier—sturdy cables woven from high-tensile steel wire that span across the flight deck. Once the hook engages with the wire, the aircraft is then arrested to an immediate stop. In 3.5 seconds, the plane goes from 220 miles per hour to zero—and so do its passengers.

Several people who'd experienced an arrested landing described it as extremely violent. After listening to their stories, I decided to eat only crackers before the flight, and I found myself almost dreading the experience. But landing on the carrier deck and "taking the hook" turned out to be exhilarating, and I realized that the stories had been overly dramatic.

After we briefed the admiral and his staff, they gave us a tour of the ship. The flight deck of a carrier is a dangerous yet exciting work environment. It was fascinating and impressive to watch the Sailors on the flight deck. It was like watching a well-orchestrated performance: wearing different colored shirts that signified separate skill sets, the teams worked seamlessly with each other to launch and recover the aircraft. Watching the flight operations alone was well worth the trip.

While on the flight deck during launch and recovery operations, I was amazed at how close we were to aircraft that were catapulting off the deck and taking the hook. One had to be extremely careful and obey instructions. If not, a person could easily be blown over the flight deck and into the ocean by the sheer force of the jet blast. The professionalism and expertise of the flight deck team was a vision to behold. They were truly "the best of the best."

After watching flight ops, we had the opportunity to sit in the Admiral's chair for a photo op. I knew my husband and stepson would be envious of that honor. The most senior enlisted Sailor on board the carrier, a Command Master Chief Petty officer, took me to the Chief's Mess, a dining facility reserved only for E-7 and above enlisted Sailors. While in line to get food and coffee, I engaged in conversation with a young female Sailor. She was so proud of her work in the Chief's Mess, and her eyes lit up when she talked about the special dessert she had made for my arrival—a monster cookie ice-cream sandwich. Although I had given up ice cream and sweets for Lent, I enjoyed a few bites and appreciated her efforts. I then presented her with one of my challenge coins for excellence. It became another one of those moments that reminded me how incredible the young men and women are who serve our nation.

In preparation for our departure, we were once again briefed before the catapult off the deck of the carrier. A catapult assists an aircraft to get up to high speeds in a very short distance, which allows the aircraft to take off from the flight deck. If all goes well, the aircraft is airborne. If things do not go well, there is a high probability the aircraft will be hurled into the ocean. I understand this rarely happens, but the risk is always there, and that was not comforting to me. The entire catapult process takes about 2.8 seconds to propel an aircraft from zero to 180 miles per hour. Needless to say, it was another anxious moment for me after watching a film that in my opinion was way overexaggerated. This time, I tried my best to not let the film or the opinions of others influence my thoughts. After the catapult launch, I thought, *Was that it?*

Much like a roller coaster, when we left the flight deck, we dipped low before the climb, and my stomach had the sensation of rolling downhill. The experience of flying in the C-2 Greyhound, taking the hook, and catapulting off the carrier was a phenomenal experience—one that not many Airmen get to do.

⨝

Back in the CAOC, our routine continued until it was time for me to return to the United States. On our days off, we could sign up for trips into Doha, Qatar. I took full advantage of this opportunity and signed up as often as I could. It was quite an experience looking from the outside at how the people of Qatar lived and shopped, the topography, and their homes. My entire group and I shopped in the local businesses in Doha, and I purchased many different articles that represented the country and area. In one store, I had selected several items to purchase. When I went to pay for the items, the store owner shook his head. I was clothed in civilian attire, with long pants and a blouse with short sleeves. Although no other shop owner had turned me down, I knew why he had refused. He was not going to sell his wares to an American woman, inappropriately dressed. I respected this, returned the items to their original place, and left the store.

On another excursion, I shopped in a local marketplace. Many local Qataris shopped there for food, spices, household goods, and clothing. It was interesting to watch the people coming and going and observe a piece of their culture. I enjoyed the smells, especially the perfumes, oils, and spices. We purchased figs, nuts, and dried fruit from the open market, which I enjoyed back at the base.

During my time at Al Udeid, it was interesting when other service members inquired about the duration of my tour and learned that it was only half, or 64 days, of an AEF rotation, typically 120 days for Air Force members. Instantly, there was disdain in their voices and an attitude that I wasn't pulling my full weight by only doing a half of an AEF deployment. Many active-duty personnel did not understand how National Guard members could split an AEF rotation, and no one knew why Master Sergeant Murakami and I had split our AEF tour.

One particular female Army Colonel belittled me about the duration of my deployment as well as my deployed location in Al Udeid, which was also a place for R&R. This was somewhat disconcerting, as she was making judgments without full knowledge of what my deployment entailed. Rather than get upset, however, I did my best to educate her about Guard and Reserve assignments. I explained that Guardsmen don't get to pick and choose the assignment or location, and some military jobs are limited in the number of deployable slots in specific locations. I also explained that not every Guard and Reservist gets the opportunity to deploy, but I knew most would if given the chance.

Not every service member "humps the hills" of Iraq or Afghanistan. Many service members perform their duties in office spaces. Combat Airspace Management happened to be a job that required us to reside in a secure and classified structure. The CAOC at Al Udeid was one of several locations where combat airspace managers were assigned. I made it very clear to the colonel that I was equally proud of my time at "the Deid" as she was for her time spent at other deployed locations.

After several similar conversations with other deployed members about the duration of my rotation, I chose my words carefully. I cautioned my replacement about the attitude toward anyone serving less than a full AEF rotation. I would have been proud to serve longer and more frequently, but there were only so many Air Guard AEF positions for combat airspace managers. Splitting the AEF with

Master Sergeant Murakami enabled him to get his training and for both of us to deploy. If I had to do it over again, I'd make the same decision, as it was for the greater good and the overall readiness of the HIANG organization.

As my time in the CAOC was nearing an end, the officer in charge of combat plans awkwardly broached the topic of an award.

With sixty-four days on site, I had done nothing above and beyond to warrant a decoration. I quickly put him at ease by declining even the mere suggestion of a decoration. I came, did my job, and when my tour was over, I would return home. As far as I was concerned, there was no recognition earned or deserved. I completed the handoff with Master Sergeant Murakami and headed back to Oahu. It had been an honor and privilege to deploy in support of Operation Iraqi Freedom and Operation Enduring Freedom to Al Udeid Air Base, Qatar. I felt as though, for a short time, I was able to support the daily air battle, the coalition, and, in a small way, help protect the United States of America.

As I transitioned back to the States, I had planned to surprise my parents with a visit. Apparently, I should have given them a heads-up, as the shock of me walking into the house nearly stopped time. My mom and dad were sitting in the living room at the time. Mom gasped when she saw me and hugged me for the longest time, not completely believing that I was physically present.

It had been at least six months since I'd seen them, and although I'd been deployed far from enemy lines, Al Udeid was in a combat zone. My mother was extremely relieved to know I'd made it home safe and sound. I spent the next few days with my parents, brothers, and sisters, and shared some of my deployed experiences.

While visiting with my sister Shannon, my cell phone rang. It was Major General Robert Lee. He welcomed me back to the States, then told me he'd selected me to be his Senior Enlisted Leader (SEL) for the Hawaii National Guard (HING). The conversation caught me completely off guard. His selection would make me the first-ever HIANG Airman to serve in this position *and* the first female SEL in the history of the HING. It also meant I would be dual-hatted as the State Command Chief for the HIANG and the State Senior Enlisted

Leader—having oversight of both the Hawaii Army and Air National Guard enlisted corps.

"Yes, sir," I said, still a bit surprised. "Thank you for your confidence, and I look forward to the opportunity."

When I got off the phone, the TAG's words began to hit me: I would now have oversight for the entire Hawaii National Guard enlisted corps. *Oh man*! I had much work to do.

# Chapter 38

# Returning Home

In March 2007, after returning from deployment, I went back to my federal technician position at the 201st CCG. The TAG wanted me to leave my full-time position at Hickam AFB and move to the HING State Headquarters just outside Diamond Head as his full-time SEL. He authorized my transfer and assignment to the State Headquarters as a federal technician until an Active Guard and Reserve Title-32, E-9 authorized grade became available. This all happened very quickly, and I found myself in unfamiliar territory. There was no continuity handoff with my predecessor, no current continuity book, and I did not know many of the Hawaii Army National Guard leadership. I reached out to my predecessor and received his message loud and clear: I would have to figure things out on my own.

Not having worked with our Hawaii Army National Guard (HIARNG) brethren, I didn't know all the Army rank insignia, the organizational structure, or the overall Command mission. I made flash cards to learn the enlisted ranks (particularly the junior ranks) so I could properly address every Soldier appropriately. Whenever I had a break or was at home in the evening, I ran through my flash cards, and soon I had the enlisted ranks committed to memory.

My enthusiasm was not reciprocated. The State Command's Senior Enlisted Advisor had always been a male command sergeant major in the Army National Guard, so I was both the first female *and* the first Air Guard member in the position. The Army side didn't exactly welcome me with fanfare. Since most of the HIARNG enlisted corps had never worked with the Air side of the house, many of the Soldiers didn't know what to call me—much of the time I answered to "Sergeant Major." Overtime, though, I educated the Soldiers. It was a good opportunity for Army and Air to learn from each other. I told Soldiers I was proud and honored to be called Sergeant Major, but the appropriate term of address was simply "Chief." From then on, that's what they called me.

Early after my assignment as the HING SEL, HIARNG Command Sergeant Major Robert Inouye took me to his various Army units. He introduced me to senior leaders and enlisted Soldiers and provided background and relevant information on the HIARNG units and mission. Command Sergeant Major Inouye was extremely helpful, and I considered him a great ally and partner. For some time, he was my "go-to" person for HIARNG enlisted matters, as he had the history and knowledge of the enlisted Soldiers and the organization.

During my first few weeks, I learned about some HIARNG enlisted issues pertaining to the unauthorized promotion of enlisted Soldiers. I consulted the JAG about this issue and then briefed the TAG about what had been occurring. The TAG then had a conversation with HIARNG leadership, which was not well received. As a matter of fact, at my first HIARNG Commander's meeting, I was confronted about this situation minutes before the official meeting began. I sat in my seat embarrassed and fuming to have been berated in front of others and not given the opportunity to discuss the situation. I could feel my face flush to red hot. Totally caught off guard, a moment later, I was introduced as the new SEL and asked to say a few words. Still reeling from being berated, I'm sure I stammered a bit, made a few comments, and sat back down. With every second that passed, I got more furious about the confrontation. I got up, used the restroom, splashed cold water on my face, and stuffed down my anger. Then I rejoined the meeting.

After the meeting, a couple of Soldiers who'd overheard the confrontation asked if I was okay, and I acknowledged that I was. Time passed, but the tension did not go away. The TAG and I had a conversation about what had occurred at the meeting, and with his support, I continued to stand on principle and do what was right for the enlisted corps and the good of the organization.

Weeks later, I learned from a HIARNG Lieutenant Colonel that she stood up for me to the senior officer and supported my position. She had explained to him how the original conversation had come about, my role in bringing it to the TAG, and my right to seek JAG counsel. I appreciated her efforts. Ultimately, the situation resolved itself.

As the State SEL, I had a direct line and access to the TAG and only brought what I considered important matters to him. One of my most important roles was to ensure that the TAG was never caught off guard or blindsided by enlisted matters. I never wanted him to ask me, "Did you know about this?" or "Why didn't you tell me?"

It took about six months of reading and learning before I grasped the bulk of the Army acronyms, understood HIARNG capabilities and who the key leaders were, and was able to speak Army language. The Army Guard had a different culture than the Air Guard, and I had to learn, respect, and understand it to prove myself and to establish a level of credibility.

Initially, many times I showed up at HIARNG meetings or at training exercises uninvited. It was important to be there for our enlisted corps. Overtime, I gained the support and respect of the HIARNG officers and senior enlisted corps. I fostered professional relationships by ensuring I was present at various events, visited units, and took time to talk with the Soldiers about their concerns, military and civilian jobs, education, available resources, and their families. I believe I demonstrated through word, action, and deed that the HIARNG Soldiers were as equally important to me as were the Airmen under my purview.

I was able to spend more time on the HIARNG side because we had a strong Wing Command Chief. Shortly after my selection to the state level, the Wing Commander held an interview board to select the new 154th WG CCM. My good friend Chief Master Sergeant Robert S. K. Lee III was selected. Chief Lee was highly regarded across the HIANG. As an SNCO, he upheld the highest of standards, lived the AF core values, served on the HIANG Honor Guard, and his dress and appearance were impeccable. Service before self and serving the state of Hawaii and our country were the ideals he lived by.

# CHAPTER 39

# JMARC

JMARC was a foreign acronym to me. When the TAG said, "Chief, we're going on a JMARC trip to Afghanistan to visit HING Soldiers and Airmen," I had no idea what he meant. I soon found out that JMARC stood for Joint Monthly Access for Reserve Components. JMARC is a Commander US Central Command (CENTCOM) program that periodically provides area of operation access for Reserve Component and Distinguished Visitor leaders to visit Kuwait, Afghanistan, and Iraq.

A JMARC trip allowed us to visit our people so we could touch base with them and heighten morale. We brought with us local Hawaiian foods and cards of appreciation made by the children, as well as sentiments from the Command and families.

Once again, there was no playbook in my office spelling out what needed to be done in preparation for the JMARC trip. I soon learned there were many requirements for both the TAG and me to complete prior to our trip. Most of the items were training-related as they pertained to our personal safety and security. Everything needed to be coordinated with and through the National Guard Bureau.

One of the items we needed to complete was small-arms training. Even though we were both current and qualified, we needed to requalify prior to the JMARC trip. On the day of the small-arms training, I met the TAG at the respective unit where the training would be held. It seemed odd to me that so many Soldiers were observing our training. Having never fired this type of equipment or been exposed to such a realistic simulation, I listened intently to the instructors. We went through the various scenarios and soon were handed our training completion documentation. I had always been a good shot, and I once again qualified as an expert marksman. I later learned that the Soldiers observing the training wanted to see how well the Air Guard female CCM could shoot.

The HING had never had an Airman as their SEL in its history. How to fund my travel soon became a big topic of conversation and, at times, a heated one. The fifteen days of annual active duty that Guard members perform were quickly used for temporary duty trips. Because I was an Airman and there was no such thing as "joint" or purple money (it's either Army or Air—what we called blue or green dollars), the HIANG side didn't anticipate that it would create an additional and significant financial burden when I came on board as the HING SEL. Starting my tour midfiscal year meant that the HIANG had not budgeted monies for my travel.

Therefore, when I went to the Headquarters (HQ) HIANG with a sizable bill for travel to the AOR for the JMARC trip, it was met with significant resistance. Initially, there were no funds allocated for my travel with the TAG, or for travel most anywhere. The bottom line was that the TAG wanted me to go with him, and HQ HIANG needed to reallocate dollars to make it work. Funding dollars for travel continued to be a point of contention between the HIARNG and HIANG as to who would fund what travel on my behalf. From day one, the HIARNG drew a hard line of not providing any funding for travel for my position, which meant that HQ HIANG had to do some creative budgeting and reallocation of funds.

The pop-up trips, such as the JMARC, were the most financially difficult, due to the nonbudgeted costs and timing of the overseas visits. This was new for all of us, and for the next several years, we held regular discussions about priority of travel for all HQ HIANG staff members. While I worked directly for the TAG, my funding continued to come out of the headquarters HIANG budget, which was controlled by the HIANG Commander.

꒷

In the fall of 2008, the leadership and Soldiers of the Twenty-Ninth Infantry Brigade Combat Team (IBCT), Hawaii Army National Guard, were in full training mode for its upcoming deployment to Kuwait. There were many long periods of training preparation and extended drill weekends. As senior leaders and through the HING Public Affairs Office (PAO), we kept the families, the public, and employers informed with updates and the details pertaining to the deployment. It had been a few years since we'd had a deployment of this magnitude, and Soldiers, families, employers, and the citizens of Hawaii had many questions.

Since a large contingency of the Guard was being deployed, there were concerns about what would happen in the event of a state emergency. The governor and TAG were able to ease the concerns by explaining that the remaining Army and Air Guard were fully prepared to handle any state emergency.

Knowing we would have Soldiers and Airmen deployed over the holidays and away from home, the TAG wanted to do something special for them. As a regular guest on KHVH (830 AM) talk radio, Major General Lee announced "Operation Gift Lift." The community was invited to donate Hawaiian treats and gifts of aloha to be delivered to our deployed Guard members. Soon, boxes and boxes and boxes of chocolates, coffee, Spam, rice, mochi (Japanese rice crackers), CDs, DVDs, toiletries, books, and warm clothing arrived. We had boxes stacked in several locations with a drop-off point at the state headquarters and the 442nd Veterans Club in Honolulu. Fortunately, the Deputy Adjutant General (DAG) had recently relocated his office, and it was vacant. We were able to store all the gifts of aloha in the DAG's old office. This room was quite large, and over the course of several weeks, it became stacked full of items with small paths between the stacks.

The next task was to box everything for transport. Major General Lee is an amazing man and leader. He is highly regarded and respected throughout the United States and around the world and has many high-level connections—the right connections. He worked out an arrangement with United Airlines to transport boxes to Kuwait and later to Afghanistan and Qatar. I had the task to get the items prepared for our trip. Having no staff, this was a huge undertaking. While the office was full of goodies, they were not organized in categories. To pack boxes for transport, we had to first organize and separate the gifted goodies by type of item. This made it much easier to take an empty box and fill it with a variety of items.

I sent a message to the headquarters staff and the human resource office that anyone wanting to help and donate their time to pack boxes was welcome to do so. Fortunately, there were good people who came to help, both military and civilian. We packed about thirty boxes for one particular JMARC trip, and they hardly made a dent in what had been donated to the HING. The people of Hawaii were so generous, and we were grateful for all they did in support of the deployed Soldiers, Airmen, and for Operation Gift Lift. These were gifts of aloha given from the heart.

The look on the faces of our deployed members as they opened the boxes was sheer joy. The goodies represented a piece of home brought to them in a remote and desolate location. I believe they felt the aloha spirit all the way in the Middle East. Items like sticky rice, Li Hing Mui powder, cracked seed, arare crackers, dry seaweed, mochi, and other local Hawaiian delicacies were all things they deeply missed and thoroughly enjoyed.

Trips to visit Soldiers and Airmen in Kuwait and Afghanistan were among my first JMARC trips, and I really didn't know what to expect. As we deplaned from one journey to Afghanistan, we got on our "battle rattle," which included body armor, Kevlar helmet, eye protection, and weapons. We were then ushered into SUVs and transported to base. This was not a typical ride in a vehicle. The driver drove extremely fast through local village areas, and the security detail was on high alert. Being my first time, it was a bit disconcerting, and I thought about all the service members in harm's way.

I was in a protected hardened SUV, not in an exposed foxhole with bullets whizzing by my head, which certainly put things in a different perspective for me.

While in country, we traveled mainly by helicopter. It was fascinating to fly over villages and rural communities of Afghani people. Although above them, I still got a real sense of their daily life. When I saw a flock of sheep and a herder in the middle of nowhere, it was hard to understand where he was going or how he and the sheep survived. Clearly, there was no food or water close to where the herds of sheep were located. Out the helicopter window, I also saw Afghani women beating the dust out of rugs. Why bother? I thought, puzzled. The homes appeared to be made from clay or mud and were surrounded by sand. It appeared that there was no escaping the sand and dust.

While I had seen video and pictures of Afghanistan's mountain ranges, it was quite different to actually see and fly in and around them. The mountains were jagged, and the terrain extremely rough. I thought about our US and coalition forces in full gear, humping up those mountains, carrying their packs, weapons, and other equipment. I wondered how they fought on those mountains with all the gear they carried. Once again, I was grateful for those who serve to protect us. Looking at the terrain gave me a deep and profound respect and appreciation for the Green Berets, Special Forces, Reconnaissance Marines, SEALs, Tactical Air Control Party community, and all military members who fought and continue to fight in these locations.

Subsequent trips to Iraq and Afghanistan were similar. As part of Operation Gift Lift, the TAG and I always brought boxes of goodies and gifts of aloha for the Hawaii Soldiers and Airmen. Our time and every movement were well planned and scheduled. On a particular trip to Iraq, we were driven through an area where young Iraqi women were glamorized and used as escorts. I remember thinking how tragic it was to grow up in this country where women didn't have a voice and were viewed as objects and someone's property. I had a humble upbringing, but at least I was free to make my own choices—these women were not so fortunate.

At some point, the driver pulled over, and we exited the vehicle. In front of us were the bombed-out homes of Uday and Qusay Hussein, Saddam Hussein's sons. I stood for a moment, awestruck. It was a surreal moment for me to stand there and think about the blood and treasure lost in the Iraq War. How many lives were sacrificed at this very location? I didn't know, but it gave me pause to think about it.

Inwardly, I was somewhat pleased that the homes were destroyed. Later on that trip, Major General Lee and I stopped for meetings at one of Saddam Hussein's palaces. It was the same palace where many service members had their photos taken while sitting on Saddam Hussein's chair. As I sat on this throne for a photo, for a brief moment, I pondered all the heinous acts this dictator had done to his people and to the country of Iraq. It felt odd to sit and smile for a photo while contemplating the man and the terrible things he had done.

# CHAPTER 40

# The Cost of War

During my tenure as the HI SEL, we lost a deployed female HIARNG Soldier in a noncombat accident. Like so many of our casualties, she was young. This was very difficult on her immediate family, her unit, Guard family, and on the entire organization. Major General Lee and I went to visit the family and offer our condolences and to see if there was anything we could do. The family had been assigned a Casualty Assistance officer, and all was in order. We could both see that the mother was really struggling. Losing her daughter in a tragic car accident was devastating. A young woman with so much potential and promise, who had deployed to Kuwait—a nonhostile combat zone—and not been directly in harm's way. I went to her mother, hugged her, and just sat and held her hand. There were no words—nothing more needed to be said. The loss was finite, and their lives would forevermore be changed.

It felt as if I were sitting next to my own mother, remembering how we sat and cried during Jeff's initial days in the hospital. This could have been our outcome, yet Jeff's life was spared. I fought back tears as I remembered our family's experience. A mother and father's pain of losing a son or daughter is indescribable and something parents hope to never experience.

The subsequent funeral ceremony honored this young Soldier's life and career. As I followed Major General Lee to pay our final respects and render our salute, both of us choked back tears. It was extremely difficult to maintain my composure. Looking back, I've often wondered why I felt such a strong need to do so. Was it because leaders are not supposed to show emotion? Was it because this was still a man's world and girls didn't cry? I can't say for sure, but I suspect part of it was my upbringing—we were told to not cry. But she was one of ours, a part of our National Guard family, and it hurt deeply to lose a Soldier and a member of the HING. My heart ached for her family, friends, and for her fellow Soldiers.

# CHAPTER 41

# The Philippines

HIARNG Soldiers were part of a Joint Task Force (JTF) that deployed to Jolo, Philippines, for six months. The task force was called JTF-PI. Jolo was considered a very dangerous area; Abu Sayyaf, a violent jihadist group, had carried out bombings and kidnappings in the region. Abu Sayyaf was responsible for the Philippines' worst terrorist attack, the bombing of SuperFerry 14 in 2004, which killed 116 people. They were known to be ruthless.

JTF-PI rotated every six months between the Hawaii and the Guam Army National Guard. Because many Hawaii and Guam Soldiers spoke various dialects of the Philippine language and still had family in the Philippines, it was a tactical advantage militarily to have the ability to connect and interact with the local Philippine population. This was essential in acquiring human intelligence on the operations of Abu Sayyaf.

After landing in the Philippines, we were transported mainly via a civilian contract helicopter. We made a stop in Zamboanga and met with local leadership who briefed us on terrorist activity and some of the challenges in the area. As we traversed miles and miles of the Sulu Sea and entered the Sulu Archipelago, it was amazing to me how many small islands there were in the middle of nowhere. Many of these islands were inhabited, and I wondered how the people were able to feed and clothe themselves, let alone receive any form of communication.

Upon landing in Jolo to visit our Soldiers, they gave us a tour of the deployed site. It was a beautiful site with lush green foliage. However, we knew extreme danger and the Abu Sayyaf could be lurking around any corner. The TAG and I held a town hall kind of meeting where Soldiers were provided current information and could ask questions. Among the topics discussed were upcoming deployment opportunities, local news, family readiness group activities, leadership changes within the HIARNG, and concerns we needed to take back to their command. We enjoyed a local-style meal prepared by the Soldiers and ate with them before departing back to the Philippine mainland.

While the soldiers realized they were in a dangerous area, this was a deployment that in general they enjoyed. In some way, they felt a sense that they were helping to protect their families in the Philippines from terrorism.

ॐ

After our visit with the Hawaii National Guard Soldiers in Jolo, Major General Lee and I had an afternoon free before heading back to Oahu. He suggested we take a charter boat to the island of Corregidor, located at the mouth of Manila Bay. I didn't know much about the history of Corregidor, but I was very interested to learn more.[10]

Corregidor, the largest island in a group of five islands, is a four-mile-long rock formation—hence its nickname "the Rock." It's shaped like a tadpole whose head is turned westward toward the China Sea and whose tail curves around and points back in the same direction. Corregidor's topography is a quilt of contrasts, and I found it breathtakingly beautiful.

"Fortress" Corregidor guards the mouth of Manila Bay, the natural harbor that surrounds the capital city. The Philippine Islands divide the Pacific Ocean from the South China Sea and are situated in the critical trade routes to Southeast Asia and north to Japan. Ferdinand Magellan first claimed the islands for Spain in 1521; in November 1542, Spanish explorer Ruy Lopez de Villalobos renamed the islands "Las Islas Filipinas," in honor of Philip II, then Crown Prince of Spain. The Spaniards soon realized the strategic importance of the island and in 1795 began building docks to repair their warships and store naval supplies.

As time went on, they built a lighthouse and expanded the fortifications to not only discourage Western colonial powers but also pirates who had for centuries looted ships and terrorized villages along the coasts. For most Americans, Corregidor is most notable for its importance during the Spanish-American War and World War II.

On February 15, 1898, after the battleship USS *Maine* mysteriously sunk in Cuba's Havana Harbor, the United States declared war on Spain. The first major battle took place half a world away when Admiral Dewey sailed the American fleet into Manila Bay and engaged the Spanish fleet, which were greatly outnumbered and outgunned by the larger, more modern, and more powerful US ships. Admiral Dewey avoided potential deadly fire from the huge guns on Corregidor by sailing past the island at night and surprising the Spanish gunners.

After a series of other battles with Spain, the war came to a close on December 10, 1898, with the signing of the Treaty of Paris, which transferred possession of the Philippines to the United States. Meanwhile, however, Filipino nationalists led by Emilio Aguinaldo had begun a fight for Filipino independence that lasted three years. In 1909, US Army forces began a fortification campaign that turned Corregidor into a powerful fortress protecting the entrance into Manila Bay. At the same time, the Navy planted minefields in both channel approaches to the harbor. When the Japanese assaulted the Philippines in 1941, it was no surprise that "the Rock" became the stronghold for its defenders.

Upon arriving on the island, we were ushered to an open-air streetcar that looked much like those used on the island in the early 1920s. We drove around the island, stopping at significant sites where the tour guide explained the history and significance of what we were seeing. The streetcar took us all over the island. We stopped at the ruins of the "Mile-Long Barracks," now a mere skeleton of the three-story concrete building that housed enlisted personnel during

World War II. We also stopped by the three-story ruins of the Middle Side Barracks, Battery Geary, Battery Hearn, and Battery Crockett, as well as the parade grounds.

On March 11, 1942, shortly before the fall of the Philippines to the Japanese, President Franklin D. Roosevelt ordered General Douglas McArthur to Australia. A bronze statue of General McArthur now stands on the beach in General Douglas MacArthur Park. Here is where he, his family, and essential members of his staff presumably departed Corregidor on board motor torpedo boat PT-41, accompanied by three other PT boats, and began their journey to Australia. The journey continued from the island of Mindanao on board a pair of Boeing B-17s, the Flying Fortresses. The statue of General MacArthur is engraved with a famous message to the Filipino people: "I shall return." He would fulfill that promise almost two and a half years later when he returned in October 1944, as the US forces fought to recapture the Philippines.

Mariveles Mountain on the Bataan Peninsula could be seen from the lighthouse on Topside. Looking out, it was chilling to reflect on what happened to so many men during the Bataan Death March in 1942. I was overlooking this historical site and the land where so many suffered and died under the brutal hands of the Imperial Japanese Army, as sixty thousand to eighty thousand Filipino and American troops were forced to march sixty-five miles to prison camps. Thousands perished due to the intense heat and brutal and inhumane treatment by Japanese guards.

The most significant historical stop for me was the Malinta Tunnel, which was built under Malinta Hill. We experienced firsthand what took place in the Malinta Tunnel through a vividly staged light and sound show called the "Malinta Experience." The show is a reenactment of World War IPs dramatic events.

The Malinta Tunnel was General MacArthur's final command post and where he and Philippines President Manuel Quezon sought refuge during the Japanese attack on the Philippines. The construction of the Malinta Tunnel began in 1922 and was completed in 1932. The tunnel complex consisted of an east-west passage measuring 836 feet long by 24 feet wide, with thirteen laterals on its north side and eleven laterals on the south side. The tunnel was reinforced with concrete walls, floor, and overhead arches with blowers to furnish fresh air and a double-track electric car line along the main tunnel. Malinta provided bombproof shelter for the thousand-bed hospital, MacArthur's US Army Forces Far East (USAFFE 1941–1946) Headquarters, shops, and a vast labyrinth storehouse during the siege of Corregidor.

As I walked through the large double doors and into the tunnel, it smelled musty, and the air was thick with aromas that told the story of what it would have been like to be secluded in the tunnel during the bombings. Our tour guide explained that the tunnel today is open to tourists and was designed to capture the essence of what it was like to be in the tunnel during wartime. As the large doors closed behind us, the tunnel went dark. The guide provided a detailed explanation of everything we were about to see. Dim overhead lights appeared as we were ushered to a corridor off the main tunnel.

The area was furnished with tables and chairs, an old typewriter, and other items that would have been found in an office of that era. Sculptures were strategically placed to give viewers a sense of the compact space people worked in. The room was smoky, and the lights flickered. Overhead, you could hear the sounds of planes and bomb bursts. This setting was reenacted to give tourists a glimpse of what it would have been like to work in an environment under attack. Without notice, the flickering lights went out, and we were in near-darkness once again.

In another corridor, lights went on, and we moved to that area to see a makeshift hospital area. Originally, the Malinta Tunnel was home to a thousand-bed hospital. Statues depicted wounded Soldiers, and doctors and nurses attending to the wounded with archaic equipment. As we looked on, the air was thick, and the stench was stifling. I could only imagine trying to operate or care for the wounded in a setting like this. Clearly, it was not sterile, it was poorly lit, and they operated knowing that the few lights they had could go out at any moment. The sounds from planes overhead continued, as did the bomb bursts and shelling.

At the end of the long corridor was an area where gas was stored. The stench of fuel filled the air. At the time, it made me wonder if the Japanese knew there was a large storage of gas in the tunnel.

Malinta Tunnel is said to be bombproof, but one can only imagine the type of explosion and devastation there would have been had it been bombed.

It didn't take long to realize why the tunnel smelled as it did. Described as poorly ventilated, the tunnel swarmed with little black flies, bedbugs prickled the flesh, and dust hung in a pall despite continual mopping by the inhabitants. The tunnel dwellers surely felt suffocated, helpless, and trapped. There was no privacy for anyone. At the height of its occupancy, more than four thousand occupants stayed there, including women, nurses, civilians, and army wives. Between cigarette and cigar smoke, wounded personnel, antiseptic, bodily odors, gas fumes, and the musty dampness of the tunnel, I wondered how they endured that environment. At the end of the tour, I was grateful that Major General Lee had suggested we visit this most historic island.

# CHAPTER 42

# Making a Difference

One of my favorite memories as the Hawaii Senior Enlisted Leader was during the first Soldier of the Year competition to take place in many years. Six HIARNG Soldiers competed. Soldiers were selected to compete based on their overall performance related to military job skills, dress and deportment, and, most importantly, their willingness to participate and prepare. Due to the demands of the competition, Soldiers had to spend an inordinate amount of time learning a broad scope of material for the written portion of the evaluation and honing their skills for the hands-on demonstrations, including dissembling and assembling an M-16 rifle, finding coordinates via land navigation, and dialing in radio frequencies and transmitting via a mobile radio. In addition to their commitment and hours of preparation, the commitment of the family was equally important, as spouses and their children engaged to help Soldiers prepare.

A rucksack march over rough terrain was one of the components of the competition, the distance of which was unknown to the competitors. Without knowing where they were going or how long they would march, Soldiers had to carry a thirty-five-pound "backpack" along with their rifle, pacing themselves by running and/or walking. The leadership followed behind the competitors in a military vehicle to ensure everyone's safety.

During the march, a couple of Soldiers were obviously struggling and falling farther behind. I asked the driver to stop the vehicle so I could get out to motivate and encourage them. As we walked together, I engaged them in conversation. One of the Soldiers broke ahead of us and gained some distance. The other soldier wanted to quit the competition. He said he could not go on because he had several blisters and was just plain worn out. I continued to encourage him to keep going. I knew we had to get his mind off the pain and his fatigue, so I began to ask about his family, education, and favorite foods. This kept him talking.

Suddenly, the finish line was in sight and he took off running. His face said it all: "I can do it, and I'm gonna finish strong!" It was as if a surge of energy came through him as he realized all he'd overcome. I was very proud of this young Soldier for finding the inner strength, perseverance, and fortitude to keep going. It was a *hooah* kind of moment!

Making a difference in the lives of Airmen, Soldiers, and families has always been in the forefront of my mind. One evening, I was working late. It was about 7:00 p.m. when the phone rang. I answered, and it was a Senior Enlisted Soldier calling from Afghanistan. He said my number was the only one he could find for the Hawaii National Guard. He went on to explain that he had a Guam ARNG Soldier assigned to him who was being sent to Hawaii on emergency leave. This Soldier's wife and baby were being air-evacuated from Guam to the Tripler Army Medical Center (TAMC) on Oahu, as the baby needed heart surgery. He was trying to get assistance for his Soldier. I told the caller I would pick up the Guam Soldier myself and get him to the hospital and ensure that his wife had everything she needed.

That night, I picked up fruit, breakfast bars, snacks, and water and took them to where the wife would be staying. The next day, I picked up the soldier from the airport and took him to join his wife and baby at TAMC. I escorted him to the baby's room, where his wife was sitting. As I watched them embrace and saw their baby who was awaiting surgery, it brought back memories of Ashley's emergent hospitalization when she was five days old. It was a great feeling to know I was able to help a fellow Guard member and his family during a time of need. After ensuring they had my contact information and were settled in, I went back to work. These are the types of things senior leaders "get to do."

⟋⟍

As the HING SEL, I very much enjoyed attending the Recruit Sustainment Program (RSP) and Student Flight events that had been established for our Soldiers and Airmen to make use of the lull between their enlistment and the start of Basic or Technical Training. Rather than have them become unmotivated or quit before they ever began, these programs gave them a head start. While in the RSP and Student Flight, these future Army and Air Guard members were introduced to and learned the respective Army and Air Force Core Values, the Soldier and Airman's Creeds, the rank structure, and drill and ceremonies. Additionally, they performed physical fitness training and were exposed to leadership who provided information and motivation for their future careers.

It was always an honor to speak with these young men and women, to share my humble beginnings, and to encourage them to reach high, believe in themselves, and to always give a little bit more. I would explain that the opportunities were endless in the Army and Air Guard and available to everyone, and I encouraged them to do their very best to achieve a high level of success. I emphasized with a foot-stomp that they could choose to be and do anything they put their mind to.

Future Soldiers and Airmen who completed the RSP or Student Flight many times were the honor graduates of basic and technical training schools. Why? Because they had been set up for success from day one!

# CHAPTER 43

# Riley the Wonder Dog

In early 2009, a painful family event happened when we lost our thirteen-year-old family pet. In 1996, Gary and I had been spending a good deal of time building our network business, which meant many evenings and weekends away from Ashley. As a mother, our absence began to weigh heavily on me. Ashley was eight years old at the time and had been asking for a dog for quite a while, specifically a black Lab, and I kept saying no.

Gary and I had very different views on what it meant to have a dog. Gary had grown up with indoor dogs, which were part of their family. My only experience with dogs was based on what I'd seen growing up. Being raised on a farm, a dog was an animal that needed to remain outdoors—it was not a pet or part of the family. On the farm, when a dog got sick or old, it was taken to the woods to never return. Dogs and cats were not taken to vets. When it was time to replace a dog, my dad would often get a new dog from a friend or neighbor.

Based on my experiences growing up, I did not want an animal in our home. I didn't consider that a dog would become part of our family. *If* we ever got one, it would have to live outside. I didn't want to clean up dog hair or anything else that might get left behind by a dog in our house. For the longest time, Gary and I were at an impasse.

I began sharing with our network leadership my concerns about being away from Ashley so much, and some of the key leaders suggested we get a pet for her. No doubt I rolled my eyes, thinking, *Not you, too, trying to convince me to get her a dog*. After a meeting one particular evening, on our way home, Gary and I talked more about our current situation and finally agreed that we would get Ashley a dog, but it would be an *outdoor* dog. We also agreed that we would not purchase or spend money to buy the dog.

One of our business partners, who had also become a friend, offered us a puppy. He had a female dog that was pregnant. The momma was a chocolate Lab and the daddy was an Anatolian shepherd. The daddy dog was very large—Anatolian shepherds can weigh anywhere from 120 to 150 pounds and are fiercely loyal guard dogs. Concerned about the size of the male dog, I asked our friend if we could take the runt of the litter. He agreed. Once the puppies were born, we visited a few times, and Ashley got to hold her puppy. She was overjoyed, full of smiles, and began counting the days until we could bring home her precious puppy.

We let Ashley name the puppy and pick out the doghouse and all the puppy toys. I was still not thrilled about having a dog, but as long as the dog remained outdoors, I felt that I would be able to tolerate the situation. Six weeks later, we brought Riley home. I don't know why or how it started, but I often referred to her as *Riley the Wonder Dog*...and the name stuck.

It was amazing to witness the joy that Riley brought to Ashley. Rarely did she complain that we were gone too much, as she had a new friend and pet to care for. Riley became the center of her universe, and she loved that dog unconditionally.

On evenings when we had thunder and lightning storms, Ashley, with her big brown eyes, appealed to her mom's softer side and convinced me to let Riley come in on the lanai. Although Riley had a doghouse where she could remain dry, we'd block off an area, lay down towels or sheets, and let Riley come in from the storm. Riley was visibly frightened and shook because of the loud claps of thunder. We even had to tranquilize her each year during the Chinese New Year's celebrations when firecrackers went off for hours.

Gary and I made it clear that Riley was Ashley's dog and her responsibility. She was responsible for caring for her, feeding her, and picking up after her. This was not a job I was going to take on. Ashley did a good job of caring for her beloved Riley and spent countless hours in the yard throwing balls to her and petting her. I tolerated having the dog but did not spend time with her—to me, she was still merely an animal.

When we moved from Aiea to Waikele, naturally, Riley moved with us. She, too, got a new doghouse and continued to be an outdoor dog. On moving day, Riley got into and ate rat-poison pellets. Upon discovering what had happened, I thought this would be the end of Riley, as on the farm, we never spent money for a veterinarian to care for a dog. Immediately, Gary turned to me and said, "You have to take her to the vet." Here we were in the throes of boxes and unpacking, and I thought, *We're not spending money on this dog*! I maintained that thought until our now-teenage daughter came to me with tear-filled eyes. To her, this was her sister, not just an animal. I couldn't deny Ashley a chance to save her beloved pet, so off to the vet we went.

After the examination, the doctor came out and said that Riley's stomach had to be pumped, or she would most likely not make it. He also recommended that she stay overnight for observation. His next question was, "Do you want an estimate of the cost?" I stood there for a brief moment and thought about the times when Dad took a dog to the woods. That was just how it was then—you didn't spend money on vet bills. But Ashley stood next to me with big tears in her eyes, as if she already knew what I was thinking. She looked at me and gave a long drawn-out wail, "Mom...!" In an instant, I told the doctor the estimate was not necessary and to do whatever he needed to do to save Riley.

⁓

Years passed, and soon it was time for Ashley to go to college. She had been Riley's caretaker, so now what would happen? Up to that point, I'd had very little to do with Riley's daily care. On occasion,

I walked her, brushed her, and picked up after her, but only when I was in grungy yard work clothes or when no one else was around. It was a "have to" duty for me versus something I wanted to do for our pet.

The days leading up to Ashley's departure for college were sad for all of us. She spent a lot of time outside with her beloved Riley and mourned the impending separation from her home and her pet. I was dreading the day we would leave to take Ashley to college since we had never been separated for any great length of time. This was a new chapter for Ashley and, frankly, for Gary and me, too, as we became empty nesters. Ashley hugged Riley for a final time, and tears poured down her face. It was sad for me to watch her say farewell to her dog. It was as if she was in terrible pain, and no mother wants to see their child in pain. The emotion of it stabbed me in the heart as Ashley asked me to take care of her dog. Of course, we would, I assured her, yet deep inside what I really thought was, *Gary will take care of her.*

We got Ashley moved in and settled at California State University–San Bernardino, where she would attend college for the next four years. After she moved into her dorm room, it was time to say goodbye to our daughter. *Where had the time gone? How could eighteen years have gone so quickly? Did we adequately prepare her to be successful in college? Did she really know how much we loved her?* There were so many emotions, and I had not adequately prepared myself for this moment—I'm not sure there actually would have been a way to do so. We all sniffled a bit and hugged, and then it was time for Gary and me to leave for the airport. As we drove off campus and waved a final goodbye, we both bawled like babies.

Coming home to an empty house was difficult, to say the least. I sat in Ashley's room, lay on her bed, and had another good cry. My baby was gone, and I had a huge ache in my heart. Although this was the new norm, I didn't like it one bit.

The days and weeks got easier as time passed, and we had regular communication with Ashley. Almost from the first moment she was gone from our home, we began making plans for her to come home for Thanksgiving. I could not wait. At the end of our calls, there was always an instruction from Ashley to pet Riley for her and to tell Riley that she loved her. Most of the time, I did as she asked, but admittedly, I did it begrudgingly.

The Christmas of Ashley's junior year, I noticed that Riley was changing. She had slowed down a great deal, and there was just something different about her. I had the sense that the end was near but not imminent. During a call to Ashley, I told her to plan to spend extra time with Riley and to be ready to say goodbye because I didn't think Riley would be around when Ashley returned for summer break. It was a special time for the two of them that Christmas as Ashley spent a lot of time outside brushing, petting, and talking to Riley.

A few months later, in March 2009, Ashley was back in college, and Gary was in Illinois visiting his father who had been hospitalized. I came home one day, drove into the yard where Riley typically greeted me with her tail wagging—but Riley lay lifeless, and I thought for sure she was dead. I approached her cautiously, called her name, but she hardly moved. I quickly changed my clothes and tried to coax Riley to get up. Her eyes were gray and looked dead. After much effort to lift her, I managed to get her on her feet. I thought if I could get her to walk a few steps, she could at least relieve herself. She stood there, shaking for a few brief moments, as though she didn't know where she was and couldn't see.

I got scared, really scared, and selfishly thought, *Why me, why am I the one with Riley at the end, having to take care of her?* For the previous couple of days, Riley had been pooping a coffee-ground-type substance, and I knew something was wrong. She was now twelve and a half and had had a good life. I called Gary, told him what was happening, and explained it was time to put her to sleep. It wouldn't be right to let her suffer. He agreed, but insisted we fly Ashley home before we took any action. Knowing there would be a vet bill in our future, we were on polar opposite sides of this discussion. I had told Ashley to say goodbye at Christmas, and she had.

"No," I told Gary. "I'll take Riley to the vet and be done with this." Needless to say, I lost the argument, and we made reservations for Ashley to come home from college. Gary stayed in Illinois with his father. I discussed the decision with Ashley.

That evening, I sat outside with Riley, brushed her, petted her, and talked to her about what a good dog she had been to Ashley and to our family. I began to feel bad for all the times I hadn't petted her or wasn't more attentive to her. I told Riley that Ashley was coming home the next day and asked her to hold on. She remained lifeless, and I don't honestly know if she understood what was happening. I called Ashley and told her to talk to Riley so she could hear her voice. As I held the phone to Riley's ear, she lifted her head ever so slightly, and I knew she recognized the voice on the other end. Ashley and I both cried. It was an emotionally draining evening for the two of us. Before going to bed that night, I went out one last time to check on Riley. There was no change. I repeated to her, "Ashley's coming tomorrow... Ashley's coming tomorrow... just hold on, Riley."

I went to bed and cried myself to sleep.

Morning came, and I made the vet appointment for two hours after Ashley's plane arrived. I wanted her to have time with Riley, but not too much time. As I walked to the window, I thought, *How will I ever lift Riley into the car myself?* Imagine my surprise when I looked out the window and there stood Riley on all fours, wagging her tail. I rushed downstairs and out the garage door. I could not believe my eyes. She was walking around, her eyes were bright, and I wondered, *Have we made the right decision?* Before heading to the shower, I gave Riley water and placed some food in her bowl. I still needed to get to the airport, pick up Ashley, and go to the vet after that.

When I came back out of the house to leave for the airport, I saw several piles of that coffee-ground substance. Something was definitely wrong, and I knew in my heart that it was just plain time. I got Riley in the car, and all the way to the airport she looked around, her tongue hanging out with excitement as I repeated, "We're going to get Ashley. We're going to get Ashley."

Before I let Ashley see and pet Riley, I explained what had unfolded and that we were going to the park before the vet appointment. We stopped and purchased a lei for Riley and then proceeded to the park that was near the vet. Riley was on an extended leash, where she could walk around, but most of the time, she just lay by Ashley. We gave her some water and ice chips, and soon it was time to go. Perhaps it was a blessing in disguise, but before we got back into the car, Riley passed more coffee-ground-looking poo. Ashley was able to see that her dog was truly sick and suffering.

When we met with the veterinarian, he said he could do a full workup, X-rays, and an examination, but he believed that based on her symptoms, she most likely had stomach cancer. We moved forward with the appointment. Ashley wanted to be with Riley as they put her to sleep. *What could I do?* There was no question, of course—I'd be with the two of them. Never did I think I'd be in this position—this was something Gary was supposed to do. After all, he had experience with this kind of situation. I sat with Ashley as she hugged her dog and told Riley goodbye. We placed the lei around Riley's neck, and it was time. Fortunately, the process was fast, and it appeared painless. The vet left the room and told us to take as much time as we needed. Ashley and I sat there bawling, holding and petting Riley for what seemed like a very long time. It was over, and we left.

Riley was cremated, and Ashley has her ashes in a special urn in her bedroom. Gary and I had a koa wood shadow box made in her memory that includes Riley's collar, favorite ball, and the lei she wore around her neck, as well as special pictures of Ashley and Riley in Hawaii.

Ashley and I spent that weekend in our jammies, parked on the couch. We watched chick flicks to try to take our minds off what we had just gone through. Soon it was time to head back to the airport so Ashley could return to school. Driving back home by myself was especially daunting. Gary was in Illinois, Ashley was flying back to California, and I was going back to an empty house with no dog wagging its tail to greet me.

It took me a long time to fully understand why God had laid things out as he had in those final days. This was Ashley's dog. I thought I didn't care for her and that she was just an animal and, frankly, an inconvenience. How wrong I turned out to be. It wasn't until Riley's final days when I spent time alone with her, and then with Ashley and her at the very end, that I realized…I really *did* love Riley the Wonder Dog, and she most definitely had been part of our family.

# CHAPTER 44

# Deployment Recognition

The Army National Guard holds statewide ceremonies called "Freedom Salute" that recognize Soldiers who have deployed to Operation Iraqi Freedom (OIF) and Operation Enduring Freedom (OEF). During the ceremonies, Soldiers are recognized for their contributions and sacrifice while serving in a combat zone. Families are also recognized for their sacrifices; we know that families also serve in many forms. It's important to the National Guard senior leadership that our Guard families be recognized and honored.

In Hawaii, the Freedom Salute was a very patriotic event and well attended by Soldiers, families, state, and civilian leaders. The HIARNG's 111th Army Band complemented each ceremony by playing before, during, and after the event. Because of my past involvement with our high school band, I knew and understood the level of effort and commitment that went along with playing in a band—the practice, the setting up and tearing down for each event, and the performance itself. Some of the band members had played together for decades and were professional musicians in their own right. It was evident by the reaction of the crowd what they thought of each performance—all eyes focused front and center stage. The songs the band performed reached the hearts and souls of those listening and many times resulted in a standing ovation. Whenever singer Staff Sergeant Samuel Hesch performed "Hero for Today" with the band, you could see glistening eyes in the audience as they listened to the passion and pure sound of his voice, and the lyrics that told the story of Hawaii's military heroes.

୬

The Director of the Air National Guard believed it was equally important to recognize our Airmen and families for their contributions and sacrifice as well. As such, the Hometown Heroes Salute Program was instituted to accomplish the recognition of all Airmen who deployed to OIF and OEF. Program implementation at the state level fell under the purview of the State Command Chief. On December 6, 2009, we were to hold our first Hometown Heroes Salute event. It was also an election year.

We began the planning with volunteers from the HIANG Top-3 (SNCO) Council. We planned for months to make this a very special event and developed teams to execute specific tasks. We held the event on Hickam AFB in Hangar 17, a new C-17 aircraft hangar. I was grateful for the volunteers who helped with the planning and those who came to set up and tear down. It was like watching a well-oiled machine operating at its finest: everyone did their part with minimal direction.

Hawaii Governor Linda Lingle was unable to attend the event, so Lieutenant Governor Duke Aiona was scheduled to be the honored guest speaker. At my direction, the Public Affairs Office made clear that this would not be a political speech but one to honor and recognize our Airmen and their families. The Hawaii Army National Guard Band would play prelude and patriotic music. State Senators and members of Congress were invited. The media was also invited to cover this newsworthy event. Two days before the ceremony, I was on Hickam AFB when I received a call from the State Public Affairs officer (PAO), Lieutenant Colonel Charles Anthony. Our offices were in the same building. He asked that I stop by his office when I returned.

I had a pounding headache that day and managed to politely agree to make time to stop by his office.

"Congressman X wants some talk time at the Hometown Heroes Salute ceremony," the PAO said.

"No!" I exclaimed in a nanosecond, firmly and curtly.

The PAO stared at me with a shocked look on his face, and my military bearing kicked in.

"Excuse me, sir. I meant, 'No, *sir!*'" I explained again that this event was not going to be a platform for any political speech or political remarks.

Obviously, this did not sit well with the Congressman. On the day of the event, everything was going smoothly. Airmen and families filled up the seats as planned, the band played, the decorations were patriotic, and all was on schedule. The event started with the National Anthem and the state song, "Hawai'i Pono'i." The emcee acknowledged the dignitaries, greeted everyone in attendance, made opening remarks, and introduced Staff Sergeant Samuel Hesch, who was going to perform a solo.

The entire hangar went silent as every attendee listened intently. Staff Sergeant Hesch was in the middle of his performance, singing "Hero for Today," the hangar was quiet, and you could have heard a pin drop. Staff Sergeant Hesch had the audience mesmerized with the meaningful lyrics of the song and his beautiful voice. All of a sudden, leadership got my attention as the Congressman who had requested "talk time" made a commotion and got up to leave. We were seated in the front row, so it was obvious to all that there was movement. Standing up in the middle of the solo, he lifted his white Panama hat off his head and began waving it as he spanned the crowd. I could not believe the disrespect this Congressman showed to everyone present. I escorted him out of the hangar, bid him good day, and returned to the ceremony.

The rest of the event went as scheduled. The joy and look on the faces of the families and Airmen made all the effort worthwhile. The Hometown Heroes Salute ceremony is a significant, meaningful event that continues to recognize our Airmen and families for their contributions and sacrifice.

# CHAPTER 45

# Leaving the Hawaii National Guard

The state level of activity was as hectic as the Wing—just different. As the State SEL, I attended joint initiatives, state-level activities and exercises, meetings and events at the US Pacific Command (PACOM) and Pacific Air Force (PACAF) levels, and national-level activities with the ARNG and ANG.

The breadth and scope of responsibility at the state level, of course, was wider and deeper. At the Wing, the WG CCM had oversight for about 1,800 enlisted Airmen. The State SEL had oversight of all enlisted Soldiers and Airmen assigned to geographically separated units. In Hawaii, the combined enlisted strength was about three thousand Soldiers and Airmen who were spread out in many different locations throughout the entire island chain. Trying to be at as many training exercises, drill weekends, family events, meetings, ceremonies, etc., as possible was a balancing act. No matter the reason for my presence, my favorite times were spent with Soldiers and Airmen just "talking story" and encouraging them to do more and to reach higher.

After being selected as the HING SEL, I knew my time in service was limited. I believed there was no going back. Having been selected for the highest enlisted position in the state, my career would end there. Although I "could" find another position and continue to serve, I believed that would take an opportunity away from someone else. I'd had my time, and it would end as the HI SEL. I was good with that—what more could one ask for? I anticipated serving as the HI SEL for three to five years and retiring around 2012. For nearly twenty years, I had planned to retire from my Guard state and home: Hawaii.

ॐ

In the US Armed Forces, roughly 80 percent of those serving are enlisted. To provide the service chiefs and the Chief of the National Guard Bureau (CNGB) a complete picture of the health of the force of their particular service, each of the active-duty components has a senior-enlisted person who reports directly to their respective service chief, the senior enlisted person for their particular branch. Within the Joint Chiefs of Staff (JCS) and throughout the military, this team of advisors is referred to as the "Senior Enlisted Advisors." Specifically they are, in service seniority, the Sergeant Major of the Army (SMA), the Sergeant Major of the Marine Corps (SMMC), the Master Chief Petty officer of the Navy (MCPON), the Chief Master Sergeant of the Air Force (CMSAF), the National Guard Bureau Senior Enlisted Advisor (NGB SEA), and the Master Chief Petty officer of the Coast Guard (MCPOCG).

Like the active services, the National Guard Bureau (NGB) has a Senior Enlisted Leader (SEL), later designated in 2012 as the Senior Enlisted Advisor (SEA). In 2009, the current NGB SEL's tour was ending, so his position was to be advertised nationwide. The sitting NGB SEL reached out to potential State Command Sergeants Major and Command Chief Master Sergeants to inquire about their interest. I was approached but relayed that I was not interested. I was content being in Hawaii, had always envisioned retiring from the HING, and believed we still had much work to do within the Hawaii enlisted corps. I assured my boss that I was with him to the end.

I had several subsequent conversations with State SEL colleagues about applying, but my answer was always the same: "No thanks. I'm good where I am." Work in DC at the Pentagon and leave Hawaii? I could not even imagine that. There was no way I was leaving paradise!

Truth be told, I did not believe I was fully qualified at the time. Being a Hawaii Guardsman, I doubted I would even be considered. What did I know about the DC area, the beltway, or the NGB at that level? I didn't know any of the key leaders within the NGB organization, and they didn't know me. Based on my perspective, I disqualified myself before even applying—something many of us do all too often. Although I believed that if individuals meet the qualifications, they should apply and let someone in a higher position make the decision; at the time, I did not practice what I believed.

Confident in my decision to stay in Hawaii, we pressed on with the business of the day. The NGB SEL position came open but then closed a short time later without filling it. Some months later, the NGB announced it was reopening the position. Still confident in my decision to not apply, I dismissed it.

During this time, I was in the middle of an online college course. The class assignment was to take a job announcement and write a résumé for that particular job. I used the NGB SEL position description and announcement, wrote a résumé that was a perfect match for the job, and submitted my assignment. As soon as I hit the Send button, I thought, "Dang, I could have done that job." But it had already closed. Time went on, and I learned that the announcement had been pulled for a second time. This stuck in the back of my mind, as I now wondered about the possibilities, yet I was certain that I was supposed to remain in Hawaii, and I assured the TAG I would.

Months passed, and the NGB SEL position was announced for a third time. It was then that I began to think more deeply about applying, and I spent a great deal of time in prayer. After having completed my class assignment and considering the job requirements, as well as my joint Army and Air qualifications, it had become apparent that I truly was qualified for this position. As a State SEL, the sense of obligation to apply and make myself available to the Chief of the National Guard Bureau could no longer be denied. As a qualified

Chief, I had a sense of duty to apply and let General Craig McKinley decide who he wanted to select.

For nearly twenty years, Hawaii had been our home. I had deep ties to the HING and responsibilities to the enlisted corps. Gary had a phenomenal job at KHVH News / Talk Radio, we had many close friends, and were very active in our church. Although there was a nagging itch to apply, I had given my word to the TAG, and I remained committed to the enlisted corps and to the state of Hawaii. During the announcement period, however, I continued to pray about whether to apply or remain in Hawaii. At the time, it wasn't so much a strong calling as it was a sense of obligation to apply, which left me uncertain about what to do. I had always trusted that God would show me the way, yet His path still wasn't clear to me.

During this same time, Major General Lee and I were on a trip to the Philippines, visiting our HIARNG Soldiers who were deployed for six months to Jolo. After the visit and on the plane ride home, I continued to silently pray about whether or not to apply, asking that He show me a sign because I just didn't know what to do. I asked that if He was calling me to apply for the NGB SEL position, He needed to show me, as I trusted His path for me. It was at that very instant I knew I had to apply. It was almost scary as a sense of His presence washed over me, and my path became crystal clear. That inner voice and intuition kicked in, and I felt the calling to make myself available to serve at a higher level at the National Guard Bureau in DC. After returning home, I took a day of leave and sat quietly by myself in our home, continuing to pray and think about this decision.

I had not said anything to Gary or Ashley about my experience on the airplane. That evening, the three of us discussed the opportunity and what it would mean to our family. Gary had an equal voice in the decision for me to apply for the NGB SEL position. He had a career and worked for a great business, was well established, and his clients trusted him. His six-figure salary was clearly a key factor to consider. It was a huge financial decision with a daughter attending college out of state, and admittedly, I was a bit anxious about completely losing his salary. Fortunately, we had made smart financial decisions throughout most of our marriage and were in a position where we could make things work financially.

Although Ashley was away in college, I asked both of them if they could support my decision to apply. We discussed what I envisioned the pace and the schedule to be. Both Gary and Ashley agreed that I should apply and supported my decision. Actually, they had wanted me to apply the first and second times the position was announced. They believed strongly in my abilities and leadership qualities. Most importantly, they understood my devotion to our enlisted corps and believed this was an opportunity for me to continue to serve our country.

The next day, I went in to see my boss. It was an awkward conversation to broach because I'd assured Major General Lee that I would be with him to the end. There was no hesitation—he immediately gave me his full support. Next came the process of gathering the necessary documents to submit for the package. Gary helped me make separate binders for potential board members and mailed them to the NGB. Once the application was submitted, it was in God's hands, and I trusted that whatever happened would be His will. My faith and His calling to leadership were clear. I did my part by putting my name in for consideration and believed strongly that as a Chief and State SEL, it was the right thing to do. Now came the hardest part: the waiting.

Time ticked by, and one day, I was notified that the Chief of the National Guard Bureau was considering me as a candidate for the position. Soon after, I received a telephone interview date and time. The interview was going to be held during an ANG Enlisted Leadership Symposium I would be attending. By now, I had read everything I could about the NGB and refreshed myself on the Joint National Guard Programs. I anticipated questions and developed answers. In preparation, and as I'd done in the past, I made index cards with key points about the Employer Support of the Guard and Reserves, Youth Challenge Academy, Family Readiness Programs, State Partnership Program, and several other topics. I studied, rehearsed, and prepared.

On the day of the interview, which would take place after lunch, I was nervous and anxious. The ANG Enlisted Field Advisory Committee Command Chiefs were having a special luncheon with the Director of the Air National Guard, Lieutenant General Harry "Bud" Wyatt. At the time, I was serving as an alternate on the Enlisted Field Advisory Council and attending the meetings. As we waited for Lieutenant General Wyatt, I stepped onto the balcony to check my voice messages. There was a message from Ms. Carol Lagasse (CNGB's administrative assistant) in General McKinley's office informing me that my interview time slot had been moved up. The interview would take place in five minutes!

With index cards in my bag and my heart pounding, I raced to the elevator as I called Ms. Lagasse to let her know I received the change and was headed to my room. Hurried, anxious, and not having my cards laid out in preparation of the call was nerve-racking, to say the least. I had prepared, rehearsed, and was very methodical about how this interview was going to go—and now chaos ensued. As I approached my hotel door, I could not locate my room key. I dumped out my entire bag on the floor, grabbed my key, and kicked the remaining articles that were in my bag inside my room while simultaneously dialing the number on my Blackberry.

As one can imagine, I was superfrustrated with how this was unfolding, but there was no time to think or change the current circumstances. Once I'd been introduced to General McKinley, I walked back to the door to retrieve my index cards off the floor. Horrified, I realized I'd lost the connection. I quickly redialed the number and was connected to a staff member who didn't know who I was or why I was trying to contact General McKinley.

*You've got to be kidding me*! I thought, frantic.

After reconnecting with General McKinley and the board, the phone interview began. Although I made no further attempts to retrieve my cards, we were once again disconnected after a couple of questions. In a state of panic, I called back a second time and was immediately reconnected to the interview board. After that, I stayed glued to the window for better cell reception.

*Why didn't I call on the landline?* I thought, mentally kicking myself.

The interview continued, and I longingly looked at my index cards and notes that lay just a few steps away from me by the hotel door. *The best-laid plans* was all I could think. I answered every question to the best of my ability, and as quickly as it began, the phone interview ended.

As I hung up the phone, I was flustered and extremely frustrated. *How could this have happened the way it did?* There was no way I would be selected. Not because I didn't answer the questions well, but the entire interview was messy and disjointed. Here was the most important interview of my entire career to date, and I had to run from one floor to another, could not recover my dropped note cards, and lost our connection twice. To me, the organized and perpetual planner, I was not at my best. Frustration turned to anger, and I spent the rest of the afternoon inwardly beating myself up. After that, I pretty much figured it was over, and while extremely disappointed in myself, at the end of the day, I tried to grab on to the silver lining. I still lived in Hawaii, I loved everything about being the state's SEL representing and serving the enlisted corps, and I had an incredibly supportive boss. As I'd told him previously, "There is still a lot of work to do."

After returning from the conference to Hawaii, I got reengaged with the work at hand and enlisted matters. I kept my application for the NGB SEL position fairly private, meaning few people knew about it—or so I thought. It was at a town hall meeting with enlisted members when an Airman asked whether I'd applied for the DC position. Caught off guard by the question and still not believing I'd be selected, I responded, "Yes, I applied, and if selected, I'll be honored to serve in that capacity, representing all National Guard enlisted members."

# CHAPTER 46

# She's Doing What?

During the long wait, I had received an e-mail about a Special Olympics event being held at the Sheraton Waikiki called "Over the Edge Waikiki." This was an event to raise money for Special Olympics. Those who signed up could participate by rappelling—harnessed and connected to ropes—down the side of the thirty-three-story Sheraton Waikiki. Some of our HIARNG Soldiers were participating as volunteers and helping with the event. By now, many of the Soldiers knew me quite well, and we had strong professional working relationships. I had decided not to attend or participate in the Special Olympics event as my schedule was jam-packed. One day out of the blue, I received an e-mail from one of the Soldiers who was in charge of VIP timeslots within the event.

"We have set aside a number of slots for the command staff to participate—unless you're chicken," the e-mail read.

*What? Chicken?* I was being called out by one of my enlisted Soldiers. Needless to say, I cleared the calendar and sent a quick e-mail back:

I'll be there!

That evening at dinner, I told Gary that one of my Soldiers implied I was too chicken to rappel down the side of a building, so

I was determined to do it. Gary stopped chewing and put down his fork.

"Excuse me?" he said, his eyes wide. "You've never rappelled before, and you're going to do your first one from thirty-three stories up?"

"I was called out!" I explained, shrugging.

"Aah," he said, grinning. "Now it makes sense."

Participants were told not to leave any articles or items in our pockets that could potentially fall out. As I left my car, I took nothing with me, including my bag, Blackberry, or my personal cellphone. Before taking the elevator to the rooftop, we signed waivers that outlined all the life-threatening and life-ending scenarios and were briefed on safety and rappel procedures. At the top, as the Soldiers hooked my harnesses and strapped me in, I went over in my mind the technique for letting out the rope a little at a time. As one individual began his descent, and the next was ready to go, I took a moment to look over the edge. Anticipating that I was about to rappel down the side of this building, my heart skipped a beat. It was a mixture of exhilaration and trepidation. However, I was not about to flinch even a little or show any sign of fear or anxiousness. I listened carefully to the final instructions and waited my turn.

My heart leaped with the first step or two over the edge, but then it was sheer elation. Going down at a methodical pace, I was able to take in everything around me. The view rappelling down thirty-three stories of the Sheraton Waikiki was breathtaking. The ocean sparkled like diamonds and the view of Diamond Head was spectacular. Although I'd climbed Diamond Head a multitude of times and stayed in rooms at the Sheraton in the past, the perspective was completely different. It punctuated the beauty of this island on which we'd lived for almost twenty years.

After talking with HIARNG Soldiers, other participants, some of the Special Olympic kids and staff, I headed to my car and planned to get back to work. Sitting in my car in the parking structure of the Sheraton Waikiki, I began to check my voice messages. As the young kids say, my phone had "blown up" with messages from NGB, the HITAG, HIANG Commander, and Gary. I kept repeating, "Oh my gosh, oh my gosh," because I knew what was coming. With my heart racing, I knew this was it. I dialed the number to the Chief of the National Guard Bureau's Office.

General McKinley informed me that he had selected me to be the next NGB SEL and said that I should talk with my family and get back to him with my decision. I told General McKinley that the decision had been made before I applied, and I graciously accepted the position.

I called Gary next and learned that Carol from General McKinley's office had called him earlier looking for me. He had just concluded an early-morning sales meeting with a new advertising client when he got the call. Gary explained to her that I was rappelling down the side of the Sheraton Waikiki. With that, Carol shrieked, "She's doing what?"

I suspect they questioned my sensibility at that point. The rest of the day was a complete whirlwind.

As a side note, Gary's day was crazy too. He had just finalized a fifty-thousand-dollar annual contract for KHVH radio station. After solidifying the deal, he walked in and told his boss, "I have good news and bad news. The good news is I just closed a new annual advertising contract…the bad news is I'm quitting in a month because Denise was just selected for a position at the Pentagon, and we're moving to DC."

Gary had been working for ten years at Clear Channel Communications, KHVH (830 AM) talk radio as an executive account salesman. He was at the top of his career, making a six-figure income and having broken and held all the sales records at Clear Channel. His departure was going to be a significant loss for them. Knowing he was about to lose his top executive salesperson was a huge blow to his boss and the entire company. They would have to do some significant maneuvering to find a replacement for Gary. Ultimately, it would take two people.

# CHAPTER 47

# The Announcement

About six weeks later, I was asked to attend the NGB Joint Senior Leadership Conference (JSLC) in DC in November 2009. Approximately two thousand people attended: adjutant generals, senior officers, and state senior enlisted from the fifty states, three territories, and the District of Columbia. I understood General McKinley would make the announcement of my selection at the conference, so Gary came with me, and we flew Ashley to DC from California, where she was attending her final year of college. It was important to me to have them both at my side.

I had prepared remarks in the event I was called upon to speak, but General McKinley chose to make the announcement from the podium and not have me address the audience. When it was break time, as I was about to leave the table, Staff Sergeant James Greenhill came up with microphone in hand to conduct my first interview.

I was not prepared for an interview and later wished that I had given more polished answers. I really don't remember much else about the day or the conference other than lots of congratulatory handshakes and well wishes. The announcement at the conference really made it official. I had just become the first woman to be selected as the Senior Enlisted Leader to the Chief of the National Guard Bureau.

Upon returning to Hawaii, it was apparent that the news had hit the street. Many congratulatory e-mails and telephone messages awaited me at my office. In my mail, I also found a note from a Hawaii US senator. As I attended various meetings and visited units in the first couple of weeks, I was often greeted by words of congratulations.

Before leaving Hawaii and moving into the position, there was much to be done, including military orders to coordinate our household move from Hawaii to DC over the subsequent three months. We had not done a PCS (permanent change of station) move for nearly twenty years. The process had completely changed during the prior two decades and much had to be done online. Our prior move had been done when Gary was still on active duty, so he'd managed the move. Now I was the one responsible for transitioning back to the mainland. We had to prepare our house for sale and sell a car. Additionally, Gary and I had job transitions to consider, which for me included convening and participating on a selection board for my replacement, interviewing candidates, and doing a handoff to my successor. While still in the position and until my replacement took the reins, certain meetings and programs required my attendance and oversight.

Shortly after my selection, I was fortunate to receive a coveted slot to attend the Keystone course at the National Defense University in Washington, DC. Although I was excited to have received a slot— very few senior enlisted leaders are given the opportunity to attend— the timing could not have been worse. The Keystone course is offered twice a year, and about forty senior enlisted are selected to attend each time. Keystone is a Command Senior Enlisted Leader Course that spans two weeks and encompasses travel to several locations. It is designed for currently serving or slated senior enlisted to serve in a general or flag officer level joint headquarters or Service headquarters as a joint task force. Because of my new position, I was now selected to attend. As I departed for the Keystone course, I looked at Gary and said, "Handoff! You have the ball now."

Keystone was an eye-opening course, which I believed would have been even more beneficial had I been given the opportunity to attend earlier in my career. We heard from many senior leaders learned key concepts related to joint operations and were exposed to joint strategies on a level I had never previously experienced.

General James Mattis was a guest speaker. His leadership philosophy and key points were exactly what SELs at our level needed to hear. I also met key enlisted leaders, including Sergeant Major of the US Army Kenneth Preston, Master Chief Petty Officer of the Coast Guard Michael Leavitt, Command Sergeant Major Mark Ripka, US Joint Forces Command / United States Africa Command and senior Keystone mentor, and Sergeant Major Bryan Battaglia, Senior Enlisted Leader of US Joint Forces Command, who was later selected as the Senior Enlisted Advisor to the Chairman of the Joint Chiefs of Staff. Prior to my departure to Keystone, our house was sold, and during Keystone, Gary packed up the contents of our home. I figured it was only fair that he got to experience a PCS household move himself, as I had managed our prior moves from Illinois to California and California to Hawaii.

Upon returning to Hawaii, it felt odd to walk into our empty home. We loved our little 1,477 square feet of a house in Waikele and had many wonderful memories of our life in our home and neighborhood. It was where our little girl had blossomed into a teenager, graduated high school, and went on to college. It was where her precious dog Riley had passed over the Rainbow Bridge into doggie heaven. We had great neighbors and cul-de-sac cookouts that were nothing short of a blast. But now it was time to start a new chapter and transition to billeting on Hickam AFB for a few days before leaving for Washington, DC.

# CHAPTER 48

# Aloha

The Hawaii National Guard sent me off in grand style by hosting a farewell dinner at the Enlisted Club on Hickam Air Force Base. My good friend Chief Master Sergeant Robert Lee III spearheaded the event with the assistance of an incredible team of Airmen and Soldiers. Once more, the Hawaii Army National Guard Band played prelude music and gave a stellar performance. Having heard them play so many times in years past, it was really special to me to have them there. I was honored by the songs they chose, as each one deeply touched my heart.

Ashley flew in for the event. Many of my Hawaii National Guard *ohana* were there, along with close friends and family. It was quite an evening with gifts of leis that stacked up and nearly covered my eyes. At times, leis had to be removed and placed at my table so more could be presented. As much as I wanted to leave every single lei on to show my love and respect for those who gave them to me, the sheer weight and bulk of them made it necessary to remove some.

There were so many memories that flooded my mind as HING members gave me hugs filled with their aloha. It was a huge honor to have Governor Linda Lingle attend and make memorable remarks. I had watched her for several years and learned a great deal from her words, mannerisms, and how she interacted with the people of Hawaii. That evening, as in the past, she connected with the audience and spoke from her heart. Her words and the way she delivered them resonated with me. Unbeknownst to her, she had been a mentor to me from afar. When asked to speak in subsequent years, I've put into practice all that I observed and learned from her.

There were several other highlights of the evening. Gary had helped the planning committee by gathering photos for a slideshow. I had not seen some of the photos in decades...and perhaps they should have stayed in hiding! For instance, there was one photo from my brother's wedding in the early eighties. There I stood in a high-collared dress with a neck ruffle along with permed hair and poodle bangs.

Another highlight of the evening was a video that members of the HING made. My good friend Chief Master Sergeant Bridget Komine, HIANG (ret.), played me and did a great job. Even my successor, Command Chief Lee, who was most likely the impetus for the movie, was in it. The video was a spoof on some of my idiosyncrasies. It couldn't have been more spot-on! They managed to capture the essence of my personality and the standards I upheld all too well, such as dress and appearance and my personal deportment. There was one especially humorous part in the video where an Airman and Soldier walked by me, and I noticed their dress and appearance violations. I stopped a "G-14 classified conversation" (a made-up term used in the movie *Rush Hour*) to approach and correct the violators as the music from *The Terminator* played in the background. Everyone laughed especially loudly at that scene. Gary acted in the video as well and had managed to keep it a secret, which was difficult for him to do. I knew something was up but had no idea about the extent of their trickery. The video got many laughs.

I was humbled and honored that night when the HIANG leadership presented me with a koa canoe paddle. Koa trees only grow on the Big Island of Hawaii, and Hawaiians cherish all things made from their wood. Brigadier General Stanley Osserman, a master craftsman and friend as well as a superior, made the paddle for me. Previous paddles had only been made for General officers, never an enlisted member. The beautiful koa paddle was a steersman's rudder, the key position in an outrigger canoe that guides or directs the vessel. The steersman keeps the canoe on course and provides direction. Brigadier General Osserman said he chose the steersman position because I was going to the NGB to guide, direct, and steer our

National Guard enlisted corps. Words could not express the emotion and deep meaning of this gift and the many other thoughtful gifts of aloha that I was blessed to receive that evening.

The night ended with my comments in expressing my deep gratitude, appreciation, and the privilege for having been able to serve in the Hawaii National Guard. I had been blessed with many opportunities and was proud to have served alongside the finest National Guard Soldiers and Airmen in the country. I expressed my sincere love and appreciation to Gary and Ashley for their unwavering support and for always standing by my side. As one does at a wedding, I had the opportunity to offer a table favor to each of my Hawaii *ohana*. With the help of Chief Lee and the planning committee, we created a CD of motivating and uplifting songs to give to each person in attendance. After nearly two decades of service in Hawaii, it was a deeply moving and emotional evening—one I will always cherish, as it is forever etched in my heart.

Leaving Hawaii was as difficult for Gary and Ashley as it was for me. Hawaii had been Ashley's home—it was all she'd ever known since we moved to Hawaii when she was two and a half. Ashley was raised in Hawaii and learned that people are people no matter their color, ethnicity, or where they've come from. Hawaii is a melting pot of rich culture and extreme beauty. Although she was away in California to attend college, she'd always known she had a home to come back to. Now that home was sold and we were leaving Hawaii lock, stock, and barrel. Saying the words, "Hawaii will always be your home" felt like empty words to us at the time. There was a gaping hole in all our hearts as we prepared to leave. The next time Ashley would come home, it would be to DC and to a new house.

Departing Hawaii was one of the most difficult things I've ever had to do. While Minnesota is where I was born and raised, Hawaii was where I spent most of my adult life. We were leaving paradise as well as lifelong friends in Hawaii who were *ohana*. I loved nearly everything about the islands, especially the aloha spirit and warmth of the people.

The few things I knew I wouldn't miss were the traffic, congestion, and poi. I knew I would always remember our church community, neighbors, and my Hawaii National Guard family. These were people I had spent the majority of my military career and adult life with, working side by side every day. We shared our work life, setbacks, struggles, and our achievements. So very much of what I became as a professional Airman and leader I owed to them. Leaving them just plain hurt. Hawaii is where I had endless opportunities to learn, grow, and excel. I was proud and grateful to have served in the Hawaii National Guard and will always have a deep and profound respect for my Army and Air Guard *ohana*. Although I was anxious about this new endeavor, I trusted that the Lord would walk the journey with us—He always had.

The night we left, Gary and I took a red-eye flight from Honolulu to DC. Filled with mixed emotions, we were excited about what my new position and living in DC would be like and the new things we were sure to experience. We boarded the plane and got settled. Sitting in a bulkhead row, we faced two United Airlines flight attendants in their jump seats. While we waited on the taxiway, I imagined the air traffic controller clearing us for takeoff and almost hoped there was a delay. I was not ready to leave Hawaii and all that it meant to us.

As the plane began to roll, there were no words. Gary and I grasped each other's hands as if to say, "This is it." We stared out the window and watched the twinkling lights of Oahu become smaller and more distant. With tears rolling down our faces, we kept our eyes fixed on the island until we could no longer see its outline or the lights. The pain was real, and we were not ashamed to sit there and cry like newborn babies. The ache in our hearts was gut-wrenching.

No doubt the flight attendants were wondering what was going on and why we were crying. As the tears subsided, we felt the need to explain our behavior to them. Their words reflected that they understood how difficult it was to leave one of the most beautiful places on earth.

This was one of those moments that will remain in my mind and heart forever. I often think of that flight and am immediately filled with the aloha spirit, remembering our cherished friends, the countless experiences, and a lifetime of memories. Hawaii will forever be home.

Ashley, eighth-grade graduation, St. Elizabeth, 2002

The 154th Wing Commander, Colonel Peter Pawling,
pins new Wing Command Chief, 2004

USMC Ball, Waikiki, Hawaii, 2005

New State Command Chief, December 2006

Hall family in California, 2005

Visiting Airmen at Al Udeid Air Base, Qatar / Operation Gift Lift, 2007

On Saddam Hussein throne, Iraq, 2009

Uday and Qusay Hussein homes, Iraq, 2009

In Waikele with Riley the Wonder Dog, Christmas, 2009

Flying with the HITAG, MG Robert Lee, 2007

Chief's Jelinski-Hall, Lee, and Rafael, Change of Responsibility, 2010

Cutting the farewell cake, 2010

# Part Four

## The Pentagon Years

# CHAPTER 49

# Washington, DC

We arrived in Washington, DC, on February 18, 2010. Although I had previously visited our nation's capital, I found myself in awe as we drove around that first weekend. In Hawaii, I only traveled on a couple of major roads; DC had four major freeways. I called it "navigating the 95s": I-95, I-295, I-395, and I-495. Initially, driving anywhere was overwhelming, and I worried that I'd get myself lost.

Navigating the halls of the Pentagon was similarly daunting. The enormity of the five-sided building was intimidating, and I wondered how I'd ever find my way around.

By the middle of March, we had moved into a home on Andrews AFB. We had a court full of fantastic neighbors, including the Chief Master Sergeant of the Air Force, James Roy, and his wife, Paula. Jim and I had been colleagues in Hawaii when he was the US Pacific Command (PACOM) Senior Enlisted Leader and I was the Hawaii SEL. I was looking forward to working together again as well as becoming closer friends.

From the very beginning, everyone welcomed us to the neighborhood and included us in social gatherings, rotating from home to home. Everyone watched out for each other, whether it was a snake in someone's yard or a plumbing issue. Throughout the three years we lived there, Gary and I enjoyed the comradery and sense of community.

As Key Spouses, Gary and Paula Roy worked closely together on family initiatives. They also attended various meetings, conferences, and events, including meetings at the White House for Joining Forces with the First and Second Ladies. As the only male spouse, Gary was typically the only man in the room—which was just fine with him.

⸮

The Chief of the National Guard Bureau (CNGB), General McKinley, hosted a welcome-aboard ceremony for me in the Pentagon. My good friend Chief Roy was there, along with Sergeant Major of the Army (SMA) Kenneth Preston and many friends. Just before General McKinley and I were about to enter, members of the Hawaii Air National Guard walked in with leis in their hands. I hadn't expected any representation from the HING and was deeply touched by their presence.

I'll never forget walking into my office for the first time: except for a desk and chair, computer, and a binder, it was empty. It wasn't located in the Pentagon, but in JP1, an office building in Crystal City, Virginia, that housed many Army and Air NGB personnel.

Having come from an island state as far from the beltway as you could possibly get, the question was, "Where to start?" One of the first things I did was walk the halls, meet everyone I could, and introduce myself. I decided to go floor by floor and meet the Soldiers and Airmen who worked in JP1. When I stopped at one particular section, a female Master Sergeant asked where I was from. When I told her I was from Little Falls, Minnesota, she asked if I had worked in the local bank. It took me just a second to recognize her, and then I exclaimed, "Joyce!"

Master Sergeant Joyce Hanson was the Soldier who had said to me, "I see so much more potential in you than this. Why don't you join the Air Force and get out of this town?" She had driven me to the Air Force Recruiter's office, and she had changed my life. Now, almost twenty-six years later, we reconnected in Washington, DC, as

Airmen serving in the National Guard. I owed her so much for seeing something in me, encouraging me, and believing in me.

⟋⟍

With no playbook or continuity handoff, I did what any senior enlisted leader would do—I figured it out. I started by meeting with key staff members, received briefings from them, and then I began to network within my circle. In early March, my office was moved from JP1 to the Pentagon so I could be in closer proximity to my boss. Walking into that imposing, historic building, I reflected on the many important military strategies and decisions that had been developed there. The history that lined the halls and told the story of our nation, including pictures of significant leaders, was nothing short of magnificent. Then I had another thought, *How will I ever learn my way around this building?*

The Pentagon is virtually a city in itself. Approximately twenty-three thousand employees, both military and civilian, and about three thousand nondefense support personnel contribute to the planning and execution of the defense of our country. These people arrive daily from Washington, DC, and its suburbs, over approximately thirty miles of access highways, including express bus lanes and one of the newest subway systems in our country. They ride past two hundred acres of lawn to park approximately 8,770 cars in sixteen parking lots, and climb 131 stairways or ride nineteen escalators to reach offices that occupy 3,705,793 square feet. They tell time by 4,200 clocks, drink from 691 water fountains, use 284 restrooms, and consume 4,500 cups of coffee, 1,700 pints of milk, and 6,800 soft drinks served by a restaurant staff of 230 and dispensed in one dining room, two cafeterias, six indoor snack bars, and one outdoor snack bar.

Thankfully, I had an executive assistant who escorted me to my office on the first day and explained how to get around the building.

"If you get lost, go to the 'A' Ring in the center of the building and follow the windows," she said. That one small piece of advice saved me many times.

On the first day as we walked around, my eyes were as big as saucers as I tried to take in everything. I was overwhelmed with the mammoth size of the building and the sheer number of people walking in the corridors. I was surprised to note how many walked with their heads down, seemingly oblivious to the great privilege of working there.

*I will never be one of those people,* I thought to myself. *It's an honor to work in the Pentagon!*

I began greeting anyone who approached me with their head down. I'm sure many were surprised when I said hello, but no matter what they thought, I intended to acknowledge them and make them look up. How could anyone take working there for granted? Many people grumbled about working in this five-sided building, but not me. It was almost unbelievable that I had the privilege of working in this historic building with our nation's finest military and civilian leaders. Every time I entered or exited the Pentagon, that feeling of awe was present.

❧

Walking in and out of my new office every day kept me grounded and reminded me where I had come from. Outside the former CNGB's office on the "A" Ring of the second floor hangs a display of the Hawaiian Islands that shows the devastation and destruction on Kauai after Hurricane Iniki. I'd had the privilege of deploying to the island the day after the hurricane struck and was proud to have served my state in its aftermath. Now, in the Pentagon, I got to pass by the display many times throughout the day and feel the aloha spirit and warmth of the Hawaiian people.

# CHAPTER 50

# My Team

When I came on board as the Senior Enlisted Leader, my team consisted of an Army National Guard Executive Assistant (ARNG E-8) and an Air National Guard Executive Assistant position (ANG E-7). I had an ARNG executive assistant when I arrived, but the ANG executive assistant position was vacant. Quickly, the vacant Air Guard position was advertised nationwide throughout the entire ANG.

One of the best and most important decisions I made early on was to hire the Air Guard Executive Assistant, Master Sergeant Jason Hisaw. Through his exemplary work ethic, superb attention to detail, and integrity, Master Sergeant Hisaw soon became someone I relied on implicitly. Whether he was getting me to and from meetings or something more complex, like managing my demanding travel schedule, I was confident I would show up at the right place, at the right time, and on the right day. Master Sergeant Hisaw always took that extra step to ensure that everything ran smoothly. For instance, when I had a meeting in another part of the Pentagon, he would do a dry run to identify the most direct route.

Master Sergeant Hisaw was among the select few over the course of my career in whom I felt comfortable confiding, knowing that anything we discussed would be held in complete confidence. He was an extremely valuable member of the team and always provided the utmost candor and objectivity, consistently taking into account what was best for the organization. Throughout his tenure of service, he truly was the glue that kept the office and me together. Master Sergeant Hisaw had been in the DC area for some time, knew his way around, knew many of the key staff, and was extremely resourceful. I greatly appreciated his loyalty and dedication.

He saw me at my best and worst and handled each situation with great finesse, dignity, and grace. One of "the worst" occurred while we were on a trip back from Maxwell-Gunter AFB, and I was sick as a dog. I slept on and off during the ride to the Atlanta Airport and threw up before the flight. Master Sergeant Hisaw made sure I got on board the plane and home safely.

I was saddened to lose Master Sergeant Hisaw when he left for a phenomenal civilian job and a position in the Florida Air National Guard, but I was extremely happy for him. He left the Pentagon with my deep appreciation and profound respect. It was no surprise to me that those sentiments were echoed by everyone who knew him.

During Master Sergeant Hisaw's tenure, I submitted an administrative package to upgrade the ANG Executive Assistant position to an E-8/SMSgt, equivalent to the ARNG position. It was important to me to resolve the disparity in the pay grade between the Army and Air, as I believed the positions needed to be equal. Ultimately, the position was upgraded.

When he departed, I was fortunate to have Master Sergeant Bryan Rotherham, ARNG, and Senior Master Sergeant Darren Burnett, ANG, assigned as my executive assistants. Together they made a phenomenal team. Both were extremely professional and dedicated, and they represented the office in a highly dignified manner. We got the work done, but we also enjoyed strong and cohesive friendly relationships.

⌇

The role of an executive assistant is crucial and can elevate or discredit an office or the principal in that position. I was privileged to work with a number of outstanding executive assistants in the Pentagon, but I found that it was not easy to identify the right person to serve at such a high level of responsibility. The position of executive assistant was extremely demanding. Working in a structure as immense and complex as the Pentagon often made the assistants' duties even more challenging. Not only did they keep the office running, maintain my daily and travel schedules, and get me to and from meetings and events, they also fielded calls, answered the mail, accompanied me on travel, and often worked long hours to meet the mission requirements. At this high level, they needed to be resourceful, take initiative, have high standards of personal deportment, be highly organized, and be able to interact with senior enlisted and senior officers, including four-star generals, and senior civilian personnel. One day, the Secretary of Defense appeared in my office unannounced, and I was not there. Thankfully, my executive assistants were prepared to represent me.

Early in my tenure at the Pentagon, however, many scheduling errors occurred. For instance, on one occasion, I missed a meeting with the Chief Master Sergeant of the Air Force. On another occasion, I showed up for an appointment on the wrong day. The worst mistake happened when I had instructed my executive assistant to accept an invitation from the Governor of Hawaii to speak at the International Women's Leadership Conference. After not hearing from the governor's office, I made a phone call to her executive to confirm the day I would speak, and I was informed that my office had not responded. I was mortified.

Embarrassing errors like these reflected poorly on me, my office, and the National Guard as a whole. Although I understood that mistakes happen, it's imperative that senior leaders have confidence in their executive assistants to ensure important details don't fall through the cracks. Regardless of how long the various executive assistants served on my team, however, I deeply appreciated the contributions and service of each one. Their efforts and commitment to the job and how they represented my office and the Chief of the National Guard Bureau were a reflection of the entire National Guard.

# CHAPTER 51

# The Best-Laid Plans

I learned early on that things don't always go as planned. One of my most embarrassing moments happened within weeks of arriving at the Pentagon. Gary and I had just moved from billeting on Joint Base Anacostia-Bolling to our quarters on Joint Base (JB) Andrews. General McKinley was flying to North Dakota to assess the spring flooding—which was not uncommon for the state—and the North Dakota National Guard's response, and he asked me to accompany him. I was wearing my preferred service uniform (blues) that day but needed to be in the Airman's Battle Uniform (ABUs).

A Colonel who was driving to JB Andrews offered to take me home so I could change my uniform. I called Gary and asked him to get my ABU uniform, jacket, and boots out for me since I would need to change quickly. All my uniforms were in a separate closet so they would be easy to find. To my surprise, Gary called me right back.

"There are *no* ABUs in the closet!" he said. "Your boots and jacket are there with your blues, but that's it."

"What?" I responded, a little anxious. "They have to be there. Can you look again? Maybe I put them in another closet."

The colonel and I pulled into the driveway, and I ran in to change. Gary hadn't found the ABUs, so I frantically ran from closet to closet and pulled drawers open. Just as Gary had told me, there were no ABUs. With my head lowered in shame, I e-mailed General

McKinley and explained the situation. I was humiliated and mortified to tell the boss I couldn't accompany him on our first scheduled
trip together. Not a great first impression!

It turned out I had left my uniforms hanging behind the bathroom door in billeting since closet space was tight. From that day
forward, I kept extra ABUs, blues, a service dress uniform, hats, and
boots in my office. I was never in that embarrassing situation again!

# CHAPTER 52

# The Joint Chiefs of Staff

The chief of the National Guard Bureau is a four-star General Officer and can be selected from either the Army or Air National Guard. In November 2008, General McKinley became the first four-star general to lead the National Guard. The CNGB position had previously been filled by a three-star Lieutenant General, but legislation in 2008 elevated the job to a full general's billet. The CNGB was not yet a full voting member of the Joint Chiefs of Staff, however, when the National Guard Bureau Senior Enlisted Leader (NGB SEL) position was announced in 2009.[11]

The Joint Chiefs of Staff (JCS) are the senior General officers (four stars) of each service branch: the Chief of Staff of the Army, the Commandant of the Marine Corps, the Chief of Naval Operations, and the Chief of Staff of the Air Force. The Chairman And Vice Chairman of the Joint Chiefs lead the JCS. The Chairman reports directly to the Secretary of Defense, who reports directly to the Commander in Chief, the President of the United States.

The members of the JCS represent the most powerful military men in the world. At the time, I became the Senior Enlisted Leader, the CNGB was an "invited member" to the JCS but not a full voting member. The Commandant of the Coast Guard—which is part of the Department of Homeland Security and not part of the Department of Defense (DOD)—was in the same position. Both could present information, discuss strategies, procedures, policies, and provide counsel and guidance, but neither had a vote on the final decisions made within the JCS.

These dynamics changed in December 2012 when the National Defense Authorization Act (NDAA) was signed into law. The act made the Chief of the National Guard Bureau a full voting member of the Joint Chiefs of Staff on equal footing with all the service chiefs. This was the first change to the makeup of the JCS since 1986 when the Commandant of the Marine Corps became a full voting member.

Although the National Guard ultimately received enough support from Congress to pass the bill, five of the service chiefs had testified at a Senate hearing that it was unnecessary for the CNGB to be a full voting member. The only chief advocating for full membership was my boss, General McKinley.

The service chiefs for the US Army and the US Air Force fully understand the Title-10 federal policies and provide guidance to all components (Active, Guard, and Reserve). On homeland missions (Title-32), however, no one is better versed to discuss these matters than the CNGB. The National Guard is the only military component that has a dual federal and state mission. When federalized, Guard units fall under the same chain of command as active duty and reserve forces, ultimately answering to the president of the United States. For the state mission in peacetime, the National Guard falls under the jurisdiction of the governor for each respective state or territory. Each state and territory has an Adjutant General (TAG). The District of Columbia has a Commanding General appointed by the president of the United States. The fifty states, three territories, and the District of Columbia are commonly referred to within the National Guard as "the 54."

The 450,000-plus men and women that made up the National Guard in 2010 represented one of the largest components within the US military. In the early years of Operation Iraqi Freedom (Iraq War) and Operation Enduring Freedom (Afghanistan War), tens of thousands of National Guard members deployed to combat zones. Thousands of others were on active duty in their home states supporting the war efforts in logistical, administrative, and financial matters. For all these reasons and more, it was appropriate and necessary for the CNGB to be on equal footing with the other service chiefs in the JCS.

In the US Armed Forces, roughly 80 percent of those serving are enlisted. To provide the service chiefs and the CNGB a complete picture of the health of the force of their particular service, a senior enlisted person reports directly to their respective service chief for each of the active-duty components. Once the CNGB became a full member of the JCS in 2012, I was invited to attend their meetings. Even though the National Guard Bureau Senior Enlisted Leader was not yet officially recognized as part of the JCS SEA group, the other Senior Enlisted Advisors welcomed me into their fold. I was able to bring the voice and perspective of the National Guard, particularly as it pertained to our traditional enlisted Guard members and the state missions of the 54. Overall, my participation offered an increased awareness of enlisted issues at the highest level of government.

# CHAPTER 53

# Joining the SEA Team

About a year and a half after I began working in the Pentagon, General Martin Dempsey became the Chairman of the Joint Chiefs of Staff (CJCS). His first official act as CJCS was to select and name a Senior Enlisted Advisor to the Chairman (SEAC). This was significant because the previous chairman did not have a SEAC, which was unsettling to the enlisted corps, particularly the senior enlisted. General Dempsey saw the importance of having an SEAC to provide him with critical feedback from our enlisted members of the Armed Forces.

Sergeant Major Bryan Battaglia, a Marine, was chosen as the SEAC. He was a consummate professional and highly respected. Sergeant Major Battaglia embraced my office, viewing it as equal to the other services' senior enlisted Advisors. During the early days of his tenure, I scheduled an office meeting with him. What struck me most that day as I approached his office was the location and proximity to the Chairman of the Joint Chiefs of Staff. As I stood feet away from the office of the CJCS and in the office of the SEAC, I felt humbled to think about where my journey had taken me, once again wondering, *How did this happen?*

At the time, the most significant difference between the other services' senior enlisted and my position was that the NGB SEL was not listed on the Department of Defense Order of Precedence list. This document determines the order of precedence for seating arrangements at official functions, assignment of government quarters, and so on. The senior enlisted advisors for the other five services were on the list, but the National Guard SEL was not. This caused some consternation at certain events, and initially, it was an issue for my staff to have me included and seated with the other SEAs. Even after the CNGB became a full voting member of the JCS, my position was still not recognized because it had not been included in the original legislation. Before anything could change, a representative had to introduce a bill in the House, a House committee had to approve it, the House had to pass it by a majority vote, then the process had to be repeated in the Senate, and finally, the president had to sign it into law. Once that happened, my position would be authorized within the National Defense Authorization Act. This process would not happen for quite some time.

Although not on the protocol and precedence lists, I was fortunate that early on, the SEAC and the other SEAs recognized that the NGB SEL position brought a different perspective and was an integral part of the overall team. They involved my office and included me in meetings, events, and important enlisted discussions.

As much as I appreciated the inclusivity, there were still differences in how our offices were staffed. For example, when I was asked to speak at conferences and various other events, I did not have a speechwriter as the other SEAs did. I spent nearly all my free time or flight time writing the next speech, as I typically did not use the same material twice. Most of my speeches had their own themes, and my comments reflected the nature of the event and audience. This was the most difficult part of the job for me, as I spent countless hours preparing those speeches. It was important to me that the words and intent be carefully selected, edited, and reworked again and again. For that reason, I often spent a full day researching and writing a twenty- to thirty-minute speech.

Impromptu speaking was never an issue. Getting in front of Soldiers and Airmen in the field or in their offices was no problem, as the focus was on them and the key senior NGB leadership messages were the talking points. Yet the words for formal speeches did not come as easily. I had to internalize what I wanted to say and the message I wanted to deliver so that it came across as authentic and relatable to the audience. I envied General McKinley and other leaders who were able to get up in front of a microphone, face an audience, and speak without a written speech. I, on the other hand, prepared and practiced every word, even going so far as to annotate in the written speech where to include appropriate hand gestures as well as voice inflections. By delivery time, I knew my speech almost verbatim, as I had practiced it in front of a mirror countless times.

During peak travel, I typically spent the few weekend days I had at home in front of the computer writing the next speech. As I wrote and spoke more often, I learned one of my strengths was speaking from the heart about what I had learned and experienced. It was always my firm intention to not only teach and motivate those in the audience but to leave them with a "life lesson" they could someday apply to their personal and/or their professional journey. Many times, this included examples of mistakes I had made and how I'd recovered and learned from them.

Most leaders will tell you they learn much more from their mistakes than their successes. I hoped that being open and honest would allow my listeners to relate better to the messages I wanted to convey. I also believed it was important to use appropriate quotes from world-renowned leaders. I spent many hours reading leadership quotes from people like Sir Winston Churchill, John F. Kennedy, Abraham Lincoln, Dr. Martin Luther King, Eleanor Roosevelt, General Douglas McArthur, General George Patton, Doctor John C. Maxwell, and many, many others.

My favorite quote, popularly attributed to Winston Churchill, urges each of us to find our reason for being, to identify our gifts and talents, and to put them to the best use possible. I have shared this quote frequently to inspire others; it has most definitely been a cornerstone of my life's work:

> To each there comes in their lifetime a special moment when they are figuratively tapped on the shoulder and offered the chance to do a very special thing, unique to them and fitted to their talents. What a tragedy if that moment finds them unprepared or unqualified for that which could have been their finest hour. (Unknown)[12]

Early on, I realized that humor was not one of my strengths. Some people can pull it off and others can't. I fell into the latter category. For example, I prepared a "Top 10 List" PowerPoint presentation with funny photos and accompanying sounds for my first speech at the Enlisted Association of the National Guard of the United States (EANGUS) conference. It bombed. Initially, the sound didn't work. The pictures were there, but the accompanying soundtrack didn't come through. That's a real problem when you're trying to be funny. I quickly moved on to my prepared remarks and never again attempted humor.

# CHAPTER 54

# People First

Most Air National Guardsmen and Noncommissioned Officers (NCOs) from across the nation complete their professional military education at the Training and Education Center (TEC) for their Airman Leadership School (ALS) or Noncommissioned Officer Academy (NCOA). It was always an honor to be asked to speak at the Air National Guard, I. G. Brown Training and Education Center (TEC) graduations. The graduates are the future of the USAF, ANG, AFR, and our country. To spend time with them, engage in conversation, and share a few words of wisdom gave me great pride, and knowing that my message had the ability to shape and influence their future decisions gave me a sense of purpose. It was always encouraging to see the professional and outstanding Airmen who would return back to their states and do great things for our country. There was a strong sense that the Air Guard was in good hands with these up-and-coming young leaders.

One time, I was the guest speaker for an NCOA graduation in Knoxville, Tennessee. As the flights lined up to be recognized on stage, I took note of one particular female NCO. She looked like she was carrying the weight of the world on her shoulders. Her head remained down, and a look of despair was on her face. What should have been one of the happiest days of her ANG career appeared to be one of significant and deep duress. Something was definitely wrong. I made a mental note to find her after the graduation.

In a crowd of hundreds of Airmen all dressed alike and a roomful of guests, the odds were not in my favor of finding this Airman. I believe it was through divine intervention that she happened to walk by me. I excused myself from the conversation with other Airmen and approached her, introduced myself, and went out on a limb to explain what I had observed. Most Airmen are not going to open up to a Chief, let alone a Chief who is a stranger and happens to be the NGB SEL, but she did. That morning, her ex-husband had called and said he was taking their daughter and filing for sole custody. Clearly upset and overwhelmed, the Airman didn't know who in her state she could contact for assistance. I got her cell number and name and told her I would contact her State Command Chief. I also spoke with her flight leader at the TEC so he could check in with her before she left for home.

Later that week, I followed up with Staff Sergeant Winner to make sure she was okay. Her State Command Chief had coordinated with her Wing Command Chief and First Sergeant, who connected her with the Wing Family Readiness Program manager and the Director of Psychological Health. They assisted her with resources to deal with the legal and psychological situations.

It deeply troubled me that no one else had approached her when Staff Sergeant Winner was clearly not okay. This served to reinforce one of my core beliefs, which I have stated many times over the years to make a particular leadership point:

"You must always be engaged with people—this means all service members and civilians in your charge, or with whom you come in contact, because you never know what is going on in their lives or in their minds. Make eye contact, notice body language, ask questions, and ask and ask again."

A few years later, I saw Staff Sergeant Winner in Washington, DC. I had retired and was serving as a Board of Trustee for United Through Reading (UTR). I was attending an event called "Tribute to Military Families" (TMF) at the Andrew Mellon Auditorium. Staff Sergeant Winner saw my name listed and decided to attend the event for the ANG. In a happy coincidence, she was seated at my table. She had volunteered to attend the TMF so she could tell me how her life had changed. She wore a bright, big smile and said she now had custody of her daughter, a new job, and had been promoted to Technical Sergeant. She looked and sounded confident and happy. It was such a blessing to see how she had changed and how strong and resilient she had become.

About a year and a half later, Gary and I were delighted to visit with Technical Sergeant Winner at the National Guard Gala in Washington, DC. Her life and career were both still continuing on the right path, and she was clearly happy. At the next UTR Tribute to Military Families, she brought her daughter to meet me. I was deeply touched by her gesture and the opportunity to see them together.

I asked Technical Sergeant Winner if I could share her story. To my surprise, she not only agreed but wrote the following letter chronicling her experiences. I'm including it here only to show how a leader can make a huge difference by simply reaching out and showing compassion.

> It is with great pleasure I write to you and offer my sincerest gratitude for your thoughtful and kind actions. The impact of your kind words and compassion has made me a more resilient Airman and a stronger woman both professionally and personally.
>
> I first met you in 2011. I was graduating from the NCO Academy at McGee Tyson in early February. To backfill, I just finalized a divorce agreement that took nearly eighteen months due to custody conflicts. The timing for the NCO Academy could not have come at a worse time, but with my mind fearful of my future and taking on new challenges, I left for training right after the winter holiday. Mentally, I felt prepared for the training. Emotionally, I was scattered, not stable, just not myself. My confidence was low, and participation and interaction with others was gradual. I encountered sleepless nights worrying

about home. I was devastated but tried to stay focused on training.

Come graduation day, I was filled with anxiety as I anticipated the challenges to come. So there I was…receiving my certificate with my NCO classmates. As the ceremony finished up, family members, unit leadership walked around congratulating their Airmen and loved ones. I didn't have anyone there, but I wasn't alone in that respect. I was just about ready to depart the building as you approached me. You grasped both my hands and congratulated me, introduced yourself, and said you watched me walk up with my class and receive my graduation certificate. You saw within me something that concerned you (and you continued), "I want you to know that whatever it is that you are going through right now, I am here for you. I will be your wingman, and we will get through this."

The irony of that moment is that I couldn't immediately tell you my response other than the tears that filled my eyes then and fill them now.

I drove home to Pennsylvania, ten hours, thinking about what you said, wondering how in the world you could see in my expression the challenge and despair in my life at that time. Our paths crossed at a very specific and critical time in my life. Your compassion gave me strength and the drive to get back to my civilian life and take on the challenges to come. Your actions are a proven example of a wingman and have provided me with a true model of professionalism to live by.

In many ways, our encounter was a turning point for me. Sometimes all it takes is someone telling you exactly how they see it, knowing that they believe in you and hearing someone else say we will get through this...because for some time, I was contemplating, "Will I get through this?"

Time passes, challenges come and are resolved, and opportunities arise. I find myself on a tour at the Air Guard Readiness Center, attending workshops, seminars, ceremonies, and Galas. Really a proud moment for me...not only to see you at my first gala but to be seated at your table. I am overwhelmed with emotion. To see you is such a pleasure, an honor. And it would be some time before I would see you again, but I do. If I'm not merely at the same place at the right time, you're reaching out to me through a call or e-mail.

You wouldn't know this in passing, but you seem to pop up at my highs and lows. We met at what I felt at the time was my all-time low. We would meet again at points in my life where I had some accomplishments to be truly proud of, and just recently when you reached out through e-mail, I was going through some tough times. In my mind, I refer to you as my guardian angel. When I'm overly stressed, I try my best to seek out friends, some type of support. But life gets in the way, and before I know it, I'm on the verge of crumbling. A couple weeks ago, when I got your e-mail, it came to me as a reminder, a reminder that someone cares and that I can get through this.

Ma'am, you've instilled within me the hope and desire to be strong and provide others strength when they are faced with challenges, be it embarking on a new journey or facing a hurdle to the finish line. I have been told on several occasions that I am silent but strong, and what takes one person twenty words takes me five. I am reliable, professional, and dedicated. There is a leader within me. I know that now.

I am forever grateful to have met you. To share this small piece of gratitude is an honor. In the simplest of phrases that could possibly capture the magnitude of your kind gestures, you saved my life.

My sincerest gratitude,
TSgt Patty Winner

I was elated to see the mother and leader she had become, and I was humbled by her gratitude and kind words. Everything we're taught as Airmen and leaders about the importance of caring for our people was evident through her story. As I write this, Technical Sergeant Winner has once again reached out to invite me to attend her promotion ceremony to Master Sergeant.

The motto "People First" signifies the importance of taking care of each other. It's the responsibility of every service member and civilian to reach out and ask the tough or uncomfortable questions. We never know how our interaction and concern will help someone—maybe even save their life.

# CHAPTER 55

# On the Road

Like many senior leaders, I had the opportunity to travel extensively domestically and internationally. It was one of my greatest joys to visit National Guard Soldiers and Airmen who were either deployed or serving in their home state. As the top senior enlisted leader of the National Guard for the entire United States, it was my goal to carry the priorities, key messages, and gratitude from the Chief of the National Guard Bureau to the field. It was important to me that I represent the Chief and my office with great dignity and respect for the enlisted corps.

I made a point of visiting locations where many senior leaders tended not to visit, such as Duluth, Minnesota, in January, or North Dakota in March, or New York during a snowstorm. I wasn't trying to make travel painful or punish the staff; it was just important to show support to all National Guard enlisted men and women, regardless of location or weather.

On one trip to Landstuhl, Germany, I accompanied the Chief of Chaplains for the National Guard to visit wounded warriors. Chaplain John Ellington prepared us for what we would perhaps see and experience while visiting our Guardsmen in the intensive care unit. I felt prepared after my experience with my brother and having spent time visiting wounded service members in Hawaii at the Tripler Army Medical Center. Gary, Ashley, and I had visited wounded service members regularly, especially around Thanksgiving, Christmas, Fourth of July, and Veterans Day.

Our first day in Germany, my executive assistant and I were off to our first meeting when I slipped on the ice and slush. I rolled my ankle and fell hard on the ground, and the pain was severe. To make matters worse, I fell close to the security guard gate and in full sight of many personnel. I ended up in the ER for X-rays and pain meds, and I hobbled on with the day.

The next morning, I painfully put on my boots, sucked it up, and did what needed to be done. I visited one Soldier who had just been wheeled into his room after undergoing hours-long surgery. He was still unconscious, and his family surrounded him. Every part of his body was bandaged, except for his head, and lacerations covered his face. For me, it brought back traumatic memories of my brother, but I knew I couldn't think of myself—the soldier's family needed hope and comfort. The chaplain and I prayed with them and did our best to console them. Having gone through a similar experience, I understood the importance of having someone put an arm around your shoulders. As I reached out and held this Soldier's wife, she cried in my arms, and my heart ached for her.

That evening, my ankle and foot were black and blue, severely swollen, and painful, but I forced on a dress shoe for dinner. The wounded warriors we'd visited were in significantly more pain, had more severe injuries, and would have gladly traded places with me. A high ankle sprain was *absolutely insignificant* compared to the sacrifice and injuries our service members suffered.

# CHAPTER 56

# Israel And Egypt

One of the most interesting trips from both a professional and personal perspective was the trip I took with General McKinley to Israel and Egypt, an area rich with ancient history. Religious conflicts have defined this land for thousands of years, and it's one of the most dangerous areas in the world today. I had read about the Middle East, heard discussions on the news, and received briefings about the ongoing conflict, but I'd never traveled there.

I was elated to have the opportunity to travel to this region, yet I did have some concerns about safety. For instance, I understood that it would be best to not venture out alone. As long as I traveled with the CNGB and our team, we would all be relatively safe.

Thankfully, members of the CNGB's team prepped us on customs, courtesies, and various meetings and events. First, we flew to Tel Aviv, where senior Israeli military leaders had invited General McKinley to observe an exercise that included their military, hospitals, fire, police, and other departments that would be involved in a large-scale crisis.

Walking through the hospital and the surrounding area, it looked much like exercises in America where the National Guard and first responders come together and simulate their response to a large-scale domestic crisis. Patients on gurneys were dressed in simulated injuries with "blood" on them, many crying out as if they were seriously injured. It was a very realistic exercise, and the doctors, nurses, police, firefighters, and other first responders worked quickly and professionally as if it were all real. It was obvious that everyone involved took terrorist attacks and their responsibilities seriously. Numerous journalists documented the event, and several news organizations swarmed General McKinley, getting a quick interview.

Staying in Tel Aviv was an eye-opening experience. The hotel was on the water with a beautiful sandy beach, and the Mediterranean Sea was breathtaking. Being the only woman in the group, I opted not to go for a run alone but enjoyed the view from my hotel balcony. The water, sand, and warm breeze took me back to Hawaii.

Our Israeli hosts gave us a tour of an "up-armored elementary school." This may have been one of the most culturally shocking visits I have experienced. As we drove to the school, we took in the countryside, and it was unnerving to see hardened bunkers in nearly every yard. The area was just a few miles from the Gaza Strip or mere minutes from the launch of a Qassam rocket to impact. I could not imagine living with the fear that a missile attack could occur at any time.

As we toured the school grounds, I noted more outdoor bunkers in the schoolyard. Our hosts told us that the children knew they had nine seconds to run to a bunker if they heard a siren. The interior ceiling and walls of the bunkers were brightly painted, and artificial grass carpeted the ground, making the bunkers feel homier. This way of life was normal to the children—they didn't know any differently. We visited a classroom and learned that teachers and children routinely practiced getting under their desks to seek cover even though the school was reinforced to withstand missile attacks. As we stood in front of the classroom, I saw a little girl to my right sitting alone, an empty seat beside her. She locked eyes with me, and I smiled at her and gave a little wave of my hand. She placed her hand on the empty chair and patted it as if to say, "Come sit down." I placed my hand to my chest as if to ask, "Me?" She nodded, and I sat down beside her.

After a moment, I reached into my pocket and gave her one of my challenge coins. The girl beamed as she held the coin. She reached into her backpack, pulled out a book, and flipped to a page that showed a gift box wrapped with a bow. She pointed to the coin and then to the wrapped box and then to herself, as if asking, "Is this a present for me?" I nodded my head and smiled. I asked the interpreter to translate my words and explain to her that I had given the coin as a sign of friendship, and the little girl was radiant with smiles as she clutched it. We exchanged no words, but we were able to communicate through facial expressions, hand gestures, and a simple book.

That little girl put a face on the conditions the Israeli people face daily. I think about her often. Her living environment is not one that any little child or adult should have to endure, constantly in fear, but it's all they know—that's their life.

We left the school, and our driver took us to a small hill. We climbed to the top, and the driver pointed at the horizon.

"Look," he said, "that is the Gaza Strip."

We were about a mile from one of the most hostile and deadly areas in the Middle East. That is where the missiles would most likely be launched, the ones that would trigger the sirens to alert the children we had just visited. This area is what they live in fear of on a daily basis. So many times on that trip, I thought to myself how fortunate and blessed I am to be an American and live in a free country where our children can grow up and not live in constant fear. That little girl's face seems to haunt me when I least expect it, and I often wonder how her life turned out.

One day, we hired a tour guide and drove to the Holy City, Jerusalem. As we entered the Old City, the ancient walled section of Jerusalem, we stood and looked across the Kidron Valley at the Mount of Olives. Inside the Old City, we walked to the Christian Quarter and into the Church of the Holy Sepulcher. I reached my hand down into the hole where many believe the cross of Jesus Christ stood on the day he was crucified. As a Catholic, this was a surreal moment, and I felt the presence of the Holy Spirit. Being in the Holy City and walking on the grounds where our Lord and Savior walked was almost incomprehensible.

Stepping inside Joseph of Arimathea's tomb was haunting and brought a sobering sense of where I was standing, knowing he had been responsible for ensuring the proper burial of Jesus. We stood on the outside the Edicule, the structure that preserves the location of Christ's tomb, but the line was simply too long to get inside. Still, being in the presence of Christ's tomb was deeply spiritual and profoundly moving. Equally so was the Church of the Dome, also known as the Dome of the Rock, a sacred shine to both Muslims and Jews, built in the late seventh century. This is where the prophet Muhammad is believed to have ascended into heaven and where Abraham is believed to have prepared to sacrifice his son, Isaac.

I purchased some items made from olive wood—small statues of the Holy Family, praying hands, and a Bible—and placed them on a stone slab where Jesus was laid after He was taken down from the cross. It was peaceful and deeply moving to have these quiet moments alone, and I felt as though I were in His presence. The smell from the slab of stone was of perfumed oils, and it made me think about what happened to Jesus in this sacred area. The entire experience was one of the most profoundly moving religious and emotional moments of my life.

The second such experience occurred when we went to the Western Wall, or Wailing Wall. The wall is the only remaining part of the Second Temple, the center of Jewish religious life, destroyed by the Romans in AD 70. It is called the "Wailing Wall" because of the Jewish people who wept and wailed at the wall after the destruction of the temple. I placed my hand on the wall and could almost feel the pain of so many who came to pray here. It is traditional for people who make a pilgrimage to the wall to place pieces of paper that contain petitions and prayers in the many cracks in the wall. I, too, wrote a petition, placed it in a crack, and said prayers to our Lord. This was another spiritually moving moment for me.

The entire visit to the Holy Land deeply affected me. Here I was on a military visit, representing my country and performing military duties on a tour meant as a history lesson of the region. I had not expected to have a spiritual experience that took me to the roots of my faith. I hope to one day go back as part of a pilgrimage and spend several days walking in the footsteps of Jesus Christ.

We next flew to Egypt for a series of meetings with government and military officials. On one of our free evenings, a few of us hired a tour guide to take us to the Pyramids and the Sphinx. When we parked the vehicle and opened the door, a crowd of local people immediately swarmed us, trying to peddle their wares. It was a little scary for me, as it was not customary in that area for a woman to walk around uncovered. Wearing a sleeveless top and capris, with no head cover, I stood out like a sore thumb in the small group of Americans. I grabbed the arm of one of the guys and said, "You're my husband for the evening."

It was too late in the day to tour the pyramids, so our guide took us to the top of a building to watch the sunset behind the pyramids. It was a sight to behold, and I could not believe what I was witnessing. The pyramids and the Sphinx are magnificent in size and structure. I still have a hard time believing that as I stood there, I was gazing upon statues that were built more than 4,500 years ago.

# CHAPTER 57

# National Guard High Points

One of the most rewarding initiatives that my office and I undertook was developing a video highlighting the enlisted corps, filmed exclusively by enlisted men and women. The video depicted enlisted National Guard Soldiers and Airmen from across the nation who served in various military occupation specialties. We also honored National Guard families for their contributions and sacrifices. In a special section, we paid tribute to our fallen National Guard heroes with Arlington National Cemetery as the backdrop.

I was proud of this video, as it was all about our enlisted men and women, their contributions, and what they bring to the fight. It was important to me to show the National Guard enlisted corps that they are just as important as the officer corps and senior leaders. Our National Guard story—beginning with the volunteer militia in 1636—rests squarely on the backbone of the enlisted corps. Officers and senior leaders provide the guidance on a strategic level and are "in the tactical fight" every day. Their bravery and professionalism are above reproach, and they lead our National Guard team. Our enlisted corps, however, comprises about 80 percent of our National Guard, and our success, deployed or at home, falls on their shoulders. Our enlisted corps is where "the rubber meets the road," and our Senior Noncommissioned Officer Corps (SNCO) provides the key small-unit leadership component every day.

Based on their education levels, responsibilities, and decades of past legendary successes, the SNCO corps today would have been the officer corps in decades past. We do a better job today highlighting the enlisted corps, but videos in past years primarily showcased the officer corps. My office represented the enlisted side, and because of what our enlisted Soldiers and Airmen do every day and the valuable military and invaluable, often-overlooked civilian skills they bring to the fight, it was important to me that we highlight the enlisted contributions, sacrifices, and skill sets.

We showcased the video at the Enlisted Association of the National Guard of the United States annual conference (EANGUS), where it truly bolstered morale among the enlisted corps. Once the video was circulated, many organizations showed it at state conferences and within their respective units. Additionally, it was shown at various venues at the national level. The feedback from adjutants general, commanders, and other senior leaders confirmed how important it was to highlight the Soldiers and Airmen of the National Guard and what they contribute.

Another National Guard initiative I'm very proud of was the National Guard Diversity Program. At the time, a few states were shining examples of diversity in action while the majority of states only met minimum diversity requirements. Seeing the need and recognizing the gaps in the current diversity program, General McKinley dedicated considerable resources and time to developing a strong diversity program within the National Guard throughout the 54. He believed the National Guard needed to lead this initiative from the highest level. At the direction of the CNGB, we established a Joint Diversity Executive Council (JDEC) to develop and guide diversity initiatives for the National Guard. The diverse council included Soldiers and Airmen, adjutants general, officers, and enlisted from across the country.

As the NGB SEL, I served as cochair of the Council and committee chair for the Strategic Communications committee. We developed program guidance, a sample charter, products, and training aides to assist the 54 in developing their respective programs. The CNGB and JDEC members gave video recordings, live streamed updates, and a Leader's Guide to all Soldiers and Airmen. This guide explained the meaning of diversity and highlighted each individual's role to promote it. It was interesting to hear and learn what people believed diversity was. Many people still had the outdated notion that diversity was merely about race and gender; in fact, it includes diversity of thought, inclusion, opportunities, and so much more.

As I traveled across the country talking about the diversity program, I engaged with Guard members and carried the message forward that "together we are stronger"—that our individual strengths, experiences, beliefs, background, and diversity of thought represent the strength of the National Guard. All Guardsmen needed to look at the picture of top leadership and see themselves somewhere in that picture. For far too long, the leadership picture looked the same. Intending no disrespect to middle-aged White men, that is what the top leadership picture looked like for decades. Broadening that select group was long overdue.

While the JDEC developed and provided all tools necessary to implement and execute the updated diversity program, it was up to each of the fifty-four adjutants general to roll out and place priority on the program. Because this had been a focus area and initiative at the CNGB level, most states understood the importance of implementing or improving this program.

We have made huge strides and progress in this area and today see a significantly more diverse picture. More women and ethnicities have leadership positions now than ever before. People from across the entire country bring in their perspectives, beliefs, and experiences. Diversity is all about the inclusion of everyone, so all may have equal opportunities to advance and succeed. It is about providing the opportunities for everyone to grow and be heard. In this way, we expand the talent pool, acquire a larger and more inclusive perspective, and ensure that more qualified people are trained and ready to serve in a variety of positions. Air Force Colonel Ondra Berry of the Nevada Air National Guard stated it succinctly: "Strength through diversity comes from strong leadership and increasing opportunities." As a diversity team, we did a lot to introduce initiatives that made the National Guard program stronger.

On October 16, 2012, the Association of Diversity Councils recognized the National Guard Bureau's Joint Diversity Executive Council as one of the top twenty-five diversity councils in the country. The JDEC placed fourteenth for outstanding contributions and achievement that led organizational diversity processes. In October 2013, the JDEC was once again recognized as one of the country's twenty-five best diversity councils and moved from fourteenth place to seventh.

$$\backsim$$

"What's one of your keys to success?" a female veteran asked me once.

"Communication," I responded immediately. That was easy.

"How did you communicate as the NGB SEA?" she followed up.

I gave her a few examples. Most leaders state up front that they have an open-door policy, where people can stop in their office or make an appointment to meet at almost any time. I, too, had this policy. If I was in my office, I took great pride in answering my own phone rather than having my calls go through an executive assistant. It was also important to reach out to State Senior Enlisted Leaders, Command Sergeants Major, and Command Chiefs. During my tenure, there was no way I could get to every state, but it was important to reach out by telephone and check in with the state's top enlisted and listen to their concerns.

The Army National Guard has a council called the Command Sergeants Major Advisory Council, and the Air Guard has a parallel council called the Enlisted Field Advisory Council. Both councils address enlisted concerns on a national level. I attended several of these meetings and relayed the CNGB's priorities and brought back information to him. Senior leaders also communicate via email and conferences.

I had many opportunities to address large groups of National Guard members and carry messages related to top priorities and areas of special emphasis. The CNGB's top priority was always "the mission first"—state and federal, which encompassed the training and readiness of the force, including medical and dental readiness. Areas of special emphasis included suicide awareness and prevention (eyes-on leadership to know our people, as well as the resources available to help them); reducing (with the goal of eliminating) sexual harassment and sexual assault ("see something, say something" education and awareness); ethics (ensuring we are living our core values and making sound decisions); and resources available to our Guard members (such as the Director of Psychological Health, Military OneSource, financial managers, civilian higher education, civilian organizations that donate time to the military, and the First and Second Ladies' Joining Forces).

〜

At the national level, the ARNG and the ANG had well-defined recognition programs for their Soldiers and Airmen of the year. For the ARNG, this consisted of bringing their regional winners to the National Capital Region (NCR) where they attended events, toured the nation's capital, went to Capitol Hill, and met with ARNG senior officers and enlisted leadership. Their visits and events culminated in the Soldier of the Year (SOY) banquet, where the national winners were announced. The National Guard winners, the Soldier, and NCO of the year then went on to compete nationally at the US Army level.

The ANG's process consisted of selecting the Airman, NCO, SNCO, First Sergeant, Honor Guard member, and Honor Guard manager of the year from the fifty-four states and territories, and the DC award winners. The selection was done through the submission of individual packages, after which a board convened to select the national level Airmen of the Year (AOY). The AOY winners were also brought to the NCR and attended similar events, including an AOY luncheon and receptions at the Director of the ANG and ANG Command Chief's homes. The national AOY winners also went on to compete at the Air Force level.

In conversation with General McKinley, he and I discussed having a joint week where the Soldiers and Airmen came to the National Capital Region at the same time. The respective ARNG and ANG would have individual recognition events, but overall, the intent was to combine the SOY and AOY winners whenever possible. Combining resources was less taxing on senior leadership, protocol, and support personnel, and it saved money.

Although the ARNG and ANG did a phenomenal job recognizing its award winners, I was excited about the possibility of the joint week and believed that the National Guard as a whole needed to highlight and promote our SOY and AOY winners on a bigger scale. I also thought it was important to host a combined enlisted dinner and short ceremony at our home on JB Andrews for the SOY and AOY recipients. We had amazing support from the CNGB's enlisted aide, protocol, public affairs, and other offices. Having the CNGB spend time with our nation's best-of-the-best was the highlight of the evening. For me, it was also very special having my brother Jeff and wife, Barb, in attendance as well. Coming from my same rural background, they had never experienced anything like this event, and it was a pleasure for me to see the smiles on their faces.

The next year, we kept a similar format with combined joint events wherever possible. Because it was a long week for the SOY and AOY recipients, I wanted them to come to our house and relax for an evening. I decided a luau would be the perfect way to get people to unwind. The dress was "island casual": shorts, T-shirts, and sandals. We decorated the yard with beach-themed items, brought in sand and a beach umbrella for souvenir photos, had seashells and Hawaiian decorations on the tables, and even had dozens of pictures of Hawaiian fish on the garage door. Everyone in attendance received a lei, and we served Hawaiian food and drinks.

We held the culminating awards banquet in a beautiful hotel banquet room. We were fortunate to once again have the Old Guard Fife and Drum perform, as well as the Air Force Strolling Strings. Both performances were amazing. As I watched the SOY and AOY recipients, their families and guests, it seemed they were in awe of the display of military pageantry at its finest. It was an honor to have as our guests Chief of Staff of the US Air Force General Mark Welsh and Chief Master Sergeant of the Air Force James Roy. At the end of the banquet, we honored General McKinley with a gift from the enlisted corps in recognition of his decades of service, as his retirement was planned to take place that fall.

The next year, the SOY and AOY events were postponed due to the Budget Control Act. I fought the good fight on how important it was to continue recognizing our best people on a national level although I understood we might have to scale down on events or shorten the time in the NCR. I had several conversations with the CNGB and staff but in the end lost out to optics and funding.

Although I understood the financial crisis that sequestration brought to our military and country, this was disheartening. I still believed it was important to recognize our warriors who go above and beyond, compete, and distinguish themselves as winners on a national level. After two successful years of SOY/AOY joint recognition, it was disappointing to let it go and see it shelved for the immediate future.

# CHAPTER 58

# Change of Responsibility

During his tenure as CNGB, General McKinley's theme was "The National Guard—Adding Value to America." Whether testifying on the Hill or speaking to military and civilian leaders and National Guard members, he consistently recognized and gave examples of how National Guard members brought value to America and communities all across the country.

I can still clearly remember the day he called to tell me he'd selected me to be his Senior Enlisted Leader. His tone was matter of fact and his words direct. I soon came to know General McKinley as a decisive, strong leader who had a deep love of country. He was an effective communicator and a dynamic orator. He was able to get up in front of an audience with a few points listed on a note card and talk eloquently for a long period. He had a larger-than-life, charismatic personality and spoke in a strong, authoritative voice. He could speak extemporaneously, which made me want to be a better speaker. He was articulate and persuasive.

I worked for General McKinley from February 2010 until September 2012. After four decades of serving his country, he was ready to retire. During the change of responsibility ceremony, the Secretary of Defense recognized General McKinley's outstanding contributions. General McKinley was highly respected; the president of the United States, Secretary of Defense, and other top military and civilian leaders sought out his sound guidance on National Guard and other highly sensitive military matters. Mrs. Cheryl McKinley, the General's wife, was also recognized for her tireless support of National Guard families.

General McKinley had given me a great deal of autonomy to run my office. We had traveled together visiting National Guard Soldiers and Airmen and had collaborated on key initiatives. I was eternally thankful for the opportunity that he had given me as his SEL.

The Twenty-Seventh CNGB Army General Frank J. Grass became my new boss. I knew General Grass had started out as an enlisted Soldier, but I didn't know much else. Over the following weeks, I came to learn more about his stellar career and how he became a four-star General and our Chief. The more I got to know him, the more I was able to see his professional and easygoing nature that enabled Guard members to relate and respond to him with ease.

We also had a new first lady of the National Guard, Mrs. Patricia Grass. She was caring, sweet, and as down to earth as they come. I held her in high esteem. Being an active first lady of the National Guard, Mrs. Grass attended numerous events and ceremonies. Together, the Grasses were now leading 450,000 plus Soldiers, Airmen, and their families, and I was proud to be part of their team.

General Grass kept me through the end of my tour and changed my title from NGB Senior Enlisted Leader to NGB Senior Enlisted Advisor. Through collaboration with the SEAC and the service SEAs, we decided that my position should be reclassified as a SEA rather than a SEL so that all senior enlisted positions that supported members of the JCS were in parity. In addition to the change in title, my role expanded under General Grass's leadership. While I continued to have complete autonomy to run my office, I took on a more active role within the CNGB's office and consulted with the CNGB, vice CNGB, and senior staff members on a wide array of issues. His leadership style sent a clear message to the staff on how he saw his SEA.

One subtle but significant example took place at his very first staff meeting. General Grass moved my seat at the table from the opposite end to his immediate left. Whenever we traveled, held local town hall meetings, or spoke to Soldiers and Airmen stateside or at deployed locations, he always asked me to say a few words after he spoke. I felt like we made a synergistic, dynamic team, and we shared a united front.

# CHAPTER 59

# Domestic Operations

The vast majority of responders to domestic natural disasters throughout the 54 are members of the National Guard. When civilians see uniformed military members responding to floods or snowstorms or a chemical spill, they often don't realize that the Soldiers and Airmen are National Guard members rather than active-duty service members. During 9/11, some of the first military people on the scene were members of the New York National Guard. The same was true of the Boston Marathon bombings in 2013. The reason National Guard members respond to domestic catastrophes is because the Guard is responsible for the homeland mission.

One of the ways General Grass wanted his office portrayed was that we were a command team, which provided me with new opportunities to see the great work our Soldiers and Airmen were doing across the country and overseas. Hurricane Sandy was a prime example of our working relationship.

Hurricane Sandy was the eighteenth named tropical cyclone of the 2012 Atlantic hurricane season (June 1 to November 30). Sandy formed in the central Caribbean on October 22 and intensified into a hurricane as it tracked north across Jamaica, eastern Cuba, and the Bahamas. The hurricane moved northeast of the United States until turning west toward the mid-Atlantic coast on the twenty-eighth, then transitioned into a post-tropical cyclone just prior to moving onshore near Atlantic City, New Jersey. Sandy's track resulted in a worst-case scenario for storm surge for coastal regions from New Jersey north to Connecticut, including New York City and Long Island. Unfortunately, the storm surge occurred near high tide along the Atlantic Coast, contributing to record tide levels.

Approximately seven thousand citizen Soldiers and Airmen were mobilized in eleven states to respond to Hurricane Sandy. National Guard assistance to local first responders and the Federal Emergency Management Agency (FEMA) included support at evacuation shelters, route clearance, search and rescue, and delivery of essential equipment and supplies, providing food, water, presence patrols, transportation, house-to-house wellness checks on Staten Island, and running pumps and generators. The bulk of the Guard members— more than four thousand—were focused on the two worst-hit states, New Jersey and New York.

General Grass asked me to accompany him as he conducted a damage-assessment survey from a National Guard UH-60 Black Hawk helicopter over New Jersey, New York City, and surrounding areas. We saw houses off their foundations, piles of soaked possessions, and sand-covered roadways from shore to shore of narrow barrier islands. We flew over an area where many homes had burned to the ground. The devastation was vast, and as evening fell, only flashing police lights were visible.

Seeing areas hit by a hurricane from the air gives you a completely different perspective from viewing a disaster on television. Instead of looking at clips of a very small area, I saw the complete carnage all around, and my heart ached for the families affected by this devastation. Seeing the debris, the foundations where homes once stood, the demolishment of steel structures, and the sheer magnitude of destruction left me in awe at the power and force of Mother Nature. Yet at the same time, watching the work our National Guard members were doing to help relieve the suffering filled me with a great sense of pride. Some members worked eighteen-hour shifts during those initial days.

As amazing as their efforts were, however, it truly was nothing new. No matter what domestic operation or crisis happens on the homeland, National Guard members are ready to respond and help any way they can. More often than not, the Guard responds even before a governor calls them up.

Even in the midst of such devastation and destruction, it was a privilege to accompany General Grass. We thanked every Soldier and Airman we could—sometimes all we could do was shake a hand, pat someone on the back, or simply say thank you. I fully understood the sacrifice they were making, and I knew that many of them were putting their own families second. Some of the Guard members who answered the call had suffered devastation in their own homes and neighborhoods, yet here they were, helping their fellow citizens in any way they could.

As we flew to the heart of New York City, we passed by Lady Liberty standing in the harbor. I have reflected on her and what she means to our country many times, and I have often spoken of being proud to be an American and how privileged I am to live in this great nation. The Statue of Liberty not only represents freedom for those coming to our shores but also opportunity for all her inhabitants. I was awestruck and humbled to pass by her in such close proximity.

Major General Patrick Murphy, the New York National Guard TAG, met us when we landed. Flooding was everywhere. General Grass and Major General Murphy discussed how they were going to get water out of subway tunnels and off roads. Many had lost homes and were without food, water, and electricity. Major General Murphy spoke proudly of the Soldiers and Airmen who had trained for combat and, without a moment's hesitation, now served in domestic operations, working tirelessly in security, logistics distribution, and with law enforcement and their local partners.

We headed back to Washington, DC, flew past the Washington Monument and Lincoln Memorial, and landed on the Pentagon helipad—a first for me. I found myself thinking, once again, *How did I end up here*? For a farm girl from Minnesota, having the privilege of accompanying the Chief of the National Guard Bureau to witness our Soldiers and Airman respond to a disaster with all hands on deck, it was a humbling day indeed.

# CHAPTER 60

# The Hardest and Best of Times

In 2013, during an interview at the Women in Service Memorial at Arlington National Cemetery, someone asked me, "What was the hardest thing you dealt with as the National Guard Bureau SEA?"

Unequivocally, it was the all-too-frequent messages that announced the loss of a National Guard Soldier or Airman to suicide. Learning of these tragedies left me feeling hollow and helpless. I didn't know these men and women, but I felt their loss profoundly and could imagine how it would affect their comrades, parents, spouses, and children. It was hard to understand how troubled, ill, or depressed someone had to be to take their life. Although we know it is not possible to prevent every suicide, leaders at every level in the National Guard do all they can to prevent them from occurring.

During my time as the NGB SEA, I had a gut-wrenching personal experience with suicide. Ashley had befriended a Wounded Warrior at a concert, and one weekend, he drove to Maryland to visit Ashley. Because he had nowhere to stay, we invited him to stay with us. When I learned he was not an active-duty Soldier but in fact a Guardsman, I explained to Ashley that in the future, he could not stay with us. It would not be appropriate because of my position as the NGB SEA. She fully understood.

Always one to help someone in need, Ashley believed she was an anchor for this Soldier. Their relationship was strictly platonic, but he came to rely on her when he needed to talk, as he was having a hard time with his past wartime experiences. When Ashley confided in me that he had talked about suicide, I was alarmed. As a Guardsman leader, I spoke with him on the phone about available resources and assistance.

One night, Ashley woke me up.

"Mom!" she whispered urgently. "He's threatening to kill himself! What do I do?"

The Soldier had been out drinking and had texted her. Immediately, I contacted the local authorities in his area. He lived in a fraternity on a college campus, so I contacted the school authorities, then his State Joint Operations Center. I personally knew his State Senior Enlisted Leader / Command Sergeant Major, so I called his phone and left a message. During this time, the police officers located the Soldier and decided he was not a threat to himself.

Morning came, and I spoke with his State Senior Enlisted Leader. We went through the entire chain of events, and I emphasized that this Soldier was crying out for help and was in crisis. Sometime later, the Command Sergeant Major called and said he had spoken with the Soldier and all appeared to be well, but he had asked the First Sergeant and Chaplain to contact him at his school.

During the next Unit Training Assembly / Drill weekend, the Soldier received Suicide Awareness Training and spoke with his Sergeant Major, First Sergeant, Chaplain, and Commander. He received all the assistance available to him.

The following weekend, Gary, Ashley, and I were on a trip when we received the devastating news that the Soldier had shot himself. At the funeral, standing next to Ashley as her mom, but in my uniform as the NGB SEL, was one of the hardest things I've ever had to do. Trying to keep it together emotionally as an Airman and being strong for Ashley was almost impossible. I was on the verge of tears throughout the entire service, hurting deeply for Ashley and for the Soldier's family and friends. After the funeral service, we had a long conversation with the Soldier's parents, and they thanked us for trying to help their son.

Looking back on that experience still troubles me today, both as a Guardsman leader and as Ashley's mother. Could we have done more? Did this Solider get all the help he needed? Did he have a battle buddy checking up on him? Could I have saved him if I had engaged earlier? These questions continue to trouble me.

After this experience, I had a face for the suicide crisis in the military. From that point on, whenever I read the ongoing suicide e-mail notifications, they took on an even deeper meaning. I understood how far-reaching the pain of loss was to family, friends, colleagues, and any others who tried to help.

When I spoke to our enlisted corps all over the country, I often used this experience to reinforce the importance of looking out for each other. It's not just a leader's responsibility to know their people, but it's also a duty we *all* have to each other, whether we're peers, subordinates, superiors, or in another organization. As I explained to many audiences, we need to know our people and look into their eyes. Most likely, we will be able to see if something isn't right. We often think it's not our business to ask about a person's relationships, finances, or family life, yet by asking deeper questions around such topics, we may save someone's life. If we feel something is wrong, we need to trust our gut, ask the uncomfortable questions, and be there in any way we can. As one of this Soldier's favorite bands suggested in a hit song, one friend can save a life.

ॐ

Another of the hardest things I faced was the effect of the ongoing Iraq and Afghanistan Wars. The toll it took on our service members, families, friends, and America has been a huge price to pay. We can never truly measure how many fives the war affected.

As a senior leader, I believed it was important for me to connect with those who served and returned from both wars, particularly because most of these men and women were enlisted members. Their branch of service didn't matter—I still felt a connection to them. I wanted the opportunity to visit, hear their stories, and show my gratitude and appreciation for all they gave to our country. It was an honor to visit wounded warriors in hospitals and other facilities. None of them wanted pity, yet one could not help but think how their lives had permanently changed.

I could not have ever imagined that my brother's accident decades earlier would one day help me through visits with wounded warriors. Each time I entered a facility—-Tripler Army Medical Center (Honolulu, Hawaii), Landstuhl Regional Medical Center (Germany), Walter Reed National Military Medical Center (Bethesda, Maryland), and San Antonio Medical Military Center (Fort Sam Houston, Texas), were just a few—I mentally went back to seeing Jeff in the hospital. I remembered watching him lying in traction, his wounds wrapped, going in and out of consciousness. Remembering how careful our family had to be to keep Jeff calm, I mentally prepared myself for what I might see and to be fully present for our wounded warriors and their families. Sometimes just putting an arm on a spouse's shoulder or taking their hand offered them the compassion and comfort they needed in such difficult circumstances.

I'm sure we got more out of those visits than the wounded did. Although many were fighting for their lives and on the road to a very long recovery, the men and women we visited were awe-inspiring. It was apparent they were working extremely hard on their recovery, and their battle buddies and families were there to encourage them every step along the journey. Without exception, every service member just wanted to get well, recover, and rejoin their unit.

Service members with missing limbs, head wounds, burns, and other injuries repeatedly taught me a valuable lesson: no matter what happens to a person's body, the human spirit can endure. Watching how hard these wounded warriors worked to recover, strengthen themselves, and move forward was inspirational. Their continual positive attitude and desire to just "get back in the fight" touched me deeply. I went on these visits intending to encourage our wounded warriors and see how I could help, but they were the ones who lifted me. The courage of these service members and their families gave me a new perspective: no matter what I was dealing with, it paled in comparison to their challenges.

By the time we left a hospital or recovery unit, we were the ones lifted by the fighting spirit of our United States service members and their families. It will always be one of my highest honors to have visited with and witnessed the dedication and bravery of those who serve our country. America can never repay the debt owed to our military men and women.

ꝥ

While there are other "hardest things" I encountered as a senior enlisted, one of the most disheartening was the lack of proper and immediate care for our veterans. When I met with them, they often shared stories of not being properly cared for, and occasionally, a veteran would contact my office because they could not get the care they needed. I fully understand there are requirements or criteria that have to be met to receive care from the VA, but it was hard to listen to these veterans' stories after knowing how honorably they had served their country.

One example was an eighty-five-year-old man who served in the Korean War. He was extremely hard of hearing, but his doctor at the VA told him he could not receive hearing aids due to a lack of service medical documentation. Medical records in the 1950s may not have been as detailed as they are now, but you don't need a report to know that a mechanic and infantryman in a combat zone, without hearing protection, was exposed to continuous loud noises and explosions. I wrote to his local VA on this veteran's behalf, and he was able to get a disability rating for hearing.

I ache, knowing there are thousands of veterans who do not have someone to personally take up their cause. Veterans often don't know how to access resources, or they don't live near VA facilities. As a result, they don't get the help they need and have earned. They either become completely lost and unknown to the system, homeless, or seek assistance through costly civilian channels.

I know President Abraham Lincoln intended for America to take the very best care of her veterans. On the front of the Department of Veterans Affairs headquarters in Washington, DC, two metal plaques bear these words from his second inaugural address:

> To care for him who shall have borne the battle
> and for his widow and his orphan.

President Lincoln affirmed our government's obligation to our veterans in this address near the end of the Civil War. I can only pray that we as a nation do all we can to help those who have given so much for our freedom.

❧

During the same interview at the Women's Memorial, the question that followed "What was the hardest thing?" was "What was the best thing you ever experienced as the NGB SEA?" Without question, the "very best" thing was working and spending time with the Soldiers and Airmen of the National Guard and their families. These are my brothers and sisters, and there is nothing I wouldn't do for them, then or now. These men and women volunteer to serve their country and their state in over three thousand zip codes across our nation, protecting the homeland and defending our liberties abroad.

National Guard members have earned many distinguished awards for bravery and heroism in combat. One such American hero, Staff Sergeant Leigh Ann Hester, Kentucky Army National Guard, became the first female soldier since World War II to be awarded the Silver Star for valor in combat. Staff Sergeant Hester was one of the women featured in the movie *Unsung Heroes*. The enemy ambush during the supply convoy she was shadowing was caught on tape and included in the documentary. Other heroes, Specialist Alek Skarlatos, Oregon Army National Guard, with the assistance of Airman First Class Spencer Stone, United States Air Force, and Mr. Anthony Sadler, helped thwart a terrorist attack in France on a train while on vacation.

The reason Guardsmen do this is simple: to help people in need. They don't wait for a governor to initiate a state call-up or activation. They simply respond and do what must be done, which is what they're trained to do. I was blessed to meet and see National Guard Soldiers and Airmen across the nation and overseas doing what they do best. As their motto states, they are *Always Ready, Always There!*

# CHAPTER 61

# Is There a Doctor in the House?

One year, a veteran asked me to speak at the Veterans Day dinner celebration at Chantilly High School in Virginia. This event was special to me because it honored our veterans, but it also gave me the opportunity to influence young high school students.

While the veteran who invited me had overall responsibility for the event, the students made all the decorations, sent invitations, prepared and served the meal, and performed musical numbers. An honor student served as emcee, and other students greeted and escorted guests. They even cleaned up after the dinner.

The veterans in attendance were primarily the parents and grandparents of the students, and their years of service spanned from World War II to the present day. In preparation for my speech, I did much research on significant events from World War II, the Korean War, the Vietnam War, Operation Enduring Freedom (OEF), Operation Iraqi Freedom (OIF), Operation New Dawn (OND), and Operation Noble Eagle (ONE). It was important to honor each era of veterans and highlight the incredible bravery and sacrifice these men and women made for our country. I wanted the veterans to understand that I knew they had paved the way for my generation to serve and follow in their footsteps. I wanted to honor the men and women of America's "Greatest Generation," those who had fought in the "Forgotten War" in Korea as my father had done, the Vietnam veterans who came home to a divided country and had never received the recognition they so richly deserved, and our current veterans, America's new generation of heroes.

The night of the dinner, I arrived early so I could visit with the staff and students and be present as guests arrived. Gary and I met many of our nation's heroes, and we found it deeply humbling to speak with them personally. Listening to these warriors tell their stories of service and combat, seeing the pride in their eyes and smiles on their faces, showed us how proud they still were to have served our country.

One sassy and jovial WWII veteran took a shine to me and told Gary he'd better take good care of me, or he would step in. It was fun joking back and forth with him. I hugged him earnestly and thanked him for his service to our country. This veteran was a legend, a "Flying Tiger" who had flown with one of the most storied aviation units of WWII in the Pacific Theater. Flying Tigers were pilots from the US Army Air Corps, Navy, and Marine Corps who flew with the First American Volunteer Group (AVG) of the Chinese Air Force in 1941–1942. Their combat record against the Japanese in the skies over Burma and China was unmatched. They were recruited under presidential authority and commanded by Colonel Claire Lee Chennault.

I began my remarks, and the words flowed with ease as I spoke of my passion for veterans, their service, and what this day meant to our country. In some small way, I also felt like I was honoring my father for his service.

The room was silent, and I felt like I had the attention of everyone in attendance. In the middle of my comments, though, the veteran who organized the event interrupted me.

"Excuse me," he said, taking the microphone, "is there a doctor in the house?"

Given the age of some of the attendees, I was worried it could be quite serious. Someone with medical experience went to the aid of an elderly woman in distress, and an ambulance arrived within minutes. Paramedics attended to her, then quickly took her to a hospital.

Now it was time for me to regroup and try to regain the attention of the audience. I felt it most appropriate to offer a short prayer for the woman, so I asked the audience to join me in a prayer and a moment of silence, and then I picked up where I had left off. Afterward, many stayed to talk to us and take pictures. I was deeply touched by their gratitude for my comments when I was the one grateful for *them*.

On the drive home, I reflected on the significance of the event. I had never paused a speech for a medical emergency before, but that's not what had made the evening so unforgettable. I had gone to the dinner to give—to honor veterans and their families and to inspire students to fight for their goals—but I was the one who received. I thought about all the work the students had done to put this incredible evening together for the veterans, most of whom served decades before the students were born, and the service they gladly provided to the elderly and the compassion for the woman in distress. I thought about those heroes sharing their stories of historic deeds of service and sacrifice and how much they touched my heart. And I thought of how young and old veterans had come to honor each other. All this left me profoundly humbled.

Paraphrasing Dr. John Maxwell, significance comes when you take your success and give back to help others. The Bible teaches us that what we give will be returned to us "tenfold." My mind bounced from event to event, and I reflected on how much I had been blessed by meeting so many incredible people throughout my career who had unknowingly inspired me to be the best I could in service to our country. I will never forget that night—a convergence of past, present, and future.

# CHAPTER 62

# White House Events

During my tenure at the Pentagon, I attended many events at the White House and on the Hill with the members of the JCS and their SEAs. It was always an honor to be invited to the White House; it never became commonplace. There were times I had to pinch myself when I was sitting alongside our most senior military and civilian leaders.

Gary and I were able to visit and tour "The People's House" several times, and it was humbling to learn some of our nation's history through the paintings, artifacts, statues, documents, and other historic memorabilia. They gave me a more profound appreciation of what went on within those walls. To think how many of our nation's leaders and dignitaries walked the same halls and sat in the same rooms we did gave me chills.

On some visits, White House docents explained the historic significance of the items on display. As a woman, I was inspired to learn that many of what we viewed would not have been there if not for President Madison's wife, Dolly. During the War of 1812, as the British were burning most of the buildings in our capital, it was Dolly Madison who saw to it that many items were spirited away and spared when the British set fire to the White House and the US Capitol.

Two of my favorite annual White House events took place on Memorial Day and Veterans Day. For these events, the day began with breakfast at the White House for the Joint Chiefs of Staff, their SEAs, spouses, and other dignitaries. During these events, the stories I heard from Gold Star Mothers, veterans' spouses, and veterans themselves at White House events were sometimes difficult to listen to but made me feel honored to share a few moments with those who had suffered the consequences of war and service to our country.

My first White House event was on Memorial Day 2010. President Obama happened to be traveling, so Vice President Joe Biden hosted the event. We were seated for breakfast with members of various military veterans service organizations, Gold Star Mothers, and military and civilian leaders. An aide explained that Vice President Biden would be coming to each table for a photo opportunity, and we were to stand for the photo and then take our seats.

It just so happened that I was the first one in the line of people at our table as the vice president approached. With one hand cocked in his left pocket, he sauntered up to me, stuck out his right hand, and said, "How ya doin', Sarge?"

To me, it was extremely belittling and insulting. I wanted to respond, "I'm not a 'sarge,' I'm a Chief Master Sergeant."

I highly doubt he would have addressed the Sergeant Major of the Army or the Sergeant Major of the Marine Corps as "sarge."

Because I expected him to address me as "Chief," the appropriate term of address, I was taken aback. Older Veterans from the Vietnam and Korean Wars and WWII veterans sometimes addressed me as "sarge," but that was the term they were accustomed to using, and it was not meant with any disrespect.

I shook Vice President Biden's hand and quickly stepped aside, thinking, *You're the VP, the number-two person in charge of the greatest military force in the world, and you don't even know the proper term of address for your senior enlisted military members?* The moment struck a nerve. Although he came from the Vietnam era, he should have known the current-day appropriate term of address. By the end of breakfast, however, I chalked up his faux pas to his generation and believed that he didn't intend any disrespect toward me.

After breakfast, we visited Arlington National Cemetery. In the interior of the rotunda, numerous glass cases displayed gifts from foreign dignitaries who had visited the cemetery. We stood on the steps in front of the Tomb of the Unknown Soldier and witnessed the Changing of the Guard. Even though I had been there many times, seeing the tomb of an American Serviceman "known but to God" was always a moving experience. The Soldiers guarding the tomb were carefully selected, and they stood watch even during blizzards and severe storms. They were truly dedicated and outstanding service members.

During the ceremony, on both sides of the tomb stood units from the Army, Marine Corps, Navy, Air Force, and Coast Guard in their dress uniforms, holding their rifles. When the ceremony was finished, I had the opportunity to interact with many of the visitors. Veterans from World War II, Korea, and Vietnam approached me, most seemingly a little unsure how to address me, since they had never seen a female enlisted person with the number of chevrons and ribbons I wore on my uniform. During their years of service, there were very few, if any, enlisted females who had achieved my rank, and none who had achieved my position. Some saluted me, and some even hugged me. It was a tremendous honor sharing a few moments with these "grizzled" warriors.

One of the most moving events for me took place February 29, 2012, when President Obama hosted a dinner at the White House honoring our Iraq War veterans. The Service Senior Enlisted Advisors, their staffs, and my office worked closely together to ensure representation from across the nation and from every component (Active, Guard, and Reserve). The White House had invited more than one hundred veterans and one guest each to the event and called it "A Nation's Gratitude Dinner: Honoring Those Who Served in Operation Iraqi Freedom and Operation New Dawn." Gold Star families and representatives of veterans groups were also there. Gary and I were seated at a table with Iraq War veterans, some of whom were wounded warriors, and the Assistant Commandant of the Marine Corps, General Joseph Dunford.

"These rooms have hosted presidents and prime ministers and kings and queens," President Obama began. "But in the history of this house, there's never been a night quite like this. Because this evening, we welcome not the statesmen who decide great questions of war and peace, but citizens, men and women from every corner of our country, from every rank of our military, every branch of our service, who answer the call, who go to war, who defend the peace."

Touching upon veteran difficulties following the Vietnam War, Obama pledged to thank and honor the service of wartime veterans.

"You succeeded in your mission," Obama said. "[I]n your resilience, we see the essence of America, because we do not give up... [A]ll of you taught us a lesson about the character of our country."

After the dinner, I wanted to personally thank the Iraq War veterans for their service and sacrifice for our nation and their fight to liberate Iraq from the clutches of a brutal dictator. One of the young Marines I spoke with was blind in one eye, had suffered many other wounds, and was accompanied by his service dog. Shaking his hand, he thanked me for being there. Humbled and deeply touched, I simply told him, "The honor is all mine."

# CHAPTER 63

# The Tank

In 1942, the newly established US Joint Chiefs of Staff and the US-British Combined Chiefs of Staff organizations moved into the US Public Health Building on Constitution Avenue in Washington, DC. The Joint Chiefs of Staff held their first formal meeting there on February 9, 1942, in a conference room on the second floor. They continued to use this room throughout World War II.

The JCS conference room soon became known as "the Tank." A popular explanation of the origin of this nickname is that access to the staff officers' entrance was down a flight of stairs through an arched portal, giving the impression of entering a tank. In 1947, the nickname moved with the Joint Chiefs of Staff to the Pentagon. Today, the JCS conference room is located in Corridor 9 in the "E" Ring, and even though nothing in the room even remotely resembles a tank, that's what everyone still calls it.[13]

It was a surreal experience to sit in small group meetings in the Pentagon with the Secretary of Defense, members of the Joint Chiefs of Staff, Service And Undersecretaries, and Service Senior Enlisted Advisors. In the sixty-eight-year history of the JCS, I was the first female SEA to a member of the Joint Chiefs of Staff, which meant I was the first enlisted woman to be a regular participant at JCS meetings in the Tank. There I sat, representing the 450,000 plus National Guard Soldiers, Airmen, and their families. At the time, I wasn't focused on breaking any "glass ceilings," just on doing my job.

But looking back, I'm aware that my participation in the Tank was unprecedented.

The meetings and discussions in the Tank were frequently at the highest classified level. No matter the level or topic, what was said in the Tank stayed in the Tank. Much of the information we discussed was "sensitive" rather than officially "classified." Members who attend Tank meetings are free to speak their mind, and some do so in colorful ways. Some of the most sensitive discussions centered on TRICARE reform, pay, entitlements, changes in retirement, education benefits, and downsizing the military. These areas directly affected the enlisted force and their families and also fell directly under the purview of the Senior Enlisted Advisors.

In addition to the meetings in the Tank, the Senior Enlisted Advisors and I met quarterly in the Secretary of Defense's office for lunch. During these meetings, the Secretary of Defense asked us for our input on a variety of issues.

A highlight of these small-group lunches was listening to then Secretary of Defense Leon Panetta. I liked Secretary Panetta's style—he was a straight talker. Even though the SEAs represented about 80 percent of our military, it was still an honor that he asked for our thoughts and recommendations so frequently and regarded them so respectfully. On occasion, Secretary Panetta included the SEA spouses for the luncheon, and he valued their opinions on military family issues as well.

The SEAs also attended many Executive Committee (EXCOM) meetings held by senior military and civilian leaders. We considered a wide array of important issues—for example, the repeal of "Don't Ask, Don't Tell," which took effect September 20, 2011. We thoroughly discussed the effects of the decision to repeal the law and what we as senior leaders believed the impact would be on the services and their respective members. While many serving in uniform had strong feelings about the repeal, it turned out to be just a blip on the radar screen. Most of us knew or had served with gay, lesbian, or bisexual service members throughout our careers. It was time to let them be open about their sexual orientation and allow them to continue serving their country proudly without fear or shame.

When the Budget Control Act and Sequestration was the talk of the country, senior leaders met and discussed many issues pertaining to the Department of Defense budget. Military pay raises continued to be discussed at length, as well as reform of TRICARE, Basic Allowance for Housing, education benefits, and National Guard pay periods for Unit Training Assembly weekends / drill weekends. These discussions were difficult because a change in one area affected other critical areas.

What made these conversations even more challenging was that they dealt with our service members and their families. Once you put faces to spaces or faces in the uniform, budget cuts become a very real issue—not just something on paper. We knew many future decisions and cuts would negatively affect the men and women who wear the cloth of our nation, serve in harm's way, and protect our country.

What really surprised me was the power and influence that Veteran Service Organizations had in these decisions. Since the time I was an NCO, I supported various professional and veteran service organizations. Having been in those EXCOM meetings, I saw first-hand how a decision could be influenced by the strong and united voice of VSOs on Capitol Hill.

It's important to know that every voice matters in the US Armed Forces—whether you're Active, Guard, Reserve, or a Retiree—when it comes to influencing the decision-making process all the way up the chain. It's important for all service members to get involved in professional military and veteran service organizations, even after retirement. It's critical to let our voices be heard.

# CHAPTER 64

# Engagements and Special Events

As the NGB SEA, I believed it was my responsibility to have a presence on the Hill, and it was essential for members of Congress to see stripes on the Hill. I served as a reminder to our congressional delegation of the enlisted men, women, and families they represent. It was important to educate congressional members on National Guard matters, but I never asked them to promote agenda items or sought specific financial support.

I visited the offices of many senators and representatives simply to thank them for what they did to support the National Guard, its members, and their families. Many times, these visits led to other general discussions about our National Guard Soldiers and Airmen. I was extremely surprised to learn that some congressional staffers had little understanding of the missions and capabilities of their own state's National Guard. I was glad for the opportunity to educate them and to highlight the contributions and accomplishments of National Guard Soldiers and Airmen in their respective states and across the nation. It was encouraging to see staff members who were interested enough to take notes and really listen and learn.

Most everyone can tell you where they were or what they were doing when the first and second airplanes hit the World Trade Center buildings. Gary and I were in Hawaii at the time, and we can vividly recall watching, horrified, as the third plane struck the Pentagon. Our eyes filled with tears, and our hearts ached when we heard about the heroic men on Flight 93, as their courageous actions forced the United Airlines plane to the ground in Shanksville, Pennsylvania. Like most Americans, we watched the events unfold and felt helpless.

A decade later, I was invited to attend a memorial ceremony at the Pentagon. I almost felt unworthy to attend and be in the presence of the families who had lost loved ones on that tragic day. The Pentagon Memorial, located just southwest of the Pentagon in Arlington County, Virginia, is a permanent outdoor memorial to the 184 people who died as victims in the building and on American Airlines Flight 77 during the attacks of September 11, 2001. There is no mention of the five hijackers who were responsible for this heinous act. The site, which includes trees, plaques, and walking paths, features 184 benches, each honoring a victim of the crash. The benches are made of stainless steel inlaid with granite. Each bench is inscribed with a victim's name on the end and arches over a shallow reflecting pool of water, lit from below.

It was eerily quiet as President Barack Obama, Secretary of Defense Leon Panetta, and Chairman of the Joint Chiefs of Staff Admiral Michael Mullen walked through an honor cordon before the ceremony began. President Obama and First Lady Michelle Obama laid a wreath to mark the tenth anniversary of the September 11 attacks at the Pentagon. There was a moment of silence at the exact time the plane struck, then service members from all branches solemnly entered the memorial grounds carrying individual wreaths to place upon each of the benches.

After the ceremony, I offered condolences and prayers to some of the family members. As they told me stories of their loved ones, they cried and laughed at the same time. I felt uplifted by their spirit and love of our country.

꒰ꗄ꒱

One of the special places I was privileged to visit a number of times was the Marine Corps Barracks in Washington, DC, the oldest post in the Corps. It is a historic place, as all the commandants of the Marine Corps have lived there since 1806, and the Barracks have housed Marines since 1808. During the War of 1812, the British set fire to much of the capital city but spared the Barracks. Marine Corps history states the British General said, "I refuse to burn the homes of men so brave."

On Friday evenings in the summer, a special military ceremony is conducted at the barracks. It features the President's Own United States Marine Band, the Commandant's Own United States Marine Drum and Bugle Corps, the Silent Drill Platoon, the Color Guard of the Marine Corps, led by the Color Sergeant of the Marine Corps, the Marine Corps Body Bearers, and ceremonial companies Alpha and Bravo. The military "laser" precision during the parade is remarkable, and the intricate drill movements are done without a single verbal command. When we had the opportunity to sit front and center, the performance was even more remarkable, as we were able to see every meticulous movement up close. As a former Marine, Gary was filled with indescribable pride each time we attended the parade.

One evening was especially memorable when a female Marine Major was the Parade Commander for the first time in the history of the Barracks. I spoke with her after the performance and presented her with one of my coins in recognition of her special achievement.

When Gary was serving in the Marine Corps, I looked forward to a particular event: the Marine Corps Birthday Ball, held every year in locations throughout the nation on or around November 10, the birthday of the Marine Corps.

Our first year in DC, we were attending a White House springtime event when Gary met the commandant of the Marine Corps, General James Amos. The Marine Corps Birthday Ball is steeped in tradition and filled with history. For a Marine, especially a retired Marine, to meet the Commandant is more than a big deal. Gary introduced himself, and they shook hands.

"Sir, this is way below your pay grade," Gary said, "but could you tell me who I can contact to get invited to the Marine Corps Birthday Ball?"

General Amos handed Gary his personal card and told him to contact his office on 1 September. Gary took the coveted card, set it in a special place, and told Ashley and me to not touch it. You can believe that card was protected for months in anticipation of September 1. The date finally arrived, and General Amos invited us to the Commandant's Marine Corps Birthday Ball. It was a highlight of the year, and we were both delighted to be invited in subsequent years as well.

The last ball we attended in 2012 was extra special. A Master Sergeant was assigned as my escort for the evening, and we had the honor of being seated with the Sergeant Major of the Marine Corps, Micheal P. Barrett. Also seated at the table was Medal of Honor (MOH) recipient Sergeant Dakota Meyer and his guest. I had spoken with several MOH recipients in the past but never for more than a few moments. On this night, we had the distinct pleasure of engaging in a lengthy conversation with one of our nation's heroes.

Before dinner, we were admiring the decorations and table gifts when Sergeant Major Barrett and Gary began talking about the men's table gift. At most military birthday balls, items like elegant coasters, commemorative glasses, and the like were the norm for table gifts—but not at the Commandant's Birthday Ball. The table gift for the men was a Benchmade combat knife with a three-and-a-half-inch blade that flipped open with the touch of a button. *Ooragh*!

I immediately took note of the women's table gift, a pink metal pen by my plate.

"What's up with the pink pen?" I asked Sergeant Major Barrett. "I'd actually prefer the knife."

He picked up the pen and inspected it closely.

"Do you know what this is?" he asked.

"Yeah, a pink pen!" I responded with a laugh.

Sergeant Major Barrett explained that it was a Kubotan, a lethal weapon that can kill if struck at exactly the right spot in the jugular vein. He demonstrated, lifting the slender instrument into the air and striking it down forcefully, but with a soft landing, within centimeters of my jugular. Ah, so now it was cool after all! Not some lame, "foofoo" girly gift. I keep that "pink pen" on my desk to this day and often reflect back on that evening.

# CHAPTER 65

# Flagship Programs

One of the National Guard's most prominent programs, yet least known to the general public, is the State Partnership Program (SPP). A joint DOD security cooperation program, SPP links a state's National Guard with the armed forces of a partner country. The National Guard proposed the idea when nations began emerging from the former Soviet Bloc in the early 1990s. Much like the well-known "sister city" program, SPP results in a cooperative, mutually beneficial relationship between nations around the globe.

In 2000, the Hawaii National Guard became state partners with the Philippines. At that time, I was assigned to the 297th ATCS at Kalaeloa Airport and heard little to nothing about the HING's participation with our state partner. Years later, as the 154th WG CCM, I began to read and understand more about the SPP but still had no direct involvement with our partner country.

In 2006, Hawaii received another state partner—Indonesia. To me, it seemed like big news because I was assigned to Hickam AFB and heard more dialogue about our new state partner. I came to understand that the National Guard Bureau goes through a rigorous process when assigning state partners. They consider many factors, including current threats in a region, mutual interests, and military-civilian strategy. The National Guard Bureau also tries to match a country with a US state that may have the same type of military equipment, culture, languages, proximity to the partner nation, and so on.

Hawaii shares many similarities with both the Philippines and Indonesia. A good number of Hawaii National Guard members came from the Philippines and still have family living there. Having Guard members who know the country and people and speak various dialects is mutually beneficial for both countries.

Indonesia is the most populous Muslim country in the world. Made up of more than seventeen thousand islands—the five main islands are Sumatra, Celebes, Java, Halmahera, and Ceram—Indonesia is the fourth largest country in the world. The day after Hawaii Governor Linda Lingle announced the historic SPP between Indonesia and Hawaii, she focused on disaster preparedness—a key area of cooperation under the SPP that also strengthens relationships and regional security in the Asia-Pacific region.

In June 2007, Governor Lingle and the Hawaii Adjutant General, Major General Robert Lee, led a delegation from Hawaii to meet with Indonesian leaders in Jakarta. As the Hawaii National Guard SEL, I was part of the delegation. The governor and Dr. Chip McCreery from the Pacific Tsunami Warning Center in Honolulu participated in a roundtable discussion with Indonesian scientists to explore possible Hawaii-Indonesia partnerships. We had several other meetings, but the one that struck me the most was a midmorning tea that Governor Lingle and I attended. We met with high-level female leaders in Indonesia—women who were well dressed, educated, well spoken, and all about business. This was Governor Lingle's meeting, so I sat and just listened. What impressed me most was that these women seemed to influence decisions at the highest level in their government. I gathered that they were the force behind the male leadership yet because of their culture they needed to remain in the backdrop.

When I began my tour of duty at the Pentagon, I quickly discovered that it was my good fortune to have been exposed to the SPP at the state level. Not only had I taken the time to read and understand what the program entailed, I had accumulated important practical experience. While serving as the NGB SEA, during meetings, lectures, or presentations, I often had to explain and defend the SPP to active-duty military members, as they often had misunderstandings about the program. Fostering positive foreign relations is a key mission of the National Guard, and the SPP enhances the potential for a more secure and stable country or region. The partnerships are limited only by what the two partners want to accomplish; they are two-way relationships built on trust that outlive political administrations.

When SPP started in the 1990s, many officers and enlisted members in the partner nations held low-ranking positions. Today, many of them are among their nation's most significant military and civilian leaders, and the value of these longstanding relationships frankly cannot be measured. Our Guard members and their partner troops have trained together in peacetime and have fought and bled together on the same battlefields in Iraq and Afghanistan.

While interacting with foreign militaries, the consistent message I heard over and over during my time and involvement with SPP was that they wanted and needed the leadership and trust we have in our NCO and SNCO ranks. They had a strong officer corps but lacked the medium and upper levels of a professional noncommissioned officer corps. Through their respective partnerships, they saw firsthand the leadership, strength, professionalism, competency, education, and commitment that the US military has in its enlisted corps.

$\sim$

The other significant National Guard program is the National Guard Youth ChalleNGe Program, established in 1993 to turn around the lives of young people ages sixteen to eighteen who are having difficulty completing high school. This free program is open to permanent legal residents in participating states and territories.

In conjunction with the NGB, state governments, and local sites, ChalleNGe currently operates about forty programs in approximately twenty-eight states, Puerto Rico, and DC. It's a voluntary seventeen-month dropout recovery program that helps at-risk youth earn their high school diploma or GED. Some states offer credit recovery, which allows youth the opportunity to return to high school upon successful completion of the program.

There is a misunderstanding that ChalleNGe is a program for bad kids. Quite the contrary. In fact, many of the teenagers who attend the program are students who dropped out of high school to work and help support their families.

ChalleNGe empowers participants to embrace responsibility, achievement, and positive behavior. During the first phase, which lasts about six months, students take part in eight core components: academic excellence, responsible citizenship, physical fitness, leadership/followership, job skills, service to the community, health and hygiene, and life coping skills.

Upon completion of the residential phase, cadets participate in a twelve-month postresidential phase, during which mentors continue to provide guidance and support using the military model of discipline and structure. The mentors help participants enroll in college, trade school, start a career, or join the military. The top performers are awarded scholarships. More than 130,000 students have graduated from the Youth ChalleNGe Program, changing their lives in the process.

I first became aware of ChalleNGe while at the Air Traffic Control Squadron because the Hawaii Youth Challenge Academy is located at Kalaeloa. Given my own beginnings, living in a town where not many opportunities existed outside farming, the program touched my heart.

Many told me they came from a one-parent home where their parent got sick and they had to work to pay the rent or to feed their brothers and sisters. The students found themselves in Youth ChalleNGe because they got behind in or dropped out of school. Some of the stories were heartbreaking, and I couldn't imagine being in those situations. Of course, there were some who had fallen in with the wrong crowd and were going down a bad path. The Youth ChalleNGe Program provided students with a last chance to get their lives back on track.

While in Hawaii, I personally witnessed the transformation of some of these young adults. While there were honor graduates who went on to excel in four-year-degree colleges, most attended a two-year college or trade school, entered the military, or found employment upon graduation. Thanks to the mentors, invaluable life skills, and discipline, these graduates learned to believe in themselves, and they got a fresh start in their young lives.

Due to these personal experiences, I was delighted to receive an invitation to the annual National Guard Youth ChalleNGe Gala in Washington, DC, in 2010. The National Guard Youth Foundation (NGYF) puts on a gala every year as a fundraiser for the program and to highlight the significant accomplishments of the cadets and the program. TAGs, senior military, civilian leaders, and celebrities attended. More importantly, directors from each state brought two cadets.

During the social and dinner hour, I spoke with as many cadets as possible. These young men and women had faced a pivotal life choice and made the decision to turn their lives around. I told them how proud I was of what they had accomplished, and I encouraged them to continue working hard at achieving their dreams. I loved listening to their stories. They had lofty aspirations—the cadets' eyes told me how committed they were to the program and to achieving their goals.

The time I spent with them was a lot like the time I spent with our wounded warriors. Listening to their stories, I was inspired by what they had overcome. Some of their personal trials and tribulations were more than a teenage should ever have to experience.

Several of the cadets got up on stage that night and told their stories of what led them to ChalleNGe and how the program was changing their lives. Many in the audience were in tears.

The following year, I attended the 2011 Youth ChalleNGe Program Gala, where the one hundred thousandth graduate was recognized. It was a star-studded night, honoring our cadets and their accomplishments. When the one hundred thousandth graduate was announced, everyone in the audience stood and clapped with thunderous applause.

"I am proud to be representing one hundred thousand other cadets, each of us with our own story of how we turned our lives around," Tori Walston said, stepping up to the microphone. "Thanks to the program, all of us were given a second chance and a brighter future. Learning about teamwork was one of the most important things I learned while in the program because you're not always going to like everybody and it's good to learn how to deal with differences. The program is full of learning about important life skills that you can use in the real world."

One of the guest speakers that evening was Louisiana Senator Mary Landrieu, a staunch supporter of the NGYCP.

"Without the help of the National Guard and its leadership," she said, "the Youth ChalleNGe program would not be able to achieve the things it has done to date, or have been so successful."

General McKinley added, "Having one hundred thousand [cadets] graduate is a tremendous milestone. Thank you for allowing the National Guard and the National Guard Youth Foundation to do these great things."

Gail Dady, President of the National Guard Youth Foundation, also spoke.

"When you think of the National Guard," she said, "you don't think educator, you think warfighter. But when you think about it, no one is better than the National Guard to create such a successful program. The National Guard is committed to communities and in every zip code in our nation, and nothing is more important to our communities, our families, or our nation, than our youth."

Gail added that Guard members' honor, courage, and integrity serve as positive examples to the cadets who have often known only bad examples.

"The Youth ChalleNGe program is changing lives and com- munities for the better and strengthening our nation, and the Youth Foundation is very honored to partner with the Guard in achieving this," she said.

I personally worked with cadets who graduated from ChalleNGe, joined the National Guard, and went on to a hugely successful career. These men and women serve as examples of what can happen with a little guidance, direction, and having someone who cares about their future.

# CHAPTER 66

# The Fighting 69th

In the last six months of my assignment as Senior Enlisted Advisor to General Grass, I attended two unique and special events. In March 2013, New York State Command Sergeant Major Frank Wicks invited me to join the New York National Guard in their St. Patrick's Day festivities. New York City's St. Patrick's Day Parade dates back to 1761, and since 1851 has been led by the legendary "Fighting 69th," now a proud regiment of the New York Army National Guard.

I had no idea what the weekend would entail. As St. Patrick's Day approached, one of the officers from the NGB Public Affairs Office (NGB PAO) asked if I would appear on the Fox News Channel's weekday morning news show *Fox & Friends* for a taping during Women's History Month. I was happy to—I was grateful for any opportunity to tell the National Guard story.

Prior to the interview, the NGB PAO arranged for media training with the USAF. I was grilled in an in-depth simulated, taped hour-long interview. During the simulation, the media-training team occasionally paused to critique, correct, and provide recommendations for improvement. In addition to what I said, they focused on my body language, body positioning and movement, and facial expressions. It was so beneficial that I wished I'd been given that training earlier in my career.

I had the good fortune to work with several amazing NGB PAO personnel, including a former enlisted Airman named Captain

Randy Saldivar. The afternoon before the *Fox & Friends* interview, we took a train to New York City and did interview prep throughout the entire ride. Gary and Ashley joined me that evening for a weekend in New York with General and Mrs. Grass.

Since host Steve Doocy would introduce me as the Senior Enlisted Advisor for the National Guard, I wanted to honor the National Guard and my position, as we would reach millions of American homes that morning. Having my interview take place during Women's History Month, I felt a strong sense of responsibility to represent all women with dignity as the highest senior enlisted woman in the history of the US Armed Forces.

It was also a significant time for women in the military because in January 2013, the Secretary of Defense announced that 10 percent of military positions previously closed to women, or 220,000 jobs, would be open for review. Secretary Panetta stated that women would be considered to serve in these positions, including all front-line combat roles, infantry units, and in the US Army, Navy, Marine Corps, and Special Operations Command. They would also be able to serve as Army Rangers, Green Berets, Navy SEALs, Marine Corps infantry, Air Force parajumpers, and all other positions that previously were only open to men.

With this change, all standards had to be reviewed—and many members of the military expressed concerns that standards would be lowered to include women. I echoed what senior civilian and military leadership had said.

"The standards are the standards—period," I always explained. "Not a male standard, not a female standard, but *the* standard. If women can meet those standards, then they will be allowed to serve in those positions."

From the time of the announcement in January, not one woman had ever said to me that she wanted the standards lowered. The women wanted to compete as equals with their male counterparts. The standards have always been critical to the mission, as lives are often at stake.

Gary and Ashley were in the studio with me. The taping went well, and Steve Doocy was a true professional, putting me at ease from the very beginning.

Later in the afternoon, my family and I joined General and Mrs. Grass for a tour of the 9/11 Memorial and the 9/11 Museum. We would also have the opportunity to go all the way up in the unfinished Freedom Tower. I had previously visited the 9/11 Memorial years prior, and the same feelings I'd experienced in the past came flooding back this time as well. The memorial is a haunting reminder of senseless loss and a tragic and fateful day in United States and world history. Walking along the memorial and touching the names inscribed on the walls of those who perished gave me a sense of connection to that fateful day. As I walked in silence, I prayed for them and their loved ones.

At the 9/11 Museum, we learned that every volunteer there had lost a loved one on September 11, 2001. The docent was articulate and highly knowledgeable about the facts as they unfolded on 9/11 and in the days that followed. As I listened, I thought, *How could he or other family members work in this museum, reliving that tragic day over and over again?* I could not imagine looking at the 9/11 museum artifacts, giving tours, and being reminded of the loss and heartache every day. Yet the employees had smiles on their faces and took great pride in showing the museum to us.

It wasn't until the very end of our tour that we learned our docent had lost his son when the World Trade Center came crashing down. His son was a firefighter and the last "full body" to be recovered. His son's firefighting uniform coat hung in the museum. From the front, the coat looked charred but intact. From the back—well, there was no back, as his son had been completely blown out of the coat. It was while telling the story of his son that the docent and many on that tour, including me, had tears rolling down our cheeks.

I finally realized why family members continue to volunteer at the museum: our docent was honoring his son by telling his story so that others could learn and understand the horrific loss individuals and our nation suffered that day.

After the museum tour, we received safety gear and a briefing at the Freedom Tower because the floor we were going up to was not finished or secure. Orange plastic fenced off the perimeter of the top floor. The spire stood out prominently at the center of the top unfinished floor. It was haunting to actually stand on the top of the Freedom Tower and look down—it was a long way down. Our hosts gave us black sharpies and encouraged us to write a permanent message on the structure beams. Standing atop that sacred place, I wrote a simple yet heartfelt message on one of the structure beams: "God Bless the USA. National Guard Senior Enlisted Advisor." It was quite a touching experience for all of us.

❧

The following day, St. Patrick's Day, members and leadership of the New York National Guard and the Fighting 69th met at 5:45 a.m. at the armory, where General Grass joined us. When we arrived, Soldiers were bustling about preparing for the morning's festivities. At 6:00 a.m. on the dot, we gathered in the Commander's office for a traditional toast of Jameson Irish Whiskey and champagne—a tradition that began during the Civil War. We each received a sprig of boxwood to place in the top of our uniform pocket. At that time, I had no idea what the sprig of boxwood meant or that I would be marching with one of the most fabled units in the United States Army. This year marked the 162nd time they would lead the parade as they marched down Fifth Avenue.

The now legendary "69th New York Regiment" was formed in 1861 as part of the fabled "Irish Brigade." Their ranks were almost entirely made up of Irish immigrants. Their flag is a brilliant green with a gold harp below billowing clouds with the sun just peeking through. Below the harp are rows of shamrocks, and above the clouds are the words "69th Regiment, Irish Brigade." Below the shamrocks are the Irish words "RIAMH NAR DHRUID O SPAIRN IANN," which means "Those Who Never Retreated from the Clash of Spears."

During the Civil War, the Soldiers of the Fighting 69th marched into battle with a green sprig of boxwood in the brim of their hats.

They fought in the first and second battles of Bull Run, Antietam, Gettysburg, Fredericksburg, and many others. It was at the Battle of Fredericksburg that their ferocity inspired General Robert E. Lee of the Army of Northern Virginia to christen them "The Fighting 69th" for their bravery during the assault at the stone wall on Marye's Heights. Assault after assault by Union troops failed to drive off the Confederates from the hilltop and stone wall; casualties were horrible. After the battle, the dead lay across the heights. The Soldiers of the Fighting 69th lay closest to the wall—identified by the sprigs of boxwood in the brim of their hats. Since that time, the Fighting 69th has fought in World War I, World War II in the Pacific Theater, and in Iraq in 2004 and 2005. In World War I, after the battle of Meuse-Argonne, three members were awarded the Congressional Medal of Honor.

Following a brisk walk to St. Patrick's Cathedral, we attended mass. I had never been in this cathedral and was amazed by its beauty and the enormity of the structure. The Soldiers of the Fighting 69th sat in the southern part of the cathedral, a place reserved for them in honor of the regiment. The priest who said mass was from the Shrine at Knock, Ireland, and offered a faith-filled and patriotic mass. Afterward, we walked downtown with the Fighting 69th Soldiers, around the Fifth Avenue area where the parade route would begin.

Skies were gray, and the wind was crisp. It was the middle of March in New York. Soldiers marching in the parade did not wear jackets, only their Army Service Uniforms. Fortunately, I had put on a warm layer under my uniform shirt. I could see that everyone's hands were visibly cold as they shivered and rubbed their gloveless hands together. Soldiers formed up in their respective formations and stood waiting for the parade to start.

Soon it was time for the command staff and invited guests to line up. In our left hands, we each carried a *swagger stick*, made out of blackthorn and shipped from Ireland. In the early days of the parade, the officers had carried Irish *shillelaghs* made of blackthorn rather than swagger sticks. Additionally, we all placed a sprig of boxwood in our top uniform pockets. I did not know until much later that the boxwood came from the battlefield of Fredericksburg to commemorate the bravery displayed by the Fighting 69th at Marye's Heights. Sixteen hundred brave men charged up that hill. At battle's end, only 256 were not wounded or killed. The swagger stick that I carried in the parade now holds a place of honor in my office, a truly cherished gift from the Soldiers of the Army's most decorated regiment, the Fighting 69th.

As the parade was about to start, a member of the Ancient Order of Hibernians Parade Committee approached the Battalion Commander and asked, "Is the 69th ready?"

The Commander and his Soldiers shouted back, "The 69th is always ready!"

I had lost sight of Gary and Ashley long before the parade started but knew they would be somewhere along the parade route and that we'd meet up later at the armory. Light, intermittent snow began to fall, and I felt the sharp wind penetrating my uniform, but it didn't matter—I was marching with the Fighting 69th down Fifth Avenue in the St. Patrick's Day Parade in New York City. What an incredible opportunity!

The parade route ended and the command staff and military leaders remained on the side of the road to salute the Fighting 69th formations as they passed by. I remember my hands being so bitterly cold that I could not force my fingers together for a proper salute. My arm and hand were raised appropriately, but as hard as I tried to will my fingers to come together, they would not.

Once the parade ended, the Soldiers walked to a designated metro train stop where there was a special train designated to take us all back to the armory. As the train—decorated in red, white, and blue—entered the station, its whistle blared, which gave way to rousing applause from the Soldiers.

Bagpipers dressed in kilts and full regalia, playing "Garryowen," led us into the armory, followed by the Soldiers of the Fighting 69th. Inside the armory, the NYARNG leadership, General Grass, and I were seated on stage. The Chaplain gave a blessing, and the NYTAG and General Grass gave some remarks. They spoke of the glorious history of the unit and their respect for the Soldiers seated before them who were carrying on the legacy of the Fighting 69th. I will never forget the expressions of pride on the faces of the Soldiers and their families as they listened to their remarks.

Part of the tradition of the Fighting 69th is for the senior enlisted to mix a concoction of one part Jameson Irish Whiskey and two parts champagne into a large bowl, which is then offered in small cups to every member of the 69th for a toast. I was asked to help mix the traditional Regimental Cocktail. As the Soldiers of the 69th toasted, I felt privileged to be a part of this time-honored ceremony that began during the Civil War.

# CHAPTER 67

# Unsung Heroes

In 2012, Director Ron Howard produced a documentary on the history of American women in the military. *Unsung Heroes: The Story of America's Female Patriots* chronicles the story of the American fighting women in the Revolutionary War all the way through Operation Enduring Freedom, highlighting not only their bravery and courageous service but also "their fight for the right to fight."

The documentary is unprecedented—most Americans have never heard firsthand accounts from women on the battlefield, and the stories of the first female pilots of the Women's Auxiliary Ferry Squadrons, the Navy SPARS, and the first female Marines, Soldiers, and Coast Guardswomen, have largely gone untold. The history of American warriors like Staff Sergeant Leigh Ann Hester, the first woman since WWII to be awarded a Silver Star for valor in combat, and Lieutenant Colonel Nicole Malachowski, the first woman pilot in the Air Force Thunderbirds, is a moving saga of selfless sacrifice and bravery.

A member of Ron Howard's production crew asked me to participate in the filming, and I was honored to have my role in National Guard history included among the stories of such accomplished and patriotic women. Shortly before my retirement, I learned that in my position as the Senior Enlisted Advisor to the Chief of the National Guard Bureau, I had attained the highest position ever held by an enlisted woman in the history of the US Department of Defense, including all branches and components. I'm truly humbled by the responsibility to uphold the legacy of the brave American female patriots upon whose shoulders I stand.

I wish all service members and civilian men and women could watch this film to learn and understand the significant roles, contributions, and accomplishments of our military servicewomen. Boys and men need the perspective of our female warriors who show their dedication and commitment to do anything for their country by putting their lives on the line. For young girls and women, the histories of these inspiring women show that females are strong and capable of doing anything they put their minds to and demonstrate the important role women have had in securing our freedom and in defending this great nation. These were incredible women who can be role models for all of us—regardless of gender.

# CHAPTER 68

# Proud to Be an Airman

On September 18, 1947, the Unites States Air Force became the aerial warfare service branch of the US Armed Forces. Predecessor organizations, including the US Army Air Corps and the US Army Air Forces, served as the aviation arm of the larger US Army. This day is celebrated around the world, wherever Airmen are stationed, through ceremonies and birthday balls that honor the courage, commitment, and sacrifice of our Airmen and highlight the historical achievements of the Air Force.

The United States Air Force Memorial, sitting on a promontory overlooking the Pentagon and adjacent to Arlington Cemetery, honors the more than fifty-four thousand Airmen who have died in combat while serving in the Air Force and its predecessor organizations.[14] The three spires positioned at the center of the Air Force Memorial appear to be soaring skyward, evoking the image of contrails of the Air Force Thunderbirds as they peel back in a precision "bomb burst" maneuver. Only three of the four contrails are depicted, symbolizing the absent fourth of the missing-man formation, traditionally used at Air Force funeral flyovers.

The Air Force Memorial consists of four primary structures. My favorite part of the memorial is the south wall, which bears inspirational quotations and the Air Force's three core values: "Integrity first, Service before self, and Excellence in all we do."

A wreath is traditionally laid at the memorial early in the morning of the Air Force's birthday. The Secretary of the Air Force, Chief of Staff of the Air Force, Chief Master Sergeant of the Air Force, and the Air Force Association Chairman of the Board typically make up the official party who place the wreath on a stand at the base of the spires. The wreath ceremony starts the events of the birthday in a manner that honors all Airmen and their sacrifices for our nation's freedom.

September 18, 2012, was the sixty-fifth birthday of the Air Force. Weeks before, Chief Master Sergeant of the Air Force James Roy asked if I would stand in for him at the wreath-laying ceremony as he would not be in DC. The air on the morning of the ceremony was cool and crisp, and Gary and I arrived extra early so we could tour the memorial and read the placards of information. It was the first time I had ever stood on the grounds of the Air Force Memorial. Having seen the spires from the Pentagon, and while driving or flying, I was humbled to be standing at the foot of these magnificent "contrails" that rose to almost three hundred feet in the air. I thought of our fallen Airmen as I admired the four bronze statues that represent the Air Force Honor Guard. Of all the beautiful memorials around Washington, DC, this was *my* memorial. It represented my service and career, and it touched me deeply. I was nearing the end of my career, so this moment was especially poignant.

About midtour in the fall of 2011, Chief Master Sergeant of the Air Force (CMSAF) James Roy asked me to consider applying for his position. The thought of being responsible for the entire Air Force enlisted corps—including Active, Guard, and Reserve—seemed to be a big leap from my current position as I'd only been serving as the NGB SEA for about eighteen months. At the time, I didn't think I had the required depth of knowledge. Chief Roy assured me I did and asked me to give it some serious thought.

Within the ANG, I knew there were only a few qualified Chief Master Sergeants who could be considered, and the ANG would be allowed to nominate only one of them for the CMSAF position. Shortly after this interaction with CMSAF Roy, I discussed our conversation and shared my thoughts with General McKinley.

"Don't sell yourself short," he said.

The following year, in the fall of 2012, the US Air Force announced the position and selection criteria for the next CMSAF. After much discussion with General Grass and Gary, I decided to apply. I put a package together with all the required documents and submitted it for consideration. General Grass consulted with the Director of the ANG, then nominated me as the ANG nominee. I would be considered for the highest enlisted position in the United States Air Force.

Before the top five candidates were selected, the *Air Force Times* newspaper identified about twenty-five Air Force Chief Master Sergeants who were eligible for the CMSAF position and who they believed would be in the running as the top five chiefs for the position. My name was not listed. When I learned I had made the short list and was among the top five Chief Master Sergeants being considered for the position, I was floored. The Chief of Staff of the United States Air Force, General Mark Welsh, would interview me.

Words cannot express the simultaneous honor and magnitude of responsibility I felt. How does one prepare for such an interview? Truly it was a bit daunting. I could not fathom going from the NGB SEA to the CMSAF. Chief James A. Cody, my classmate in Air Traffic Control School in 1984-1985, was also nominated. Never in the history of the USAF have two people from the same technical school and the same small class been considered for the CMSAF position at the same time.

As the interview approached, I thoroughly prepared my responses to the latest talking points regarding USAF Active, Guard, and Reserve issues. My uniform was already squared away—there was nothing more to do than just be myself, remain confident and grounded in my values, and do my very best.

The interview process consisted of dinner at the home of the Chief of Staff of the Air Force (CSAF) with spouses, a town hall meeting where civilian and Air Force members of all ranks would ask questions, and finally a one-on-one hour-long interview with the CSAF.

To prepare for the dinner at the CSAF's home, Gary and I carefully went over the "Dine Like a Diplomat" PowerPoint presentation so we wouldn't make any faux pas. We discussed key talking points, family initiatives, and thoughtful answers to potential questions.

The evening at the CSAF's home went exceptionally well, and I had the town hall portion of my interview the next morning. Wearing my service dress uniform, I walked into a room where about thirty Air Force and civilian men and women were seated. The CSAF and his executive assistant sat in the back and took notes. I was not particularly nervous about the town hall meeting, as I had done many town halls across the nation with National Guard units. I enjoyed this portion of the interview process and felt confident that I had delivered solid responses.

After the town hall, I met alone with General Welsh. He showed me his office and all the historical memorabilia on display, and I remember thinking that I wished I were more of a history buff. He did not have many direct questions for me but did ask why I wanted the job. Before General Welsh became the CSAF, the Active, Guard, and Reserve components had become quite divided. There was an "us against them" attitude that permeated throughout the force, and I believed we were not operating as a coalesced Air Force organization. We needed a significant change, and General Welsh was the right person at the right time in the history of the Air Force to come in and revolutionize the way things were done. He had already begun working on bridging the gap and had an all-in inclusive mentality when it came to the three components of the Air Force.

I expressed to General Welsh that as a Guard member, I could help bridge the gap due to my understanding of each component. Additionally, there had never been a female CMSAF. As a woman, I believed I could bring a unique perspective to the entire USAF leadership team. I spoke in great detail about the advances the National Guard had made in our diversity program through the Joint Diversity Executive Council (JDEC). As the cochair of the JDEC team, I was confident I could help with the advancement of diversity in the Air

Force, which at the time was an action item of the Secretary of the Air Force. The meeting went quite well, and I felt confident that I had done my very best.

A few days later, I was home alone. I'd had a heads-up that the call would come that night, and I found myself deep in prayer. I did not pray to be selected or to not be selected, only that the outcome would be His will and not mine. I trusted that the Lord would make the best decision for the USAF.

When General Welsh called, he told me that it had been a very difficult decision. It had come down to another chief and me, and he had selected the other chief. I thanked him for giving me the opportunity and privilege to be considered for the highest enlisted position in the United States Air Force.

A couple of days later, General Welsh announced that Chief James A. "Jim" Cody, my ATC classmate, was selected as the Seventeenth CMSAF. I was happy for Chief Cody and his wife, my friend Athena, who is also a retired Chief Master Sergeant and air traffic controller. As a former air traffic controller, I understood that to have the Chief Master Sergeant of the Air Force come from the air traffic control career field for the first time was a historic event. It brought attention to our career field, and controllers across the nation were very proud about his achievement. With Chief Cody at the helm, I knew the Air Force enlisted corps would have a great future.

☙

Knowing that my tour as the NGB SEA would be ending in June 2013, and with the selection of CMSAF James Cody, my plans to retire now began to move forward.

Early in May 2013, the new Chief Master Sergeant of the Air Force, James Cody, asked me to represent the Air Force at the wreath-laying ceremony at the Women in Service to America Memorial in Arlington National Cemetery. This memorial tells the rich heritage of the women whose sacrifice, bravery, and service has had a significant role in the defense of our nation. A senior enlisted woman from each branch delivered short remarks, and it was the Air Force's turn to provide the keynote address.

For one of the few times in my career, my talk focused solely on our women service members and veterans. I spoke of the honor it was to share this event with my fellow sister Senior Enlisted Leaders and expressed how proud I was of all the women serving our nation around the world. I wanted to especially let the female veterans in the audience know that those of us serving today understood that if it had not been for their courage, sacrifice, and tenacity in decades past, the opportunities we experience today would not have been possible.

> With almost 2.3 million active and reserve component service members today, more than three hundred thousand, or 15 percent of the force, are women," I said. "For more than 230 years, American women have served with distinction on the battlefield, even when they have had to do so in secret. Well, guess what? We're not a secret anymore, and we haven't been for a long, long time.
>
> In the past, we were referred to as WASPs, WACs, WAVEs, SPARs. Today we're simply Soldier, Marines, Sailors, Airmen, or Coast Guardsmen. One in the same with our brothers in arms…as it should be.
>
> Recently, former Secretary of Defense Leon Panetta announced that the Pentagon would lift its ban on women serving in combat, [saying] that 'women are contributing in unprecedented ways to the military's mission of defending the nation.' Former Secretary Panetta was correct. We have fought, we have bled, and we have died alongside our brothers in arms in Iraq, in Afghanistan, and wherever our nation called us to serve. And we did so proudly.

The future for women in the military has never been brighter…but what we make of that future is completely up to us!

As you move forward to seize your opportunity, remember there is no separate standard for men and women—there is only *the* standard. Any woman who can meet the standard for the particular role she seeks in our armed forces can, and increasingly does, have the opportunity to succeed and to serve.

As we look to the future of women in service, we all have one thing in common: an all-encompassing love for the United States of America and a desire to serve our nation. You have put service before self and have promised that no sacrifice will be too great. May God bless our men and women in uniform, their families, and our veterans, and may He continue to bless the United States of America.

This was the last official speech I gave before my retirement—appropriately, at the same memorial where I delivered my first official speech as NGB SEL in 2010. That both had been at the Women in Service to America Memorial made those events especially poignant.

The next day, I was surprised at the morning staff meeting when General Grass commented that it was one of the best leadership addresses he had ever heard and encouraged everyone to read it. His remarks told me that I had achieved my intention to honor my fellow servicewomen—past, present, and future. *Mission accomplished.*

# CHAPTER 69

# The Final Stretch

When Gary and I left Hawaii, we sold our home and took everything with us—lock, stock, and barrel. With our move to DC, we left Hawaii several years before our original plan and knew that eventually we would need to decide where to live.

About a year into my tour in the Pentagon, Gary and I started to talk about where we were going to move and settle down after I retired. I would have easily gone back to Hawaii, but Gary felt it was too far from our children and grandkids. What made our decision easier was identifying where we *didn't* want to live. I didn't want to go north, which would be too cold, or south or east, which would be too hot and humid, or far west because we had done our time in California already. Given the political scene and laws there, neither of us was interested in moving in that direction. When we narrowed it down like that, it pretty much left us with the central part of the United States.

We wanted a conservative area with a military presence, exchange, and commissary access, four seasons, and a mild winter with lots of outdoor activities. Believe it or not, for Gary, even sports teams came into play. I had been to Colorado a few times and had spent a weekend there with friends. I threw a dart on the map and said to Gary, "Colorado Springs." That met all our criteria, and it would be easy to travel to family from there.

We flew to Colorado for a weekend, met with a realtor, and looked at houses but didn't find what we were looking for. From there, we decided to look at land. We bought the last lot we looked at and decided to build a home.

Colorado and the Colorado Springs area have ultimately turned out to be the ideal location for us to settle for our next phase of life. I've often said that if I can't live in Hawaii, Colorado is the next best place.

❧

With retirement imminent, I needed to initiate plans for my retirement ceremony and a Change of Responsibility (COR) ceremony, where the outgoing and incoming NGB SEA relinquish and assume responsibility for the office. For the COR ceremony venue, I chose the Hall of Heroes, a room in the Pentagon that I've always associated with feelings of peace, humility, and heroism. Each wall is lined with the names of our nation's Medal of Honor recipients. The Hall of Heroes is a place of reverence, and I felt blessed to be able to have my ceremony in this revered hall.

For my retirement ceremony, I selected the Women in Military Service for America Memorial (WIMSA) at Arlington National Cemetery. Unbeknownst to me, Gary and my office had been working with the Air Force and the Women's Memorial on a display depicting my military career. Because I had stored away artifacts they needed for the display, they finally had to tell me about it. I was a bit apprehensive about it, but it was clear that my team wanted to do this not only for me but more importantly to recognize how far the position of NGB SEA had come. For that reason, I agreed.

❧

Just prior to retirement, I did one last trip with General Grass overseas to visit our National Guard members. It was a high point of my career, and a great way to end it. We went to Afghanistan and to the Sinai Desert in Egypt to meet with our nation's finest, those protecting critical sites in defense of our country. As always, it was a pleasure to travel with General Grass. He was easy to converse with, and I could see how the Soldiers responded to and respected him.

At every opportunity, I told General Grass's story to inspire young Soldiers and Airmen to believe that they could follow in his footsteps.

General Grass joined the Missouri Army National Guard as an enlisted Soldier. He enrolled in college while serving his country and rose to the rank of Sergeant, spending a total of twelve years as an enlisted Soldier. He went through the enlisted ranks of E-1 to E-5 (Private to Sergeant), was selected for E-6 (Staff Sergeant) but instead was commissioned as an O-1 (Second Lieutenant). From there, he progressed through the officer ranks all the way to O-10 (four-star General).

Here was a man who enlisted in the Army National Guard, worked his way through college, got married, started a family, and became a four-star general and a member of the Joint Chiefs of Staff. While standing in front of enlisted men and women, I often said, "Only in America is this possible. If you put your mind to it, work hard, and believe in yourself, you too can achieve this success."

# CHAPTER 70

# Time to Go

General and Mrs. Grass held a state-like dinner in their quarters the evening before my retirement on June 5, 2013. General Grass's enlisted aide and the National Guard Bureau protocol team did an amazing job—from start to finish, everything was beautifully prepared and presented in grand style. It was extra special to have Gary, Ashley, my brother Bryan, my sister Shannon, and my colleagues at the dinner. We shared stories from my childhood and from my time with General Grass. Once we returned to Andrews that night, I went over the next day's events, checking everything twice. On the eve of my retirement, sleep was fleeting.

On June 6, the alarm rang at its usual time: 0415. I lay in bed briefly and thought, *This is it, my last day.* With a lump in my throat, I swallowed hard and headed to the shower to get ready. Understanding Murphy's Law, I prayed that all would fall into place. I asked the Lord to be with my family, to help me find the right words, to help me maintain my composure, and to oversee that all would go smoothly.

Driving to the Pentagon and navigating the 95s for my last official duty day was a bit melancholy. I had now driven these roads and passed by the same buildings for nearly three and a half years, but today I saw them almost as if for the very first time. I took in the details of the old brick homes with columns in the front and the beautiful trees that surrounded them as I progressed along my route. I knew I would miss that drive.

When I arrived at the Pentagon, the NGB SEA office was unusually quiet. I reviewed my remarks for the ceremonies and thought about the symbol I had chosen for the COR ceremony.

Each Service SEA has a flag that represents their respective office and position. With the recent appointment of the CNGB as a full member of the JCS, however, a flag representing the NGB SEA's position had not yet been designed. I asked the NGB Historian to research a meaningful symbol for the transfer of responsibility from me to my successor.

The item I chose was the halberd, a fearsome-looking weapon that dates back to the 1400s. The halberd combines a large flat ax head with a hook—topped with a spear—all on a six- to eight-foot-long pole. In the 1600s, the musket began to replace the halberd as its use declined although the halberd did not disappear entirely. It became a symbol of authority and was used extensively by the NCO Corps in the American militia. Since then, it has become a century-old symbol of a sergeant's badge of office. With the history dating back to the Massachusetts Bay Colony and the Revolutionary War militia, the start of the National Guard, I thought it was a perfect symbol to highlight the transfer of authority from the outgoing to the incoming NGB SEA.

During the ceremony, I couldn't help but feel a sense of sadness that my career was coming to an end while simultaneously feeling grateful for the opportunities I'd had for almost thirty years. I tied my comments to the significance of being in the hallowed Hall of Heroes that listed the names of more than 3,400 Medal of Honor recipients. The hall is a place that clearly depicts the courage, sacrifice, bravery, and service of our nation's heroes. Additionally, I highlighted the magnitude of responsibility the incoming NGB SEA now had for the enlisted Soldiers, Airmen, and families of the National Guard—I knew all would be in good hands.

Having served as the NGB SEA for Army and Air enlisted members, I thought it important to recognize two names listed on the wall, one from each branch of service. The first was Medal of Honor recipient Audie Murphy, who became a national hero for being the most decorated combat soldier during World War II. The second was Airman First Class John L. Levitow, the lowest-ranking recipient in Air Force history to receive the Medal of Honor. Both individuals are significant to our military and particularly to our enlisted corps—all Soldiers and Airmen know the names and history of these two Medal of Honor recipients. Audie Murphy and John L. Levitow represent all that we ask of our Soldiers and Airmen.

I felt a visceral finality the moment I passed the halberd to General Grass, who then passed it to the incoming NGB SEA. I loved the National Guard, I loved serving my country, I loved wearing the uniform of the United States Air Force, and I loved representing National Guard Soldiers and Airmen. Now it was over.

Many of the people who had supported me throughout my life and career, and who meant a great deal to me, were in attendance for the ceremony. Family and friends traveled from across the country, including Hawaii, and I was deeply moved by their presence. After a small reception, I went back to my empty office. The silence was deafening. I had turned in my Blackberry, my e-mail had been disabled, and I had access to absolutely nothing. As I sat at my desk, for the first time in decades, I had nothing to do. My staff was out preparing for the afternoon retirement ceremony, and I was alone in the office with only my scattered thoughts.

Outside, it was pouring rain. Gary drove Ashley and me from the Pentagon to the Women in Service Memorial at Arlington National Cemetery. I walked in and immediately was greeted by friends who had arrived early. They told me they'd just seen my career display and expressed how much they enjoyed it. I hadn't yet seen it, so Gary, Ashley, and I toured the display with General and Mrs. Grass.

Although I anticipated that it had been tastefully put together, I was taken aback by the enormity of the display. A billboard-sized poster contained many photos highlighting my career. Two uniforms flanked the display: one green utility uniform from when I was an Airman First Class and a service dress uniform with Command Chief Master Sergeant stripes affixed. A large display case covered with Plexiglas contained many artifacts spanning the nearly three decades of my career, including my first service dress (bubble) hat, my ATC pink card, coins, patches from various commands, my 154th WG CCM name plate, my dog tags, a plaque showcasing my rank insignia from E-1 to E-9, and military and family photos and other memorabilia. General Grass took note that one of the first things I did was to adjust and correct the display of one of my uniforms. Even moments before retirement, right was right and wrong was wrong!

The auditorium began filling up with family, friends, and colleagues. As the Air Force band struck a note, General Grass and I walked in the room and onto the indoor stage. Once again, and for the last time, as "Ruffles and Flourishes" played, I stood proudly and paid respect to General Grass as the senior military member. As we stood at attention during the National Anthem to honor the flag of the United States of America, I briefly thought about the infinite number of times I'd had the privilege to do so. Per my request, the flags of the fifty states, three territories, and the District of Columbia stood proudly in the auditorium. I had often spoken about the flags of these United States—about the rich culture, heritage, proud traditions, and the identity of each respective state and how the very fabric represented its citizens and the Soldiers and Airmen who served. They were individual state flags, but together they were *united* under one: the flag of the United States of America.

The emcee, a young Airman, began with introductions, and my mind started to wander to the past. I had been blessed with countless opportunities and several individuals and leaders who believed in me, starting with Joyce Hanson, who saw something in me and encouraged me to join the Air Force. During basic training, Sergeant Fox also saw something in me and planted a seed through her written words in my BMT book: "Your leadership is sound and one of the best I've seen in an AMN." At the time, hearing such words of praise and having someone believe in me was foreign. As I left basic training, I didn't want to follow her written guidance, "Don't hide behind the bushes when you leave but glow like a bright light that guides others." Ultimately, though, her words unconsciously encouraged me to excel and develop my leadership abilities even further.

The mid-1980s were a different time in the Guard. We didn't have a playbook, and little to no encouragement was offered. Somehow, without specific guidance, I figured out what needed to be done and did what I thought was right. From the beginning of my career, I believed in the Air Force core values and standards, listened to my instincts and my intuition, and trusted in the Lord to guide me. Many times, I stood on the foundation of values that my parents instilled in me. Today of all days, I wished they could have been present and seated in the front row.

Sitting on the stage and looking out at those in attendance, my mind continued to wander through flashes of my career. One of the most pivotal decisions I made as an NCO was to develop my personal and professional leadership skills. I took it upon myself to read and pursue avenues for self-development and personal growth, believing it was up to me to take charge of what happened next and being willing to go outside my comfort zone.

At another juncture in my career, I questioned a medical finding.

*What if I hadn't done that?* I thought. *I'd have been separated from the Air National Guard long ago.*

Taking a huge strategic risk by leaving the 297th ATCS as a controller and cross-training into combat airspace management was instrumental in my journey. Going from a GSU and then being assigned to Hickam AFB opened many new doors and more opportunities.

*What if I'd accepted what the General Officer said to me, "You can't be a Command Chief"? Or what if I'd listened to the commander who told me, "You won't be selected as the Wing Command Chief"? Most likely, my journey would have stopped there.*

Respectfully not taking no for an answer quickly became something I espoused. Deterring words just made me more determined.

I thought of another leader, but this example was positive. As a fairly new Wing Commander, and against advice from some of his Group and Squadron Commanders as well as many Senior (old-school) Chiefs, Major General (ret.) Peter "Skipper" Pawling went out on a limb, took a chance, and selected a Senior Master Sergeant to be his Wing Command Chief. That was another defining moment in my career.

I thought of the Group commanders in Hawaii and how much I deeply appreciated the personal and professional relationships I developed with them. I learned a great deal from each of them, and they richly blessed my life in many ways. They included me in conversations, decisions, and sought my advice on enlisted corps issues. They demonstrated that they valued my participation and input. They supported my decisions in strengthening the First Sergeant program, reestablishing the Top-3, implementing the Enlisted Performance feedback program, and so much more. As I interacted and observed the Group commanders, I had the opportunity to learn a great deal more about what it meant to be a true leader. These were the types of leaders I wished I'd had earlier in my life and throughout my career. They were role models for me, and while they may not have known it, I looked up to them and followed their words and actions. The Maintenance Group commander, Colonel Ronald Han, was also very spiritual, and I was drawn to his and his wife's sincere love of the Lord. In private conversations, I felt strengthened by their words. While the Group commanders were clearly my superiors, we were *ohana*.

Memories of serving as the HI SEL floated past, and I gently shook my head in disbelief that I'd had the great opportunity to serve our Hawaii Army and Air National Guard enlisted corps. When selected, I knew little about the HIARNG, but Major General Robert Lee (ret.) gave me the chance to prove myself. It was a steep learning curve, and I gained a deep and profound respect for the Hawaii Army National Guard Soldiers and what they brought to the fight. I was fortunate that General Lee provided me with the opportunity to gain Joint experience. He, too, took a chance on selecting the first Air National Guard member to serve as the HI SEL.

Now here I was sitting on a stage as the outgoing NGB SEA and retiring. It was a surreal moment. Feeling a strong call to apply, General Craig McKinley (ret.) responded by giving me a final opportunity to serve the National Guard enlisted corps. How do you adequately thank someone for trusting and believing in you and giving you the opportunity to serve our nation's finest Soldiers and Airmen across all communities of these great United States?

With the flags of the 54, surrounding General Grass and me, I turned to thoughts about our colors. I had carried a US flag with me wherever I traveled, a reminder of what this country stands for and the blood and treasure that have been shed defending it.

More of my life flashed before me, and I once again thought about how blessed I was to have served my country. I'd had tremendous opportunities and experienced so much. This little girl from the prairie had truly done all right. I swallowed hard to gain my composure, get my thoughts and feelings under control, and bring myself back to the present moment.

General Grass presented me with a Legion of Merit decoration for my past achievements, a retirement certificate, and a clock shaped like the Pentagon. In a later ceremony, I would be presented the Defense Superior Service Medal, culminating my almost twenty-nine years of service to our nation, along with the Minuteman Award, the highest award given by the Enlisted Association of the National Guard of the United States.

Gary was also brought on stage and recognized. He received a certificate signed by the president of the United States for his unwavering support, and later, Ashley was presented with a bouquet of flowers.

Gary, Ashley, my family, friends, and the National Guard Soldiers and Airmen were the focus of my remarks. Looking out at the audience, I was surprised and overwhelmed to see the priest who married us, Monsignor David Benz; my squad leader and friend from basic training, Senior Master Sergeant Christine Rivera (ret.); and Senior Master Sergeant Joyce Hanson (ret.), the woman from my hometown bank and reason for my joining the USAF.

The hour-long ceremony flew by, and soon I found myself in a reception line thanking people for coming out on a rainy Friday afternoon. With enough time to catch my breath, change, and regroup, my family and I headed to Joint Base Anacostia-Bolling for my retirement dinner. My dear friend and colleague Chief Master Sergeant Susanne Meehan (ret.) spearheaded the dinner event with

Senior Master Sergeant Edward Starr and Senior Master Sergeant Darren Burnett. The emcee had been hand-selected: Master Sergeant Jason Hisaw, my former executive assistant. I owe them all a debt of gratitude for making the evening one I'll remember for the rest of my life.

As the evening was coming to a close, I tried to absorb the day's events. After a pause in thanksgiving to God, who had led me through this incredible journey, I glanced over at Gary and Ashley. With a heart full of gratitude and love, I thought, *I could have never done this without you by my side.*

# CHAPTER 71

# Transitioning to Civilian Life

Gary and I packed up our car and headed west, stopping to visit and reconnect with our families. Looking out at the unending highway, I closed my eyes and started to think about parts of my career that were a bit uncomfortable to revisit. These were aspects of my professional life that weren't so easy to reflect upon, including the fear of failure, which drove me toward new opportunities and to excel in whatever role or position I served.

The fear of failure, which haunted me initially in my career, had propelled me to succeed and to do my best in every endeavor. As the years passed, my fear of failure became less apparent. It wasn't until about the last decade of my career that I understood the power the fear of failure had continued to have over me. About five years before retiring, when I was the Hawaii SEL, I had the opportunity to attend a three-day leadership course. One of the exercises we had to do was break a board on which we wrote our biggest fear. Although the fear of failure had become subtle, it was always lurking just under the surface. So it didn't surprise me when it was the first thing that entered my mind. Without any hesitation, I wrote in bold lettering: **fear of failure**.

The next part of the exercise was to break the board with an arm chop, symbolically letting go of the fear that had the potential to cripple us or, at the very least, to hold us back. I held tight to my board and did not want to take a turn. I let the other thirty participants go before me. How could I let go of the impetus for my prior accomplishments? Wasn't the fear of failure a part of me, a part of my identity? Finally, I took my turn and broke the board with one swift chop.

Afterward, we were supposed to dispose of the pieces, but I couldn't do it. I placed them in my wall locker at the office and glanced at them from time to time. When we moved and I was boxing up my things, I considered the boards for a moment before throwing them out with the trash I'd like to think that the fear of failure no longer has any hold on me, but I know it's still there. Today, though, I'm able to look it squarely in the eye and say, "No matter what you think, I'm going for it." For me, not letting the fear control me is more significant than letting it go.

꒰ꔛ꒱

As we continued driving, I thought of the question I was sometimes asked, "What was it like to be a woman in a man's world?"

As a child, my father ruled the house, and as they say, he ran a tight ship. There was no questioning his decisions or talking back; he gave his orders, and we executed them. In the Air Force, a male-dominated organization, I did well under the leadership of my male supervisors—it was a natural fit. After all, my father had been barking orders at my siblings and me our entire childhood.

I was driven to succeed and did all I could to ensure I learned the material, my job, and how to be a good Airman. After Palace Chasing into the California Air National Guard, I not only did what my supervisors asked of me, but I also went above the call of duty and maintained high standards for myself. At the time, the ground radio operations career field that I cross-trained into was also fairly male-dominant, and again, it was a natural fit as I was accustomed to having a man provide training and direction.

It wasn't until I was an NCO and at about the technical sergeant rank that I began to see a glimpse of what some people called "the good ol' boys' club." While I recognized its existence, I still didn't buy into the notion that "it's a man's world" or that "only men can get ahead." I believed that one's record should stand for itself, and I continued to be a good Airman. My uniform was always squared away and impeccable. I completed my PME ahead of schedule, volunteered, and maintained a positive attitude. I've had to stand up for myself from time to time, but I believe men have to do that as well.

As an SNCO, when it came time for promotion or for assignment into a new position of leadership, I *did* not let the fact that I was a woman enter into the equation or become part of the conversation. Even in Hawaii where I was a *haole* (foreigner) and didn't look like the majority of the Airmen in the HIANG, it just didn't matter. I let my record and what I had accomplished stand for itself. Never *ever* did I play the "woman card" or allow it to be played on me. I believe if a person does their job, completes all their required training, volunteers, and is a well-rounded Airman, then their record stands on its own merit—period.

While assigned to the Headquarters 201st Combat Communications Group as a full-time technician, I attended an off-site senior leadership day of training. I enjoyed this type of training as I always learned something new or had a principle tenet reinforced. Colonel James Townsend was leading the discussion on mentorship. He was going around the room, asking who our mentor was and why.

My mind raced to come up with a name. *What am I going to say?* I thought.

Mentorship was something that had not been part of my journey thus far. There had never been a supervisor or leader who took me by the stripes and provided guidance, direction, recommendations, or exposed me to new or future opportunities. What does one do in a case like that? You figure it out on your own! I had been doing that for most of my career—and in my life, for that matter. Although I looked up to my parents and grandparents, they had never mentored or counseled me. I had to get my parents' approval before acting on a decision, but I made those decisions on my own, taking into account the values I'd been taught.

Within a few moments, it was my turn.

"Chief, who is your mentor?" Colonel Townsend asked.

I put my head down, breathed in, and exhaled with a deep sigh. "I don't have one," I said. "I just didn't grow up in that kind of environment. But…there is someone I've looked up to and admired since I was a teenager, Mary Tyler Moore."

That got a few laughs and chuckles.

"Let me explain!" I continued. "Mary Tyler Moore's character on her TV show worked in an all-male newsroom, and she had to work harder than her peers and prove herself every day. She did this with grace, tenacity, and great poise, and I believed that if she could do it, so could I. Mary never gave up and never quit, and that was something that had been instilled in me since childhood."

Being a woman in an all-male environment sometimes had its challenges: to make my voice heard, for example, or to make a point in a meeting, I often had to interrupt the conversation. Female voices are simply not as loud as male voices, generally speaking. But I found that as long as I didn't mind getting my hands dirty, I fit in with the guys. I was not afraid to roll up my sleeves, sweat, and get dirty. If we were in the field, I had no problem with sleeping in the tent with dirt floors or be in MOPP4 gear (a full chemical training suit). I actually enjoyed the combat field condition environment.

While assigned to the Pentagon, I directed my staff to wear our service or class B uniform in the office. I believed that when I visited troops in the field or during a Unit Training Assembly weekend, I should mirror their uniform, which was most often the ABU. I made a point to wear my jacket and skirt when the service SEAs and I were together in service dress uniform. I did so because while I represented all Soldiers and Airmen in the National Guard, I also felt a sense of obligation to the female warriors. Many of them did not know their NGB SEA was a woman. I wore a skirt so I wouldn't blend in with my male counterparts. I wanted all female service members to see and understand that they, too, could achieve the highest enlisted position in their respective branch or component of service. This was not something I specifically talked to women about, but the subtlety of the skirt helped make my point.

Meetings in the Pentagon were respectful; if you had something to say, you merely had to raise your hand. From the president, Secretary of Defense, chairman of the Joint Chiefs of Staff, service secretaries, service chiefs, and senior military leaders, to civilian officials, they all wanted to hear from the SEAs. I never felt like I was shut out, stifled, or not heard.

Ultimately, it didn't matter that I was a woman. I've said time and time again that it's important to serve "pure of heart," meaning that if you serve for the good of the country or the organization in which you serve and if you do what's right for the people you lead, great things will come back to you every single time. I believe the "right person" for the job depends on your willingness to serve, not your gender.

꒦

As the car rolled along, I had one question that continued to puzzle me, though, What I would do now? As someone who was always active and fully engaged in my positions, I couldn't help but wonder, *How do I continue to make a difference and have an impact on other people's lives and my country?* Just as I had done decades earlier in the bank, I questioned, "What's next?"

As Gary and I continued to drive toward our new home, I knew I couldn't yet answer those questions. It was simply too soon. For now, I needed to focus on working with Gary to make our new dwelling a true home—one where our family would feel welcome and that would serve as a safe haven for Gary and me.

After the weeklong trip west, as we climbed to our new home situated above seven thousand feet elevation, we smiled at each other. Gary and I had arrived in Colorado and were ready to begin the next chapter of our lives.

Twenty-Sixth CNGB, General Craig McKinley

Kibbutz school bomb shelter in Israel near the Gaza Strip

Fourth of July at the White House

Youth Challenge Academy opening with Governor
Lingle and General McKinley

WWII Veterans at the Women in Military Service for
America Memorial at Arlington National Cemetery

Jelinski family time, September 2011

*Right to left*: SECAF Michael Donley, CSAF and Mrs. Mark Welsh, Mrs. and CMSAF James Roy, Chief Denise Jelinski-Hall and Gary Hall

Hurricane Sandy, New Jersey, 2012

With Secretary of Defense Leon Panetta at the 237th USMC birthday, November 10, 2012

*Fox & Friends* studio, Women's History Month 2013

Freedom Tower, 105th floor, NYC, March 2013

St. Patrick's Day with the Fighting 69th, NYARNG

Passing the halberd to General Grass

Display at the Women in Service to America Memorial

General Grass views Chief Jelinski-Hall's retirement display

Delivering retirement remarks, June 6, 2013

General Grass presents the Defense Superior Service
Medal at the EANGUS Conference, 2013

EANGUS presents the Minuteman Award in
Sioux Falls, South Dakota, 2013

# Afterword

Chief Master Sergeant Denise Jelinski-Hall's incredible story depicts the life of the woman I came to know professionally and personally. She is one of the finest Airmen and senior noncommissioned officers I have had the privilege to serve with during my entire career of almost forty-seven years. I am so glad General Craig McKinley, 26th Chief of the National Guard Bureau, selected Chief Master Sergeant Jelinski-Hall to be his Senior Enlisted Advisor. There is no doubt in my mind she was truly the most qualified and best applicant among a field of extremely talented Command Chiefs and Command Sergeants Major serving throughout the fifty-four states, territories, and the District of Columbia. I was extremely fortunate to have Denise in the position of Senior Enlisted Advisor to the Chief of the National Guard Bureau as I was sworn into office on September 7, 2012.

Denise's experience and expertise on all matters relating to the National Guard and primarily our enlisted force and their families were paramount to our credibility and success as a new joint activity. On December 31, 2011, federal legislation placed the chief of the National Guard Bureau on the Joint Chiefs of Staff. Denise had already developed a tremendous professional military relationship with the other six Senior Enlisted Advisors to members of the Joint Chiefs of Staff. This was no easy task, given the short amount of time since the chief of the National Guard Bureau position had been elevated. Additionally, prior to the Senate action there was initial reluctance within the Department of Defense to add the chief of the National Guard Bureau to the Joint Chiefs.

Her open and respected dialogue with all Senior Enlisted Advisors to members of the Joint Chiefs of Staff was absolutely essential as we discussed and debated a multitude of military policy changes in personnel, readiness, and training that affected all service members, including our Army and Air National Guard women and men, their families, and their civilian employers. Denise's experience was vital in educating and informing me—and other senior leadership and staff of the National Guard Bureau—on strategic issues so we were prepared to represent 450,000 plus Guardsmen. Her sage advice ensured that the interest of citizen Soldiers and Airmen were appropriately represented as Department of Defense and service policy decisions were formulated on topics such as Tricare Reform, pay and entitlements, Sequestration, Women in Combat, Don't Ask Don't Tell, family programs, and many other policy proposals.

The professional communication and connection that occurs between a member of the Joint Chiefs of Staff and their Senior Enlisted Advisor is essential to the success of the senior leadership of any military organization. This professional relationship is like no other—it must be an open dialogue that allows the Senior Enlisted Advisor unfettered access to the Joint Chiefs of Staff member. Chief Master Sergeant Jelinski-Hall and I had the ideal professional relationship. She constantly maintained an outstanding working relationship and open chain of communication with me as well as with the fifty-four National Guard Senior Enlisted Leaders across the states, territories, and District of Columbia. Furthermore, she had a unique ability to analyze the needs of our most valued asset, our women and men in uniform, and communicate those needs at the highest levels of our government.

Through her travels and personal engagement, she knew the issues our Guardsmen and their families were dealing with as a result of the War on Terrorism and the successful but demanding conversion from a Strategic Reserve to an Operational Force. She knew what resources, policies, and training were needed to maintain a high state of readiness within our units and was keenly aware of how personnel policies affected individual readiness.

Although my calendar was always quite packed, she understood she could walk into my office at any time to address critical issues that I needed to understand. She made sure I was always prepared to address enlisted issues in senior leadership meetings, such as the Joint Chiefs of Staff "Tank," Congressional visits, and White House engagements. Although we maintained this open dialogue, she had a solid sense of priorities and urgency to know when to use this unfettered access to my office. I could not have asked for a better Senior Enlisted Advisor to partner with me to lead the National Guard Bureau.

In the National Guard, our mission is threefold: (1) provide trained and ready warfighting forces to the Army and Air Force when called into federal service by the president; (2) provide trained and ready forces to our states, territories, and the District of Columbia when disaster strikes at home and we are called into service by our governors; and (3) build partnerships at the local, state, federal, and international levels. These missions are enabled by the incredible men and women who serve in the National Guard.

Chief Master Sergeant Jelinski-Hall and I traveled to see our National Guard women and men in action in support of these three missions. Whether visiting our Guardsmen in a combat zone or on a peacekeeping operation, observing their response to a natural or manmade disaster, or training alongside the troops of one of our amazing state partnership countries, I witnessed how Denise "got in the mud" to observe and listen attentively to each enlisted member, from the most junior to the highest-ranking Sergeant on the ground. I'm sure many young enlisted members felt more at ease conversing with a Chief Master Sergeant than a four-star General. As we conducted our after-action review of an overseas or stateside trip, Chief Jelinski-Hall would often summarize for me the issues our Citizen Soldiers and Airmen relayed to her during our travels. Her feedback allowed me to gauge the morale and health of our force.

There were two reasons I felt it was important for the Chief and me to travel together. First, I knew junior enlisted personnel would provide her with unvarnished examples of what was happening on the ground. Second, Army and Air National Guard leaders at all levels needed to see the Chief of the National Guard Bureau and his Senior Enlisted Advisor as a "leadership team."

All who read this memoir will agree that Chief Jelinski-Hall is a great American, born and raised on the Northern Plains of Minnesota by hardworking, loving parents, Betty and CW2 Willie Jelinski (ret.), who instilled in their children everything that is right about America. She dedicated her career to military service in the United States Air Force and Air National Guard, culminating her service to our country in the highest senior noncommissioned officer position possible within the Department of Defense and the National Guard Bureau. She achieved numerous "firsts" among outstanding women in our military. In her words, "Only in America is this possible. If you put your mind to it, work hard, and believe in yourself, you too can achieve this success."

Even more pronounced than her accolades are Denise's dedication and love for our service members and their families. She is a compassionate person who sets the example for all military members to live the Air Force values: Integrity First, Service Before Self, and Excellence in All We Do. Chief Master Sergeant Jelinski-Hall also enforced the "One Military Standard." I personally witnessed on numerous occasions her actions as the standard bearer for the Air and Army National Guard.

When you serve in the military and progress through the ranks to senior leadership positions, you are there to support the dedicated women and men in uniform because of the love you have for our nation and for your commitment to maintaining our freedom. In an unofficial capacity, your family is drawn into the military lifestyle and environment. Tremendous demands are placed on you and spill over into your family life. As military families, we all experience times of enjoyment enabled by military assignments. We also experience times of personal stress as a result of our military service. This was true for Chief Master Sergeant Jelinski-Hall's family as she served as the highest-ranking enlisted member of the National Guard Bureau.

Opportunities to participate in White House events as well as many other high-level social activities were rewarding, I'm sure. But along with opportunities for the family came extreme family challenges and sacrifice, as Denise pointed out in her memoirs. Without the great support of your family, it is extremely difficult to serve successfully at senior levels of any organization. It is never easy since the family must adapt to your professional demands. Denise's family is a model military family in sacrifice and support. I witnessed the tremendous backing she received from both Gary and Ashley. Our nation owes a debt of gratitude to Gary, Ashley, and all military families.

Chief Master Sergeant Jelinski-Hall was, and continues to be, an inspiration to me as well as to the women and men of the Air and Army National Guard. I attribute much of her success in the military to her ability to never quit, live the Air Force values, enforce the one standard, care for her family and those around her, maintain a commitment to lifelong learning, and a strong spiritual belief. She is an example of what is great about our nation.

Her humbly described success should be a guide for thousands of young women and men, especially women, showing that they, too, can achieve their dreams, or the highest levels of military leadership, by following her reflections and guidance in this incredible memoir of a great US Airman and military leader.

I feel so privileged to have served side by side with Chief Master Sergeant Denise Jelinski-Hall as we led the National Guard Bureau in support of the outstanding and dedicated women and men serving in the National Guard across our great nation and around the world. Pat and I will always cherish our tremendous friendship with Denise, Gary, and Ashley. I'm excited to see what the future has in store for Denise and Gary. Her potential is boundless!

Frank J. Grass, General (ret.)
A Citizen Soldier and 27th Chief of
the National Guard Bureau, 2012–2016

# Foundational Leadership Pillars

Throughout my life, both growing up on the family farm and in the military, I was influenced by certain principles and practices. Some I learned through personal and professional experiences while others I gathered from books or by listening to the wisdom of other leaders.

I also came to lean on something that can't be taught—to trust my gut instincts and my intuition, that feeling one gets in the pit of their stomach that tells you whether something feels right or wrong. Trusting my gut was an integral part of my journey.

As my military career progressed, I realized that if I were willing to work hard, help others succeed, and put these practices and principles to work in all aspects of my life, I could achieve things I had never imagined. Whenever I've spoken to audiences, my intention was that those listening would learn at least one thing that might help them along their life's journey. My desire is that these ten foundational leadership pillars will inspire you to achieve your dreams and goals.

## Have a Strong Work Ethic

From a very young age, my parents instilled this principle in my siblings and me. We worked for everything we had or wanted. Farmwork required long hours, sacrifice, understanding losses and setbacks, and knowing what it took to get ahead. Overtime, I learned that this principle also applied to having a successful career and a meaningful life. I found that to achieve my goals, they had to take priority over other desires. While I enjoyed watching television and movies and lying on the beach, those pleasures were the first things I needed to eliminate.

One has to understand and fully accept that success requires hard work. You will spend long hours and time away from family and personal interests. Sometimes, setbacks will outnumber successes, which means you may have to work even harder.

You will need to make tough decisions to achieve all you want to accomplish. Decide early on in your career that you are going to work hard, make sacrifices, and sometimes make difficult decisions. In the end, it will be well worth it.

## Maintain a Good Attitude

One of my most influential mentors in leadership is Dr. John Maxwell. Among the many things I have learned from him, perhaps the most powerful can be summed up in two quotes: "Attitude is everything" and "Your attitude will determine your altitude." One of the most important lessons I have learned in this area is that the best thing about attitude is that you have complete control over it. We choose our attitude. No one can give it to us, and no one can take it away.

A good attitude creates the tipping point: all things being equal, the one with the best attitude will win or get ahead. Carrying a good attitude into all I did was critical. I didn't let the naysayers get me down, and I always tried to look for the silver lining in every adverse situation. Generally speaking, supervisors tend to select those people in their organizations who have good attitudes, so I made sure I had the right attitude. This isn't to say I never got down or wasn't disappointed—I just didn't allow myself to *stay* down. I gave myself three days to stew on something and then made a deliberate decision to move forward with a good attitude. Dr. Maxwell calls it "failing forward." I have carried out this principle repeatedly in my professional and personal life. We all have challenges, struggles, and difficult times; there's no way around it—it's called life.

The key to a good life is to maintain a good attitude, looking for the positive even in the worst of times. This outlook will help you get through many tough times.

## Be Engaged with Continual Growth and Self-Development

Because I didn't follow a traditional path to college, I knew I still needed to learn and grow as a leader and as a person. Yet even when I was able to take classes, I feared failure. I didn't think I was smart enough to pass the challenging courses. At times, I was afraid to try, but I knew I had to face my fear of failure if I wanted to grow as an Airman and as a person.

As an introvert, it was important for me to cultivate a more outgoing and engaging personality. To grow, I had to get comfortable with the uncomfortable. Not only did I have to "get out of my comfort zone," but I also had to embrace what I feared most—failing and potentially embarrassing myself in front of others. One of the most uncomfortable things I did was volunteer to publicly speak. I was nervous about making mistakes or embarrassing the organization or myself—but I did it anyway. I came to understand that as a senior leader, I had to get comfortable with public speaking.

As I continued on my path of self-development and personal growth, I had many opportunities to attend senior leader conferences. I listened carefully to other leaders. I listened to the words they used and watched how they carried themselves and how they interacted with people.

As a bit of a wallflower, I was more comfortable staying in the shadows, but I clearly saw the need to engage with people. Initially, my interactions felt forced and difficult, but the more I engaged with others, the easier it became. As with any opportunity that required me to stretch beyond what was comfortable, I gained confidence the more I put myself out there.

Like attitude, deciding to grow in your professional and personal life is a choice, but if you want to become a true leader, you must embrace growth.

## Be Ready

Being ready requires us to look ahead, plan, and be open to opportunities. Readiness in all things is engrained in military members from the very beginning of their military service. Military readiness encompasses not only being ready to serve in your civilian and military career but also in your family life. On the military side, or on the professional side in the civilian community, annual and recurring technical training and higher education is paramount. Learning and growing consistently needs to be in the forefront of what we do. In our personal fives, ensuring that we have a family care plan, that our vehicles are in good repair, our medical, dental, and physical fitness is current, and our finances are in order—these things and more are essential to readiness.

Think about what sets you apart from your peers, then ask yourself, "What do I need to do to be ready for the next leadership opportunity?" Instead of looking for "promotion opportunities," look for those occasions that will provide you with the opportunity to lead. Those moments are not necessarily obvious—sometimes you have to look for them.

For military readiness, do you need to complete your military or civilian education? Do you need to volunteer, mentor or take extra online courses? Ask your supervisor or a mentor, or have a discussion with senior leaders in or out of the chain of command, or with civilian leaders, to get input for career progression.

There is a lot you can do to prepare and be ready for opportunities. Sometimes it's the small things that can have maximum impact: Read leadership articles and enroll in audio leadership programs or podcasts. Make your driving or running time productive. Many times, I listened to half of a leadership lesson on the way to work and the other half on the way home. I applied the leadership tips I'd gained in my interactions at work.

One of my favorite leadership programs is Dr. John Maxwell's Maximum Impact Club. I received a monthly CD that I typically listened to five to seven times so that it would really sink in. I was inspired by many of Dr. Maxwell's lessons and created several speeches based on the information I learned.

As you prepare for the next opportunity, remember that everyone needs time to decompress. Whether it's listening to your favorite music group or artist, playing sports or just plain relaxing, you deserve that time too. Creating balance in one's life is important, but be ready for that proverbial tap on the shoulder. Leaders will tap you to step up and lead when you least expect it.

## Take Strategic Risks

Going through a career and being afraid to take a risk is not only unwise, but it is also counter to what real leaders do each day. It's safe to say that most senior leaders did not follow a linear line to the top. Even in a corporate setting, a manager doesn't necessarily follow a straight line to becoming a CEO. As your career progresses, you'll find obstacles, roadblocks, deployments, family challenges, and career changes along the way. All these things help you grow, gain experience, and widen your perspective. It's important to get a broad breadth of experience and look for opportunities for growth—that doesn't necessarily mean upward mobility. You may have to serve in different capacities and positions, which could be through a parallel move or a deliberate decision to take a step back to gain another skill set.

Applying for the NGB SEA position was a huge strategic risk for me and my family. Coming from six thousand miles away, not knowing the people, the area, or how Washington or the beltway worked was risky. What if I didn't do well? The fear of failure was always just under the surface. What if Gary didn't find work? What if, what if, what if? We were comfortable and secure in Hawaii, yet making that decision turned out to be one of the best career moves of my life.

Does taking strategic risks always work out perfectly? Of course not, but I believe that typically the reward turns out to be far greater than the risk. As service members and civilians, we can't be afraid to make those hard decisions. However, make those strategic risks thoughtfully and purposefully. I believe and subscribe to the old adage of "When one door closes, another door opens."

## Maintain Your Professionalism

This seems like a no-brainer, and some may say it doesn't need to be said. Au contraire! Professionalism, standards, and accepted behavior are drilled into service members from day one. My experience has been that the vast majority of service members do an amazing job at maintaining standards and their professionalism. For some, however, something changes along the way. Sometimes standards get relaxed, minor infractions are overlooked, and personal wants and desires cloud judgment.

One such area, in my opinion, is that supervisors and senior leaders should never partake in alcoholic beverages with their subordinates other than in a social setting like a banquet. Never cross those types of lines. I remember when I was a Senior Master Sergeant and I attended an event as a volunteer with several subordinates from my unit. One evening event consisted of line dancing, mechanical bull riding, and other western-type activities. Hundreds of Airmen from throughout the Air National Guard attended. I had one glass of wine as I walked through the crowd and participated in the line dancing. I enjoyed myself and visited with many people. I then left and turned in early, having had one alcoholic beverage that evening.

Upon returning to our unit, I spoke with our Group Commander about the event and how well the volunteers performed. A Technical Sergeant overheard our conversation and said, "I saw you drinking and partying." I was aghast at her remark and her perception of my behavior. Quickly, I explained to the commander that I was not partying and had had one drink—that was it. From that day forward, I was overly cautious about consuming any alcohol where junior enlisted were present other than at an event like a formal ball. I also came to realize how important it is to set a drink down before having a picture taken. With social media as it is today, you can never retrieve inappropriate pictures, and you never know when they will come back to haunt you or have an impact on your career. Perception is always someone's reality.

I believe professionalism extends beyond the office or the end of the official duty day. The American public holds our military to a higher standard and expects that we maintain a high decorum of professionalism. This is something communities across the United States and around the world have come to expect from our nation's finest—and we must deliver. Even in civilian walks of life—whether in business, sports, entertainment, or Wall Street—others will make judgments about your performance. Someone will always be looking and making judgments based on your behavior, so live as if you're in a glass fishbowl 24-7.

## Don't Take No for an Answer (Respectfully)

This was huge for me. Many times, someone told me I couldn't do something. Those "nos" just made me more determined. Ask questions, read the regulations, seek information and assistance from human resources and the employee handbook, seek mentorship, and conduct research to find the correct answer. When someone tells you no, work harder to find a way it *can* be done. People often ask, "Can I?" The real question is, *How can I?* Adding the word "how" at the front of the question assumes it can be done. Look things up, take control of your career, and don't let anyone else determine your success. If "no" does turn out to be the answer and a door is closed, look for the open window!

## Serve Pure of Heart

For some, this sounds a little touchy-feely. Serving "pure of heart" means you serve for the good of the country, your organization, and the people you lead. Serving pure of heart is serving without regard for personal gain or without the need to do things that are self-serving. If you do what is right, with the right intent and for the right reasons, good things will always come back to you. You may fool some people some of the time, but most people around you will know if you are being genuine or if you're only in it for yourself or for personal gain. Always serve "pure of heart."

## Have Passion

I've often said, "If you don't love what you're doing, then do something else." Cross-train into another career field, volunteer for a special duty assignment, or find another position. Since our work life is long and we spend a great deal of time at the office or in the workplace, it's much more enjoyable if we love what we do.

If you love your job and the people you work with, then it's not work. Find your passion, find your *why*, and give it your *all*. Not only will this benefit you and your life, but it will inspire others, which makes for a stronger workplace and a more effective organization.

## Have Faith

There is a reason I saved faith for last because I know that what I achieved would not have been possible without it. Faith in others, faith in myself, and above all, faith in God is indispensable to me. I believe with all my heart that so many places I was privileged to see, so many wonderful people who crossed in my life's path, so many things I was blessed to experience and achieve were part of God's plan for my life. I know that all things, good and bad, joyful and painful, were put in front of me to mold me into the person God wants me to be.

The path hasn't always been clear, and many times, I wondered, *What is God really trying to tell me? Why is this happening to me, Lord? I don't understand!* As time went on, I began to realize that the more I quit worrying about me and the more I centered my life on others and the more I trusted in the Lord, no matter what happened, I could be at peace with it. My life in the military and at home became a much smoother "road to travel" because I knew I wasn't alone on the journey. He as always walking by my side.

Whenever I applied for a position, I did not pray to get the job, but rather that God's will would be done for me. When I wasn't selected, I did not fully understand why it was not my "time," but the important this is that I never gave up, never stopped doing my best, and never quit believing in my abilities. My trust in the Lord and belief in myself continued to guide me, even in the hardest of times.

I have faced obstacles and challenges, hard times, and great times. For almost twenty-nine years, I had the privilege of serving God and my country in the United States Air Force and Air National Guard. I met people from around the world, traveled to places I had never heard of, and experienced things beyond my wildest imagination. Through faith and hard work, I have achieved positions never before held by an enlisted woman. When I joined the Air Force, I had no idea that one day I would be the first woman to serve as a senior enlisted advisor to a member of the Joint Chiefs of Staff, nor could I have ever imagined that I would achieve the highest position ever held by an enlisted woman in the history of the US military. I am humbled at the life God has given me.

It is clear to me that God has always been in control of my life, and I have trusted His path. I am also eternally grateful to Gary and Ashley for their sacrifices and for encouraging and believing in me. I could never have accomplished what I did without them by my side.

Over the course of nearly three decades serving my country, I have discovered that the military offers limitless opportunities. In the US Armed Forces, you can choose to do and be anything—you just need to open your eyes and take full advantage of what lies in front of you.

Just before my retirement, I was interviewed at the Woman Service to America Memorial in Washington, DC. At the conclusion, I was asked a very poignant question, "What will you miss the most?" Without hesitation, I answered, "A chance to make a difference." That is my reason for sharing some of my story—that you will come to know that greatness lies within each of us. My hope is that something you read will make a positive difference in your life.

> Trust in the Lord with all thine heart; and lean not unto thine own understanding. In all ways thy ways acknowledge him, and he shall direct thy paths.
>
> —Prov. 2:5–6 (KJV)

# HISTORIC FIRSTS AS AN ENLISTED WOMAN

2004: Command Chief Master Sergeant for the 154th Wing, Hawaii Air National Guard.

2006: State Command Chief, Hawaii Air National Guard.

2007: Senior Enlisted Leader, Hawaii National Guard (Army and Air), serving simultaneously as State Command Chief for Hawaii Air National Guard.

2008: Received Department of Defense "Trail Blazer Award" for Women in the Military as a Hawaii Air National Guard member.

2010: Senior Enlisted Advisor, National Guard Bureau 2010—Senior Enlisted Advisor, National Guard Bureau (first Air National Guard member)

2012: Senior Enlisted Advisor to a member of the Joint Chiefs of Staff

2013: Received Hawaii National Guard Distinguished Service Order award (only enlisted member to ever receive this honor)

2013: Third Chief Master Sergeant to receive the Defense Superior Service Medal in the sixty-six-year history of the US Air Force

2013: As National Guard Bureau Senior Enlisted Advisor, received the Minuteman Award, the highest award given by the Enlisted Association of the National Guard of the United States

2013: As the Senior Enlisted Advisor to the Chief of the National Guard Bureau, a member of the Joint Chiefs of Staff, achieved the highest position ever held by an enlisted woman in the history of the US Armed Forces

# GLOSSARY OF TERMS

AEF: Air Expeditionary Force
AF: Air Force
AFB: Air Force Base
ANG: Air National Guard
ANGRC: Air National Guard Readiness Center
ATC: Air Traffic Control
ATCS: Air Traffic Control Squadron
ATCF: Air Traffic Control Flight
ATM: Air Traffic Manager

CAOC: Combined Air Operations Center
CATCO: Chief Air Traffic Control Officer
CBCS: Combat Communications Squadron
CCG: Combat Communications Group
CCM: Command Chief Master Sergeant
CENTCOM: U.S. Central Command
CMSAF: Chief Master Sergeant of the Air Force
CNGB: Chief of the National Guard Bureau
COR: Change of Responsibility
CSM: Command Sergeant Major

DSG: Drill Status Guardsman (part-time)

FSC: First Sergeant Council

HIANG: Hawaii Air National Guard
HIARNG: Hawaii Army National Guard
HING: Hawaii National Guard

JAG: Judge Advocate General
JB: Joint Base
JDEC: Joint Diversity Executive Council
JTF: Joint Task Force
JFHQ: Joint Force Headquarters
JMARC: Joint Monthly Access for Reserve Components

NAS: Naval Air Station
NCO: Noncommissioned Officer
NGB: National Guard Bureau

OEF: Operation Enduring Freedom
OIF: Operation Iraqi Freedom
Ohana: Hawaiian for "family"
ORE: Operational Readiness Exercise
ORI: Operational Readiness Inspection

PACAF: Pacific Air Forces
PACOM: Pacific Command
PME: Professional Military Education

SEA: Senior Enlisted Advisor
SEL: Senior Enlisted Leader
SEAC: Senior Enlisted Leader to the Chairman of the Joint Chiefs of Staff

SGM: Sergeant Major
SMA: Sergeant Major of the Army
SNCO: Senior Noncommissioned Officer

TACAN: Tactical Air Navigation
TAG: The Adjutant General

Title-5: DOD Civilian
Title 10: Active duty
Title-32: AGR (Active Guard and Reserve—full-time)

**USA:** United States Army
**USAF:** United States Air Force
**USCG:** United States Coast Guard
**USMC:** United States Marine Corps
**USN:** United States Navy

**WG CCM:** Wing Command Chief

# US Army Pay Grades and Ranks

E-1: Private (PVT)
E-2: Private (PV2)
E-3: Private First Class (PFC)
E-4: Specialist (SPC) or Corporal (CPL)
E-5: Sergeant (SGT)
E-6: Staff Sergeant (SSG)
E-7: Sergeant First Class (SFC)
E-8: Master Sergeant (MSG)
E-8: First Sergeant (1SG)
E-9: Sergeant Major (SGM)
E-9: Command Sergeant Major (CSM)
E-9: Sergeant Major of the Army (SMA or Sergeant Major)

O-1: Second Lieutenant (2LT)
O-2: First Lieutenant (1LT)
O-3: Captain (CPT)
O-4: Major (MAJ)
O-5: Lieutenant Colonel (LTC)
O-6: Colonel (COL)
O-7: Brigadier General (BG)
O-8: Major General (MG)
O-9: Lieutenant General (LTG)
O-10: General (GEN)

# US Air Force Pay Grades and Ranks

E-1: Airman Basic (AB)
E-2: Airman (AMN)
E-3: Airman First Class (A1C)
E-4: Senior Airman (SrA)
E-5: Staff Sergeant (SSgt)
E-6: Technical Sergeant (TSgt)
E-7: Master Sergeat (MSgt)
E-8: Senior Master Sergeant (SMSgt)
E-9: Chief Master Sergeant (CMSgt or Chief)
E-9: Command Chief Master Sergeant (CCM or Chief)
E-9: Chief Master Sergeant of the Air Force (CMSAF or Chief)

O-1: Second Lieutenant (2d Lt)
O-2: First Lieutenant (1st Lt)
O-3: Captain (Capt)
O-4: Major (Maj)
O-5: Lieutenant Colonel (Lt Col)
O-6: Colonel (Col)
O-7: Brigadier General (Brig Gen)
O-8: Major General (Maj Gen)
O-9: Lieutenant General (Lt Gen)
O-10: General (Gen)
O-10: General of the Air Force (GOAF)

# NOTES

Chapter 4: More New Schools

[1] John C. Maxwell attributes this quote to Charlie "Tremendous" Jones, a businessman and speaker.

John C. Maxwell, *Developing the Leaders Around You: How to Help Others Reach Their Full Potential* (Nashville: Thomas Nelson, 1995).

Chapter 9: Offutt AFB, Nebraska

[2] John C. Maxwell, *Leadership 101: What Every Leader Needs to Know* (Nashville: Thomas Nelson, 2002).

Chapter 10: It's Official!

[3] Each job in the Air Force has an associated "occupational" badge designed to reflect the respective Air Force Specialty Code. The ATC badge has a control tower on it, and once qualified at the five-skill level—and therefore facility-rated—the controller receives this basic badge and is authorized to wear it. Today, the badge can be worn upon graduating from ATC school.

Chapter 11: The Marine

[4] The official birth of the National Guard is December 13, 1636 when the first militia regiments in North America were organized in Massachusetts as a citizen force to protect families and towns from hostile attacks.

Chapter 14: First Deployment as a Military Spouse

[5] The Battalion Landing Team (BLT 1/1) that Gary was assigned to was redesignated as the Eleventh Marine Expeditionary Unit, Special Operations Capable (Eleventh MEU SOC). The Eleventh MEU consisted of a ground combat unit (GCE, BLT 1/1), an aviation combat element (ACE) consisting

of AV8 Harrier jets, UH-1N, CH-46 and CH-53 transport and Cobra Attack helicopters, a logistics combat element (then called a combat service support element, CSSE), and a MEU command element (CE).

In total, there were more than 2,200 Marines and Sailors deployed on the four Navy ships. Gary's ship was the USS *Peleliu* (LHA 5), an amphibious assault ship that was part of a four-ship naval amphibious readiness group (ARG) that transported the MEU. Just prior to the deployment, Gary's battalion was reinforced with additional Marine units operationally attached to them. BLT 1/1 had an artillery battery from the Eleventh MEU, a platoon of tanks, light armored vehicles, amphibious assault vehicles (AAVs), a reconnaissance platoon, an engineer platoon, and elements of a Low Altitude Air Defense platoon operationally attached to them for the six-month deployment. Additionally, at the start of the six-month training cycle, the battalion was reinforced with a fourth rifle company (a traditional Marine Battalion has three rifle companies). As part of a special-operations-capable MEU, they also trained for missions not normally associated with the standard infantry battalion. Among those missions were close quarters battle (CQB), noncombatant evacuation operations, humanitarian assistance operations, riot control, tactical rescue of aircraft and pilots, scout swimmer operations, in-extremis hostage rescue, over-the-horizon boat raids, and airfield seizure.

[6] Over the past decade and a half, with the Iraq and Afghanistan Wars and other federal and state crises, employers are more educated on the requirements of the Uniform Services Employment and Reemployment Rights Act (USERRA) law, as are our Guard members who have a responsibility to their employers.

Chapter 23: Beyond Kalaeloa

[7] An individual augmentee (IA) is a member of the military assigned to a unit (such as a battalion or regiment) as a temporary duty assignment, either to fill a shortage or to provide particular skills. IAs can include members from an entirely different branch of service.

Chapter 27: Command Chief

[8] Through the authority of the state's governor, the adjutant general (TAG) is the commander of a state's military forces. Responsible for both the Army and Air National Guard within their respective state or territory, the TAG oversees the training and readiness of all Soldiers and Airmen in the state command. In many states, the TAG provides direct support to veterans administration organizations and is the Homeland Security Advisor to the governor.

Chapter 28: 154th Wing Command Chief

[9] The Wing's mission is to provide premium air power, at home and while deployed. Comprised of nearly 1,900 part-time and full-time Airmen, it is the largest HIANG organization. The Wing consists of a HQ, four groups, twelve squadrons, and five flights. The 199th Fighter Squadron operates and maintains the F-22 Raptor. The 203rd Air Refueling Squadron equips the 135R Stratotanker aircraft, which provides nonstop air refueling for almost every type of US fixed-wing aircraft. The 204th Airlift Squadron operates C-17A Globemasters. Other groups in the Wing provide construction, security, communication, and logistical support. See https://www.154wg.ang.af.mil.

Chapter 41: The Philippines

[10] Charles M. Hubbard and Collis H. Davis, Jr., *Corregidor in Peace and War* (Columbia and London: University of Missouri Press, 2007).

Chapter 52: The Joint Chiefs of Staff

[11] In 2009, the senior enlisted position to the CNGB was identified as the National Guard Bureau senior enlisted leader (NGB SEL). In September 2012, the position title was changed to National Guard Bureau senior enlisted adviser (NGB SEA), for parity among the senior enlisted advisers who served members of the Joint Chiefs of Staff.

Chapter 53: Joining the SEA Team

[12] In a speech delivered to the House of Commons following the collapse of France during WWII, Churchill stated, "Let us therefore brace ourselves to our duties, and so bear ourselves that if the British Empire and Commonwealth last for a thousand years, men will still say, *This was their finest hour.*"
   Winston Churchill, "Their Finest Hour" (speech to the House of Commons, London, England, June 18, 1940).

Chapter 63: The Tank

[13] Bernard E. Trainor, "Inside the 'Tank': Bowls of Candy and Big Brass," *New York Times*, January 11, 1988.

Chapter 68: Proud to be an Airman

[14] The US Air Force Memorial is easily seen on the skyline of Washington, DC, and Northern Virginia. The Air Force Memorial "Soaring to Glory" was dedicated on October 14, 2006, and honors the service and sacrifices of the men and women of the USAF and its predecessor organizations, including the Aeronautical Division, US Signal Corps; the Aviation Section, US Signal Corps; the Division of Military Aeronautics, Secretary of War; the Army Air Service; the US Army Air Corps; and the US Army Air Forces.

# ABOUT THE AUTHOR

When Denise joined the Air Force and embarked on a career spanning almost three decades, she could not have imagined the journey would take her across the United States and around the world, while representing nearly 457,000 National Guard personnel and their families. She never imagined that one day she would be the sitting in the Pentagon with the Joint Chiefs of Staff and her fellow senior enlisted advisors, making her the first woman in the history of the United States to serve in that capacity.

Since her retirement, she completed her bachelor of science in business administration, earned a master's certificate in strategic leadership and received an honorary doctorate degree in humane letters. With a desire to continue to make a difference, Denise found her way to give back. She served three years as a board of trustee for the Military Child Education Coalition. She is serving her seventh year as a board of trustee for United Through Reading where she also serves on the Governance Committee. Denise volunteered with the Colorado Springs Employer Support of the Guard and Reserve; she serves as a military advisor for Veterans United Home Loans and is involved in church ministries. Denise is a coauthor of Beaching the Summit, a leadership book written in collaboration with her fellow senior enlisted advisors. She continues to speak to military and civilian groups on leadership, mentorship, and the importance of personal growth. Denise and her husband, Gary, have four children and nine grandchildren. They currently live in Colorado.